# On Nineteen Eighty-Four

edited by
Peter Stansky

Stanford Alumni Association
Stanford, California

THE PORTABLE STANFORD is a series publication of the Stanford Alumni Association. Each book is an original work written expressly for this series by a member of the Stanford University faculty. The PS series is designed to bring the widest possible sampling of Stanford's intellectual resources into the homes of alumni. It includes books based on current research as well as books that deal with philosophical issues, which by their nature reflect to a greater degree the personal views of their authors.

THE PORTABLE STANFORD
Stanford Alumni Association
Stanford, California 94305

Library of Congress Catalog Card
Number 83-62699
ISBN: 0-91638-10-8

# The Portable Stanford

published by the
Stanford Alumni Association

*Landscape with Figures* by George Tooker, 1965-66, egg tempera on pressed wood, 25½″ × 29″. From a private collection. Photo courtesy of Ronald Feldman Fine Arts, New York.

# CONTENTS

Preface                                                                    x

## I THE BOOK, THE MAN, THE YEAR

1   *Nineteen Eighty-Four*: The Book                                        2
    William Abrahams

2   Orwell: The Man                                                         9
    Peter Stansky

3   1939 and 1984: George Orwell and the                                   15
    Vision of Judgment
    Alex Comfort

## II WAR IS PEACE

4   Triangularity and International Violence                               24
    Gordon A. Craig

5   Newspeak and Nukespeak                                                 33
    Sidney D. Drell

6   The Economics of *Nineteen Eighty-Four*                                43
    Kenneth J. Arrow

7   1984: Population and Environment                                       49
    Paul R. Ehrlich and Anne H. Ehrlich

8   Economic Doublethink: Food and Politics                               56
    Scott R. Pearson

9   The Politics of Technology and the Technology                         67
    of Politics
    Robert E. McGinn

10    The Biomedical Revolution and Totalitarian          76
      Control
      *Raymond B. Clayton*

## III IGNORANCE IS STRENGTH

11    Lawspeak and Doublethink                             86
      *Barbara Allen Babcock*

12    Newspeak: Could It Really Work?                      92
      *Elizabeth Closs Traugott*

13    Winston Smith: The Last Humanist                     103
      *Ian Watt*

14    "You're Only a Rebel From the Waist                  115
      Downwards": Orwell's View of Women
      *Anne K. Mellor*

15    Television and Telescreen                            126
      *Martin Esslin*

16    Smokey Bear as Big Brother                           139
      *Marion Lewenstein*

## IV FREEDOM IS SLAVERY

17    For the Love of Big Brother: The Sexual              148
      Politics of *Nineteen Eighty-Four*
      *Paul Robinson*

18    Zamyatin's *We* and *Nineteen Eighty-Four*           159
      *Edward J. Brown*

19    The Proles of Airstrip One                           170
      *Gerald Dorfman*

20    Totaliterror                                         177
      *Robert Conquest*

21    Big Brother is Watching You                          188
      *Alexander Dallin*

22 Mind Control: Political Fiction and                      197
     Psychological Reality
     *Philip G. Zimbardo*

Reader's Guide                                               216

Appendix                                                     218

The Contributors                                            222

Credits                                                     226

# Preface

APPROACHING THE END OF HIS LIFE, Orwell wrote of the future. Even so, it is hard to believe he knew what was in store for his work, how much attention would be paid to it, and to himself, in 1984, the year that he chose for the title of the last book he would publish in his lifetime. Did he foresee that his novel would still be selling as well in 1984 as it did when it was first published thirty-four years ago—that it would become one of the best-selling books of the twentieth century? He may well have had some sense that it would continue to attract an ever widening audience.

*Animal Farm*, his brilliant fable about the perversion of socialism in Stalin's Russia, had been published in 1945. The success of that book, which over the years has sold more than ten million copies in Britain and America, not to mention sales in numerous translations, transformed Orwell from a moderately well-known English literary figure into one of the best-known writers in the modern world. The publication of *Nineteen Eighty-Four* in June 1949 compounded his fame and fortune. Unfortunately, he did not have long to enjoy his great success: he died in January 1950 of tuberculosis, at only 47.

He wrote most of *Nineteen Eighty-Four* during 1948 and simply reversed those last two digits when searching for a title. In America, its initial hardback printing was 244,000 copies. Since then, in the United States alone, more than ten million copies of the mass-market paperback—now in its sixty-fifth printing—are in circulation. A new edition has just appeared with a preface by the antithesis of Big Brother, Walter Cronkite.

Even for those who have not read *Nineteen Eighty-Four*, the title alone carries with it a suggestion of fear, of the monolithic state, of totalitarianism, of a deeply unpleasant world that we do not wish to see. The essays that follow attempt to make concrete that vague awareness of the book and to examine why *Nineteen Eighty-Four* has become one of the seminal books of our time— and what it has to do with our present world. The differing, and even opposing, interpretations presented in this collection demonstrate the complexity and richness of this extraordinary work and the power of its continuing influence on contemporary thought.

It is deeply impressive to find how powerful the novel still is and, while it is a warning rather than a prophecy, how much it has to do with our contemporary world. Its "relevance" is not merely a matter of its date now being upon us. It is a serious and terrifying book, and its continuing popularity attests to our receptivity to its warnings. It has helped alert us to the dangers of the all-pervasive and controlling state, and to rulers who wish to maintain power as much for its own sake as for their own advantage.

I thank Miriam Miller, the editor of the Portable Stanford, and her assistant, Laura Ackerman-Shaw, for their intelligence and diligence in turning a collection of essays into a book.

Peter Stansky
Stanford, 1983

George Orwell. BBC copyright photograph.

# I
# THE BOOK, THE MAN, THE YEAR

# 1 William Abrahams

# Nineteen Eighty-Four: The Novel

*It was a bright cold day in April, and the clocks were striking thirteen.*

ON MAY 31, 1941, a month after George Orwell had left London for a farm-house on the Isle of Jura, off the coast of Scotland, where he proposed to live thereafter—though one is tempted to say "where he proposed to die," since a less suitable climate for someone suffering from tuberculosis, as Orwell was, would have been hard to come upon—he wrote to his publisher, Frederic Warburg, "I have made a fairly good start on the book [*Nineteen Eighty-Four*] and I think I must have written nearly a third of the rough draft. . . . I don't like talking about books before they are written, but I will tell you now that this is a novel about the future—that is, it is in a sense a fantasy, but in the form of a naturalistic novel. That is what makes it a difficult job—of course as a book of anticipation it would be comparatively simple to write."

Novelists are not always the best critics of their own work, but in this instance Orwell had singled out early a difficulty that troubled him and that he never resolved to his own satisfaction. He sent the book to Warburg in December 1948, after a heroic struggle against worsening health, continuing pain, weeks in hospital, treatments with powerful, debilitating medications, not to speak of all the concomitant demands upon him that made the act of writing *Nineteen Eighty-Four* so extraordinary a feat in itself. This difficulty, of which he spoke so early, is one that may be recognized, or perhaps simply felt, by those coming to the book for the first time, and even by committed Orwellians returning to it for rereading—the divergence between the realistic and imaginative elements that coexist but are only seldom fused within the structure of the novel.

We are dealing here (in the summer of 1983) with "a novel about the future" that in less than a year will have become a novel of the present (coinciding with its title), and a year further into the future will have become a novel of the past—which to some degree it already was when Orwell was writing it in 1948; he could, with some justification, have titled it *Nineteen Forty-Five*. Relevance is where one finds it; here, unexpectedly, is a portion of a sentence from the obituary written in 1976 by Sir Michael Tippett for his fellow composer Benjamin Britten: "He [Britten] had to consider very seriously the question of the economics of opera in modern society, or rather the society of that time, 1945, just after the war, when as far as England was concerned, it was *a period of impoverishment*." (Italics added.) It was precisely that sense of impoverishment, of seediness and deprivation, of a greyness, sadness, drabness, and emptiness of the spirit, that Orwell projected as the atmosphere in his fantasy of the future, and which he had already projected in his novels of the 1930s, *A Clergyman's Daughter*, *Keep the Aspidistra Flying*, and *Coming Up for Air*.

That was the element he breathed as a realistic novelist, and it imparts to *Nineteen Eighty-Four* its tone of truth suffered at first hand. But imagination, so essential to a fantasist, was never Orwell's strong suit, and his difficulties in that line were compounded by a determination not to write merely a book of "anticipation." New readers, allured by its title and fame, and expecting a novel of things-to-come done up in futuristic, chrome-and-neon, super sci-fi style, will inevitably feel let down by a quintessential, deliberate greyness. This is not 1984 as the wonderworkers of the movies would have it: where are the robots and the rocket ships?

There was a further difficulty that he would attempt to deal with both before and after publication, a question that has continued to fuel the Orwell industry ever since: What did he intend the book to be? A novel of the future, of course; but as we have learned from the ever growing army of commentators, so often at war with each other, that is a phrase that can be made to mean virtually whatever one wants. Only a few weeks after Orwell had sent off the manuscript to Secker and Warburg, he was formulating an answer to the question for Roger Senhouse, a director of the firm: "As to the blurb, I really don't think the approach in the draft you sent me is the right one. It makes the book sound as if it were a thriller mixed up with a love story, & I didn't intend it to be primarily that. What it is really meant to do is to discuss the implications of dividing the world up into Zones of influence. . . . "

The notion of the world divided up among three superpowers—Oceania (the United States with Britain in a subordinate position), Eurasia (continental Europe under Russian domination), and Eastasia (presumably an all-encompassing Greater China)—is one of Orwell's best-known anticipations in *Nineteen Eighty-Four*, along with Newspeak, Big Brother, Thought Police, and the twenty-four-hour presence of the telescreen. It is a curious fact that in the actual texture of the novel Eurasia and Eastasia hardly figure. There are no

Russian, Chinese, or even (as one might expect) American characters; and the only part of Oceania to which attention is paid is Britain (or as it has become in the jargon of Newspeak, Airstrip One) and its drab, dreadful capital city, London, forever watched over from billboards and telescreens by a leader who may or not exist, the Stalin-like Big Brother.

This background is done in Orwell's best realistic manner, and its anticipations, inspired by their beginnings in a period of impoverishment, are brought to a logical grim conclusion. Whatever was most valuable, humane, civilized, decent, and irreplaceably, characteristically English has been reduced to the point of nonexistence. Power has become an end in itself, sought after and claimed by an invisible minority, under whom live and partly live the bureaucratic servants of the state. Together, they make up the privileged classes, the Inner and Outer Parties. Under them, so far under as to be almost unnoticeable—no matter that they are everywhere—are the proles, the members of the working class with a remnant of working-class virtues and forgivable vices—drinking beer, singing immemorial music hall tunes, and indulging in a bit of fornication, an activity specifically forbidden to the ruling classes. (Oddly, no one from the prole class is allowed an important part in the action of the novel—oddly, because we are made to understand that if there is a hope of salvation for this doomed world of the future, it would be with the proles.)

Granting, then, the irreproachable working out of the background—no matter that in real life, on the threshold of 1984, this anticipation of London couldn't be more off the mark—it seems fair all the same to observe that in a novel, even a fantasy of the future, background is not everything. In the foreground there shall be characters, who will act out their story, and in so doing give a kind of life to their creator's abstract theme and intention. Without Winston Smith, Julia, and O'Brien, its three principal characters, *Nineteen Eighty-Four* might have taken its place as an early polemic against totalitarianism and its consequences, of interest primarily to historians and ideologues; with their presence in a plot that horrifies us even as it rivets our attention, in spite of or perhaps because of its affinities both to a thriller and to a love story, it has become one of the most widely read novels of our time.

Yet it is not sacrosanct, and I think it worthwhile to inquire why, for all its immense and deserved popularity, and its limitless extraliterary interest, it falls short, perhaps *had* to fall short, of being a work of art of classic stature.

It begins with the assurance of a master realist:

> It was a bright cold day in April, and the clocks were striking thirteen. Winston Smith, his chin nuzzled into his breast in an effort to escape the vile wind, slipped quickly through the glass doors of Victory Mansions, though not quickly enough to prevent

a swirl of gritty dust from entering along with him.

The hallway smelt of boiled cabbage and old rag mats. . . .

Orwellians will recognize the terrain: we are in Orwell country—the vile wind and the smell of boiled cabbage are familiar landmarks. What is new here, and introduces us to the future, is the poster that stares at Winston at each landing, as he climbs the seven flights of stairs to his flat. "On each landing, opposite the lift shaft, the poster with the enormous face gazed from the wall. It was one of those pictures which are so contrived that the eyes follow you about when you move. BIG BROTHER IS WATCHING YOU, the caption beneath it ran."

Winston's name has a heroic ring—a reminder that he was born in the last year of the Second World War when babies were still being named for the Savior of Britain—though little else about him is heroic. He is thirty-nine, smallish, frail, "with a varicose ulcer above his right ankle," employed in the misnamed Ministry of Truth, where his job is the rewriting of newspapers to conform to changes in the international or national policies of Oceania. He has some vague memories from childhood of his mother and sister, who disappeared in the purges; fewer memories of his wife Katharine, from whom he'd separated after they had lived together for only fifteen months. Verging on middle age, he is a type of the colorless, minor civil servant who does what he is told to do—always. But on this day in April, he commits his tiny, brave act of defiance—he starts to keep a diary, even though he knows that the punishment for doing so is death, and it is very likely that he will be found out. Emboldened by his first step toward disaster, he takes yet another. Ever so gingerly at first, then ever more bravely, he draws closer to Julia, who also works in the Ministry, literally cranking out novels in the Fiction Department. Twelve years younger than Winston, she too is a secret rebel against the regime, expressing her rebellion through illegal enjoyment of sex. In due time, and inevitably, she and Winston embark upon an affair—also a crime against the state. They arrange for a secret trysting place in a room over an antique store owned by kindly, elderly Mr. Charrington, a survivor of the old regime who remembers it in fragments—a clutter of bright bits and pieces, like his shop itself.

To this point, reality and fantasy have been skillfully matched: in these first hundred or so pages Orwell has mastered the difficult task he has set for himself. But now O'Brien enters, and with him comes the acrid whiff of melodrama. For O'Brien is patently a higher-up in the Party. Nonetheless we are asked to believe that Winston, on the basis of an exchange of glances, a friendly touch on the arm, discerns in O'Brien a secret enemy of the state. They talk in pregnant phrases under the eye of the telescreen. Presently it is arranged that Winston and Julia shall visit O'Brien in his luxurious flat. There they are served drinks by his mysterious houseboy and told the secrets of the Brotherhood, a subversive underground organization, by O'Brien himself. But whereas Winston has the plausibility of a character one might have observed in life, and is invested with those minute particulars that transform a stereotype into an individual, O'Brien comes from stock—a man who smiles and smiles and yet is a villain. One suspects all too soon, as the confidences flow, and there are toasts to the past, which is in the process of being officially wiped out, that his friendship will lead to the undoing of both Winston and Julia. And so ultimately it proves.

O'Brien, having enrolled them in the Brotherhood, has arranged that a copy of the most forbidden of books, *The Theory and Practice of Oligarchical Collectivism*, by the archenemy of the state, Goldstein (Orwell's Trotsky-figure), shall be put into Winston's hands. One afternoon, in the room above the antique shop, waiting for Julia, he begins to read. On one level, the text itself, occupying some thirty pages of the novel, is a masterly pastiche of sociopolitical, quasi-Marxist writing, but on another level it is a massive miscalculation, utterly destructive to the verisimilitude of fiction. Julia arrives, Winston puts the book down, they make love. Then, as their passion subsides, he chooses to read aloud the Goldstein text from page one. Perhaps not surprisingly, Julia falls asleep; it is the one comic scene in the novel. Presently the Thought Police come streaming in to arrest them, "solid men in black uniforms with ironshod boots on their feet and truncheons in their hands." A moment later, their leader enters, who turns out to be kindly old Mr. Charrington: it is a touch worthy of Alfred Hitchcock.

The third and final part of the novel describes in harrowing detail Winston's suffering at the hands of the smiling O'Brien, who is now revealed as an *agent provocateur*. His aim, as he proceeds methodically from torture to torture, quite simply is to persuade Winston to abandon his attempt to be free, and to yield entirely and unquestioningly to the state. His ultimate threat is that if Winston refuses, he will be sent to the fateful Room 101. There he will be forced to undergo whatever he fears most in this world. A cage filled with rats is ready to be strapped to his face, and the door of the cage opened. . . .

Orwell's friend Julian Symons, in an anonymous review of the novel in the *Times Literary Supplement*, had much that was good to say of it, but complained of a "schoolboyish sensationalism of approach," especially in these scenes in Room 101. Orwell did not appear to be offended. He wrote Symons on June 16, 1949, "I must thank you for such a brilliant as well as a generous review. I don't think you could have brought out the sense of the book better in so short a space. You are of course right about the vulgarity of the 'Room 101' business. I was aware of this while writing it, but I didn't know of another way of getting somewhere near the effect I wanted."

One ventures to think that Orwell had proposed a task for which no satisfactory solution was available. Reality and fantasy are more likely to

June 19, 1949 ad for *Nineteen Eighty-Four.*

unite in a seamless whole in comedy than tragedy. *Alice in Wonderland*, yes. But the world of *Nineteen Eighty-Four* is essentially tragic; the vision that inspired it is tragic; the attempt to recapture it, heroic; the achievement, however flawed, remarkable. There are certain novels, and this is surely one of them, that become totems in their time: invulnerable to reproaches and criticism. Such, I suspect, is the fate and fame of *Nineteen Eighty-Four*.

# 2 *Peter Stansky*

# Orwell: The Man

*"To the Past," said Winston.*

GEORGE ORWELL WAS BORN ON June 25, 1903, in Motihari in Bengal as Eric Arthur Blair. His father was a civil servant in the Opium Department of the government of India, and Eric Blair was born into the class of those who helped rule, in a modest way, so much of the world on behalf of Britain. Like Winston Smith, the hero of *Nineteen Eighty-Four*, Orwell's father was a servant of an empire.

At the time of Eric's birth, England was at the height of its power—the Empire would actually be larger after the First World War, but it would never again be so self-assured. The Blairs were able to lead a grand life in India, as part of the ruling class, and even when Mr. Blair retired, they were not too badly off back in the Home Country. Orwell was prone to exaggerate the low financial status of his family, but his characteristically exact self-description—"lower-upper-middle class"—nevertheless places him in the very small top percentage of any population.

Orwell would appear to have had a fairly ordinary childhood, growing up in Henley-on-Thames, a pleasant riverside town, famous for its annual regatta, mixing with the "better sort" of children. As happened to most boys of his class in England, he was sent away to boarding school at the age of eight, in 1911. St. Cyprian's, on the south coast, was one of the best in the country. The Blairs could not afford the tuition, but the proprietors of the school took some boys on reduced fees in the belief that they would go on to win scholarships to grand "public schools" such as Eton and Wellington and thus enhance the reputation of the school. And so Orwell did. But at a great psychic price.

The experience of boarding school was, at least to some degree, a formative influence upon him and ultimately upon the making of *Nineteen Eighty-Four*, and so was the reading that he did there. Like most "advanced" schoolboys of the time, he was a devotee of H.G. Wells—he would stay up late at night reading Wells, hiding his flashlight under the bedclothes. Wells, a leading science fiction writer and projector of utopias, helped shape Orwell's own great *anti*-utopia. And there is a nice irony in the fact that the son of H.G. Wells and Rebecca West, Anthony West, is the leading proponent of the theory that the world of *Nineteen Eighty-Four* is Orwell's revenge upon his society for forcing him to go through the traumatic experience of boarding school. His aim in the book, according to West, is to send the world to St. Cyprian's. Orwell's memoir of the school—"Such, Such Were the Joys"—was written in the 1940s, when he was also writing his two bitter fables, *Animal Farm* and *Nineteen Eighty-Four*. In that essay-memoir, he does indeed present the school as a totalitarian system in which rewards and punishments were likely to depend on the whims of the headmaster, and particularly on the headmaster's wife.

It may seem minor compared with the great effect of Orwell's reaction to Soviet totalitarianism, but this early experience of dealing with a capricious "total" system is an important factor in shaping the nightmare vision of the book we are considering. Orwell also tells us that at this school he became convinced of his worthlessness—a counterpart to the sense of emptiness that Winston Smith has at the end of *Nineteen Eighty-Four*.

On the other hand, it does not do to exaggerate, and during these years Orwell was also well educated and imbued with a love of England that never left him—a consequence of his reading, his wandering over the Sussex downs to the sea, his experiencing the beauty of the south of England, that complacent, powerful land. Unlike many of those on the Left in the 1930s, he never lost this love of country, as captured in an essay written in the autumn of 1940, "My Country, Right or Left." His love of England, and his desire that it not become a totalitarian system, were the driving forces behind *Nineteen Eighty-Four*.

What other elements in his life shaped this book that has become embedded in our consciousness? As Ian Watt points out in the pages that follow, Orwell's education at St. Cyprian's and later at Eton accomplished its primary purposes: it infused him with a love and command of language and reinforced that sense of authority found among the English upper classes. The written record is important, and Winston Smith spends his time rewriting that canonical newspaper of England, the *Times*, so that it conforms to the party line of the moment. Orwell had an intense pleasure in language. Some of his most famous essays are on the need to protect language from jargon, and on the political power of language. That concern culminates in the role of Newspeak in the novel. There is even a certain compulsive literary quality in Winston Smith's work, as he uses language to pervert the truth. Orwell knew that language was sacred to the preservation of truth and culture and that those who control the word can control the past, present, and future. It is the word that is England's primary "art form" and the one in which Orwell excelled.

Orwell was different from many writers in that he had a more direct experience of the role of power in this world. In large part that was because of the unusual step that his career took after Eton: he became a policeman—a police officer of the Indian Imperial Police in Burma, the "Cinderella" province. In a sense he was going into the "family business," and turning back to the modest attainments of his father rather than to the university education and further advancement that his time at St. Cyprian's and Eton had prepared him for. But in the Empire, as a police officer, he exercised power and experienced the irrationality of power—the need to demonstrate power merely to preserve the face of the Empire. (This principle is dramatically illustrated in his famous essay "Shooting an Elephant.") His imperial experience taught him the need of the state for outward conformity, both on the part of its servants, such as himself, and on the part of those whom they ruled. His political experiences in the 1930s would teach him the dangers of inner conformity.

His return to England on leave from Burma in 1927 was also a return to his earlier compulsion to be a writer. He determined to devote himself to literature. These were bleak years that became only marginally better upon the publication of his first book, *Down and Out in Paris and London*, in 1933. Under his newly chosen pseudonym, this first book records his experiences as a tramp in England and a dishwasher in Paris—a first step toward the portrayal of the ugliness of existence in the anti-utopia that was to be his final book.

Although it is not particularly relevant to *Nineteen Eighty-Four*, some mention should be made of the fact that he adopted George Orwell as a pen name. He never legally changed his name—he said to his friend Anthony Powell that if he did so he would then have to find a new writing name—but increasingly he became known to friends that he made in the late 1930s and beyond as George Orwell, and signed letters to them as such. But his legal name remained Eric Arthur Blair, and his tombstone in the small Thames-side village of Sutton Courtenay is so inscribed.

Later commentators have made much of the significance of the name: George, the quintessence of an English name, and Orwell, a river in East Anglia, emphasizing its Englishness. So, too, Winston Smith can be seen as the essence of an English name: Winston taken from Winston Churchill, the lion who had done so much to win the Second World War, concluded in the year that Winston was born, and Smith, standing for everyman. Orwell gradually built up a small but solid reputation as a novelist, although he made very little money by it. And he was rapidly using up the autobiographical capital which went into his books.

Desperate world events conspired to bring him—perhaps reluctantly—to politics, so that he became one of the most influential political writers of this century. The grimness of his literary vision was being matched by outside events—the Depression and the rise of fascism. Victor Gollancz, the publisher, sent him on a trip to the north of England to look into local conditions caused by the Depression. The result, in 1937, was one of Orwell's most powerful books. *The Road to Wigan Pier*, the account of that journey, depicts both the desperate situation of the unemployed and the solid virtues of the English working class. In the second part of the book, Orwell, acting as the devil's advocate, points out the weaknesses of English Socialists while at the same time asserting his belief in a socialist society. Here too one sees a prefigurement of *Nineteen Eighty-Four*—the case for socialism put in a negative way by showing how it could go wrong, which has caused the novel frequently to be taken, against Orwell's intentions, as an antisocialist tract.

But it was events in Spain that made Orwell truly a socialist. The Spanish Civil War had broken out on July 18, 1936, while he was in the midst of writing up his experiences in the north of England. When he was free, in December, he went to Spain and discovered in Barcelona what he regarded as a socialist paradise, and a state for which he was happy to fight. This was a brief moment when he saw what an ideal world could be like. It unleashed his genius, and was crucial in bringing about the great flowering of his essays and their defense of democratic socialism and the two books by which he is chiefly remembered, *Animal Farm* and *Nineteen Eighty-Four*. But his vision of the ideal socialist society in Spain was betrayed by Stalinist elements on the Left who were primarily interested in power. They manipulated the press to support their claim that the group with which Orwell was fighting—the anti-Stalinist semi-Trotskyist Workers' Party of Marxist Unification, the POUM—were secret fascist agents rather than fighters for the Republican cause. Orwell was deeply and lastingly outraged that a man risking his life on the front line, if he was a member of the POUM, might well be arrested and imprisoned as a fascist in Barcelona. It was that vision of a socialist state and its betrayal that provided the compelling force behind *Nineteen Eighty-Four*.

In the remaining years of his life, further experiences supplied material for the novel we are considering. As Martin Esslin suggests at the beginning of his essay, life at the BBC in the early years of the war furnished much of the atmosphere for the Ministry of Truth, and certainly the building housing the Ministry of Information—the Senate House of the University of London— served as the model for the external appearance of the Ministry. The austerity made necessary by the war, combined with the somewhat natural puritanism of Orwell and his wife, helped provide the grim atmosphere of the book.

The war reinforced the experience of Spain: he saw the honor and decency of ordinary people in their fight against Hitler. He felt that a socialist revolution would be necessary to win the war, but as the war progressed he recognized that the traditional powers in England, of which he was part by birth and training, could in fact win without the revolutionary change that he had both desired and thought essential.

When *Nineteen Eighty-Four* first appeared in the United States, the novelist and critic Mark Schorer reviewed it on the front page of the *New York Times Book Review* (June 12, 1949). He made one statement which the existence of this book of essays, among much other evidence, disproves: "[The book's] greatness [may be] only immediate, its power for us alone, now, in this generation, this decade, this year, that it is doomed to be the pawn of time." But he followed that sentence with one that is absolutely correct: "Nevertheless it is probable that no other work of this generation has made us desire freedom more earnestly or loathe tyranny with such fullness."

The text must stand on its own, but Orwell was in many ways an intensely autobiographical writer. He testified in his life and his work to the humane and civilized values that the society he depicts in *Nineteen Eighty-Four* is determined to destroy.

*Yalta Conference (From a History Textbook, 1984)* by Komar and Melamid, 1982-83. Courtesy of Ronald Feldman Fine Arts, New York.

# 3 *Alex Comfort*

# 1939 and 1984: George Orwell and the Vision of Judgment

*"We sure could have fascism here, but we'd have to call it antifascism. . . ."*
"Kingfish" Huey Long

MYTHS ARE NOT LIES: they are more often than not stylized representations of the truth, or of a part of it. They are also simpler to take in than history. For any major event—say the American Civil War—there is a corresponding file card in many people's minds. Those who lived through the event, if they were still here, would read the school books and say, "But it wasn't like that"—in vain.

The West's defeat of Hitler has formed a mythology of this kind, in which a reluctant and effete Europe, having been intimidated by the Nazis, and weakened by the antiwar burrowings of liberals, was finally shocked into response and led to victory by Churchill. It has the quality of good drama: the dithering Chamberlain, the traitor Pétain, and the awakening just in time. The story is true enough: the courage of civilians and servicemen, the Battle of Britain, and the "finest hour" were real enough—and a proper source of pride. The political picture was more complicated, as we know, and less edifying. There was indeed an antifascist war, but it sprang from grass-roots antifascism.

Americans in general did not recognize what was going on while it was going on; it is not surprising if they fail to recognize it now. I think that this is one reason why they are perplexed by George Orwell. A student of his work recently wrote to ask me why he was so "arrogant and vicious" toward opponents; she wanted help in understanding his "pigheadedness and rhetoric." None of these terms would have occurred to anyone who knew Orwell.

Arrogance, viciousness, and pigheadedness were not his trademark. Certainly he enjoyed giving good knocks, and taking a few himself, but even in an exchange of political abuse at long range, he could drop the polemic to praise my poem.

While he and I were trading verse polemics in *Tribune* on the subject of writers who gave their support to the Establishment and became "instant antifascists," official style, we were exchanging friendly letters. "I'm afraid," he wrote, "that I was rather rude to you in our *Tribune* set-to, but you yourself weren't exactly polite to certain people. I was only making a *political* and perhaps moral reply, and as a piece of verse your contribution was immensely better . . . there is no respect for virtuosity these days. You ought to write something longer in the same genre. . . ." Vicious and pigheaded? Hardly. Rather a man unsparing of himself, facing excruciating moral decisions (as we all were) in the dark; detesting fascism but afraid of a sellout by the Old Firm.

Orwell and I started off badly, in an exchange of letters in *Partisan Review* (May 1942)—I accusing him of intellectual-hunting, he accusing me, when I pointed out that adversity tended to produce great literature, of "hoping for a Nazi victory because of the stimulating effect it would have on the Arts." It is a sign of the times that we assaulted one another's positions before finding out exactly what they were. I probably mistook him for a hard-line Marxist, while he mistook me for another of Middleton Murry's equivocal disciples. When we got into direct correspondence, he showed not the slightest malice, though we had publicly misrepresented one another. Thereafter we started serious if intermittent discussion, first of literature, then of the War.

It has always struck me in rereading *Nineteen Eighty-Four* how very differently it must ring to readers in America, who did not live through all this—and to those in Europe who are too young to have lived through it—compared with those of us who shared the personal choices which Orwell was facing when he wrote it, and our fears about the likely course of European history. Of course we were scared by Nazism and Stalinism, but we were even more scared by the awareness that in our own bland, manipulative democracy there were termites in the floorboards, and that the floor was programmed to collapse under our own weight, not under Hitler's or Mosley's legions. If one was not there, or was not aware of these things, choices were simple: Chamberlain was a gentleman whose error in taking Hitler for a gentleman, though disastrous, was more naive than discreditable, and once war had been declared we were all comrades in an unpleasant but necessary task; *Nineteen Eighty-Four* was no more than a rather high-pitched warning against state socialism, with a particular dig at Stalin to remind us that he was an ally only of necessity. But that was not how it felt at the time—certainly not how it felt to Orwell when he was writing his bitter forecast of a possible world only forty-five years ahead. The props in *Nineteen Eighty-Four* come from the weaknesses of all societies, but the falling into place, which would bring 1984 upon us, depended on the conviction that there were those in all societies—not only in Russia or Germany—who were mining their way toward a cancellation of European humane civilization.

I counted Orwell as a friend, but he was a friend by post, for I met him only once, in a pub in Bermondsey soon after he had published *Nineteen Eighty-Four* and I had published *The Powerhouse*. I was resident medical officer at the Royal Waterloo Hospital, and I was shocked to see how ill he looked. We talked about his book, which I took to be a political statement against dictatorship. His reply was astonishing—that it was, but that the model in his mind was also that of the neurotic's internal "thought police," with Big Brother as the superego. I asked him if the two weren't the same, but he told me he had no use for psychoanalysis. I don't recall what else was said— I was too busy fitting the pattern of Orwell's intention together. Did he have a private "thought police"? I didn't feel that that was what he meant. The sense I got from his writings was of a man who detested violence—but found it perpetually unavoidable if tyranny was to be resisted—and was agonizing over where we were going. He had fought in Spain, and would have fought Hitler if he had not been terminally ill, but the sight of plump Conservatives spouting antifascism set off all his warning lights.

He was not alone in this. British hatred of Nazism was both deep and inflexible, but it was grass-roots hatred, expressed in the doggedness which civilians displayed under attack. It was this grass-roots antifascism which Churchill embodied, with immense political effect, but Churchill did not invent it—he played along with it, and may indeed have shared it. It was difficult at the time to forget that not long before he had hailed Mussolini as the savior of Europe. Well, we all make mistakes. What is hard to convey, given the concentration on the myth of British resistance to tyranny, is the profound sense which liberals had of something afoot, of impending treason. We did not know then of the Nazi overtures for British neutrality, but we smelled them. Knowing who was at the top, and what their form had been, it was impossible not to be paranoid about the glibness of their conversion: Eden, who had stonewalled over "non-intervention" in Spain, before he resigned over Abyssinia; Halifax, who hoped to turn Hitler round and point him at Stalin, "letting Fascism and Communism destroy each other."

What exactly, modern writers on Orwell wonder when they read our letters, were we going on about? To experience the climate in which we were writing one would have to immerse oneself in the newspapers, broadcasts, literary articles, and dubious personalities of 1942—John Middleton Murry, for example, who professed pacifism but opined that Hitler was "doing God's dirty work." He was the prototypic "Fascifist" whom Orwell denounced, unpleasantly reminiscent of the religious right-wingers whom we had seen in action in Spain and later in Pétain France. There was the conventional Left, much of it still taking the Party line. There were political anarchists like myself. And there was the mass of liberal opinion, deeply disturbed if not frightened, detesting the growing tide of fascist barbarity, but even more disturbed by a gut feeling that there was dirty work going on nearer home. They were relieved by the "phoney war"—at least we had not been bombed to hell and back yet. But what were all those old British acquaintances of Ribbentrop in high places, suddenly spouting antifascist rhetoric, really up to? It was as if Jerry Falwell were to open a Christian abortion clinic—unbelievable.

Orwell and I argued this, and fought it out in print. His position, like that of many another man of peace, was that Hitler had to be fought, even if the leadership doing the fighting was flawed, and had nearly blundered into war on Hitler's side when Russia invaded Finland. Mine was that no government—least of all the one we had then—could be trusted to fight a war of principle; that war *per se*, because it let Nazism choose the weapons and the battlefield, would by its own logic turn into genocide—very possibly leaving the roots of Nazism intact, to sprout as "gallant allies" in another bout of atrocity; and, fundamentally, that no man could safely trust his arms or his conscience to a government. Orwell saw the argument but thought that its only effect would be to weaken resistance in the West; it was a moral luxury we could not afford. The debate was urgent, and it was a moral debate on which positions had to be taken—Hitler was on the other side of the Channel. It was also a debate in which not everything could be said, because to have laid out the alternative to conventional war—namely a sudden and well-planned take out of Hitler and as many of his gang as possible—would have telegraphed the punch to the point of uselessness, and possibly blown an operation actually in train. (The Nazi leadership had the engaging habit of standing in a row at parades like ducks in a shooting gallery.) Accordingly, what was written was muffled. Moreover we were all being careful—enemies closer than Hitler might well be listening.

In a recent article (*Harper's*, December 1982) Norman Podhoretz argues that if Orwell were alive today he would support the New Right, and fight against the burrowings of the same dangerous liberals, who today oppose Reaganoia and nuclear arsenals. Possibly—and possibly not. It is all strangely familiar. The ineducable Right still thinks that fascist thuggery is a venial aberration if it can be used to destroy Marxist tyranny. That was not a conviction which Orwell shared.

II

Looking back at the argument I had with Orwell, and at the background of *Nineteen Eighty-Four*, and trying to remember what we knew, did not know, and what we suspected at the time, I found a sudden and striking source of information in an unexpected place—F. W. Winterbotham's book, *The Ultra*

*Secret*. Winterbotham was the senior Air Staff representative in Secret Intelligence through the prewar Hitler years. The impact of his book lay, of course, in its revelation of the way in which the breaking of the German Enigma Code kept the Allies constantly briefed on Nazi intentions, and very possibly turned the military scale. The revelations that struck me most forcibly, however, were incidental, if not accidental; in the light of our recollections of 1940, there were things here that we were able to decode.

Two striking pieces of information emerge. One is that Winterbotham himself was running around Germany in the mid-thirties in the cover of a Nazi sympathizer (which he emphatically was not), hearing personally from Hitler, Rosenberg, Hess, and von Reichenau the complete prospectus of Nazi plans. Hitler's "basic belief was that the only hope for an ordered world was that it should be ruled by three superpowers, the British Empire, the Greater Americas and the Greater German Reich. He gave me an assurance that the Germans themselves would destroy the Communists by the conquest of Russia," he writes. In this enterprise he was counting on British neutrality. Winterbotham, of course, reported this important intelligence to a Cabinet committee in 1935. So Chamberlain, it now appears, must have gone to Munich with his eyes wide open.

The "myth of Munich," actively propagated today by the Right, is that the blindness of the Chamberlain Government arose from misguided pacifism. The overwhelming likelihood, as it now appears, and as men like Orwell saw it then, is that it arose from deliberate collusion—not blindness but policy, if not treason. Whether Chamberlain was a dupe of others or a co-conspirator with them matters very little. Much of the record is still unavailable; as recently as March 1983 the British government was still engaged in contortions to prevent the release of the interrogation of the British Nazi Oswald Mosley to the public record. The likelihood is that Mosley not only named names, but knew the terms of the secret understanding whereby Britain was to remain neutral while Hitler "liquidated Bolshevism."

The Russians outplayed the conspirators. The Hitler-Stalin Pact seems to have been a desperate play to split the Hitler-Chamberlain entente, which paid off. Confusion of counsel and disarray in the Cabinet persisted throughout the phoney war. The Hess mission—Hitler's final attempt to contact his cohorts in England—miscarried, and World War II began in earnest. The myth of Munich was highly necessary; one does not secure national unity against invasion by staging treason trials, or exposing moles in the Cabinet. The moles were silenced, or burrowed deeper: the history of the Munich years was papered over as the lamentable weakness of decent men. But at the same time there was a price to pay for national survival: "the Project," the liquidation of Bolshevism, still kept its proponents throughout Western power structures, and Stalin knew it—whence postwar history.

It makes sense: Austria, Czechoslovakia, Poland, and the neutralization of France had to be conceded if Hitler was to deliver on the Project. When Stalin threatened mate, the Project had to be suspended: our torpedo was out of control and threatening to sink us. Churchill, who had never been privy to the conspiracy, and whose sense of national interest was sharp, joined hands with the Red Army. The moles brushed off their ruffled fur and got ready for the next round.

That is how many of us assessed the situation—not now, forty years on— but then. Among those who saw it in 1940 was George Orwell. It was an agonizing choice: if we hated dictatorship, a Hitler victory was unthinkable; but a Stalin victory might be the price of frustrating him. We could not say what we thought for fear of bringing one of two intolerable conclusions nearer to reality. One could not opt for the "antifascist war"—though Orwell eventually did so on grounds of clear and present peril—without realizing that buried within the "antifascist" leadership was the personnel of the Project, waiting their chance to renew their aims, to pick up and spirit away the von Brauns and the Klaus Barbies to a milieu where they could be controlled, to set up the board again, with a divided Europe as the sand table for the next war game. Stalin saw it, and set about surrounding the USSR with provinces, denying the Project bases on its borders. The scene was set for Europe outside his orbit to panic, and to accept client status itself, and American bases, through collusion rather than force. That was where we came in. That is where we are now. That would be the background for any choice an Orwell would have to make in 1983, and it would seem painfully familiar.

Informing *Nineteen Eighty-Four* was the blinding awareness that in 1940 parliamentary democracy, the conservative establishment, all the furniture of the political room in which we had been brought up, were wormy. Orwell had no love of these institutions, judged by their performance, but he was as profoundly English as was Churchill, and Englishness imposes rules even on revolution. In sum, I think that for all his distaste for the establishment, and his awareness of its familiar forms of corruption, he had not thought it could be corrupt *in this way*, that it could actually sell out to Nazis. Even a writer as abrasive as Orwell, and as hostile to privilege, was capable of being shocked by treason. He would have been the last person to agree that politics were governed by the rules of cricket, but the unconscious assumption remained that the "bosses," the opposition, though they might commit barbarities, weren't cannibals. If that were not so, if there were now *no* limits to what Tory Britain would do to defeat change, then we were headed for political Gehenna. Churchill and Orwell make odd bedfellows, but I think that Churchill, when he too confronted the evidence as to what members of His Majesty's Government had been up to, was equally blasted by it. Things *were* falling apart, the center could not hold, and if so, the Rough Beast was on its way.

Americans like to read *Nineteen Eighty-Four* as a nightmare based on

Stalinism. To some extent it is; but Orwell's novel of Soviet Communism is *Animal Farm*. *Nineteen Eighty-Four* is rather an extrapolation of the state of Europe, and probably America, if the Project had succeeded. Unlike novels about Britain under Nazi occupation, which play up the familiar horrors, Orwell's book looks further ahead—forty years ahead—to a period when the obvious excesses had exhausted themselves, when fascism had acquired a populist, if not a human, face, and some public relations gloss; when the Old Guard would have come out of hiding, when the survivors of the establishment, British and Soviet, the privileged and the apparatchiks, would have changed sides and backed the winner—and when consumerism and high-tech would have replaced goons and gas chambers as instruments of social control.

This is a scenario far more frightening than occupation movies. A pro-Hitler Britain would not have looked like occupied Poland—or not for long. Every European right-wing party (including Stalin's) is by tradition an alliance of two elements, masters and goons, "snobbos" and "yobbos." The first uses the second—Chamberlain and Pétain and the Junker aristocracy were the snobbo or establishment element, Hitler and Mussolini the yobbo. In the second phase of counterrevolution, yobbos turn on snobbos, as Hitler turned on the Prussian and Wehrmacht establishment. Ultimately snobbo and yobbo destroy each other, leaving only the indestructible apparatchiks (who take over both the privileges of masters and the coercive apparatus of the goons) and we have the society of *Nineteen Eighty-Four*—glossy but coercive, a gigantic pretense. Hybridize the coerciveness and bureaucracy of Andropov's Russia with the glossiness and rhetoric of Reagan's America, and you have *Nineteen Eighty-Four*. If Hitler had won, this marriage might have been consummated.

By 1984 the dust would have settled. Snobbo and yobbo alike would have been absorbed into a new political technocracy. The Jews and the Gypsies would have been long dead, unlamented by the new men, as they were by the antifascist Western cabinets who fought Hitler and saw the Holocaust as a deplorable business—which should not be stopped for fear of unleashing a "flood of undesirable immigrants" (see M. Gilbert, *Auschwitz and the Allies*). Nazism, Stalinism, and possibly neo-capitalism would have merged, history would have been rewritten, the traditions of democracy and of revolution alike would have been expunged—and with them humane civilization.

This vision, to my mind, is both more realisitic and more frightening than accounts of a German occupation of Britain modeled on the occupation of Poland or the Ukraine. The mythical view of Munich and the early days of World War II deprives *Nineteen Eighty-Four* both of its context at the time it was written—when it was still a toss-up whether the British establishment would conspire with Hitler or fight him—and also of its prescience: *Nineteen Eighty-Four* has not arrived in 1984, but the danger is postponed, not canceled, and many of its features are partly in place—nukespeak instead of Newspeak, politics conducted as a manipulated media event. There are some things even Orwell did not foresee; he could have made Big Brother a Christian fundamentalist ayatollah and verisimilitude would not have been strained.

It is easy enough to expand on the political homiletics of *Nineteen Eighty-Four*. My point is rather that in reading it we need to experience the world as it was when Orwell cast his mind forward to 1984. Indeed, in the fudging of the record and the myth of the West as a sleeping giant finally and unanimously aroused to resist fascism, *Nineteen Eighty-Four* is brought a little closer. The forces which were active in 1939 and 1940 are neither dead nor sleeping, and we have let them rewrite history as Orwell feared they would.

# II
# WAR IS PEACE

# 4 *Gordon A. Craig*

# Triangularity and International Violence

*Even after enormous upheavals and seemingly irrevocable changes, the same pattern has always reasserted itself, just as a gyroscope will always return to equilibrium, however far it is pushed one way or the other.*

THE PROTAGONIST OF GEORGE ORWELL'S NOVEL *Nineteen Eighty-Four* lives in London, the chief city of Airstrip One, the third most populous of the provinces of Oceania. He does not seem to know very much about the other provinces or, for that matter, about the outside world in general, except that there are two other Great Powers called Eastasia and Eurasia, and that Oceania is perpetually in conflict with one or the other. It is only when Winston Smith turns to conspiracy against his government and is permitted to read a secret book presumably written by another conspirator, the elusive Goldstein, that he learns that the relationship between his own country and the others is more complicated than he had imagined. He discovers, in fact, that Oceania is part of a highly developed international system which, despite the violence that it condones, operates with a considerable degree of efficiency. Because Winston has no historical memory, he is incapable of doing anything but marvel at his discovery. We are in a better position to look at the Goldsteinian world system from a comparative perspective and to note its superiority in some marked respects to historical models.

## II

Since ancient times, tribes, organized communities, and states have sought to regulate their relationships with their neighbors in such a way as to assure their own safety and material advantage. When they have had confidence in their superiority in numbers, weaponry, and resources, they have tended to rely upon conquest and dominion, either destroying their victims or imposing their own laws and institutions upon them. When, on the other hand, their neighbors have possessed sufficient power to defend themselves and to inflict heavy damage upon aggressors, political arrangements have taken the place of violence, and these have assumed various forms ranging from armed truce and bilateral treaties to leagues and federations.

In the world of the modern national state, these experiments have often taken the form of elaborate international systems, based upon formal and tacit agreement, and defining, and establishing procedures to enforce, rules of intercourse or norms of behavior. The purpose of such systems has usually been to restrain the propensity of their members to violence, and the means to this end has been the principle of balance of power. As a recognized modality of statecraft, consciously applied, balance of power is generally considered to have come into existence during the Renaissance, when it served as a regulating principle in the endless contentions of the Italian city-states. But the methods of Italian statecraft were in the course of the sixteenth century transmitted to the stronger national states of the West and were soon animating their own tentative efforts to establish a basis of international order; and their experience has in turn been passed on to us.

Over the centuries, balance of power systems have varied in comprehensiveness, normative scope, and the nature and effectiveness of sanctions. In fifteenth-century Italy, the Papacy and the most powerful of the city-states (Venice, Milan, Florence), while showing little restraint in their attacks upon lesser neighbors, maintained an equilibrium of force among themselves by studiously refraining from encroaching upon each other's territories, and at the same time avoiding any alliances with external powers (France, Spain, the Empire) that might induce them to intervene in Italian politics. In the eighteenth century, Great Britain, France, Prussia, Russia, and the Austrian Empire were members of a rudimentary system in which balance was preserved by the understanding that if any single power made territorial gains by war or diplomacy, the others were entitled to equivalent additions of strength (hence the elaborate territorial arithmetic that followed the War of the Polish Succession, 1733-35, and the successive partitions of Poland at the end of the century), and in which the powers were tacitly in agreement to league together against any one of their number who sought universal dominion.

In the course of the nineteenth century, the international system assumed three distinct forms, each less effective in preserving peace than the one that preceded it. In the forty years that followed the end of the Napoleonic wars, the territorial balance was defined by the Final Act of the Congress of Vienna and was maintained by a general consensus that treaties were to be honored (*pacta sunt servanda*) and that threats to the peace and the existing equilibrium should be dealt with by the Great Powers acting in concert. When this system broke down in mid-century, it was, after a dangerous interval, replaced by one that was based upon a network of secret and interlocking alliances that contained and deterred the dangerous ambitions of the powers in the European center, while diverting their acquisitive energies to colonial areas overseas. After 1890 when this became too complicated to be efficient, it gave way to a bipolar system in which two leagues of powers, the Triple Alliance and the Triple Entente, confronted each other and sought (unsuccessfully, as it turned out) to deter each other's aggressive tendencies by manifestations of alliance solidarity in time of crisis and by constantly increasing armaments.

Since 1918, there have been other attempts to create effective international systems, either by seeking a substitute for the principle of balance of power (as in the experiment of the League of Nations) or by returning to its older forms (the cold war system, in which NATO and the Warsaw Pact powers were poised against each other). And, in the more recent past, there has been a highly imaginative attempt to overcome the inherent dangers of cold war dualism: the Nixon-Kissinger détente strategy. The ultimate objective of this experiment was a tolerable working relationship between the two modern superpowers, but it included among the tactical instruments that were designed to induce the Soviet Union to agree to a *modus vivendi* a triangular balance-of-power politics in which the United States, as *tertius gaudens*, maintained friendly relations with both the Soviet Union and the People's Republic of China, ideological antagonists not only of each other but of the United States as well.

Common to all recent experiments in system-building has been the conviction, nurtured by the military revolutions of the last two centuries, that peace was to be preferred to war. Thus, Henry Kissinger has written of his triangular policy, "We moved toward China . . . not to collude against the Soviet Union but to give us a balancing position to use for constructive ends— to give each Communist power a stake in better relations with us. Such an equilibrium could assure stability among the major powers, and even eventual cooperation, in the Seventies and Eighties." To actualize that preference, it was further believed that rationality should guide the employment of all of the expedients at the state's command, including the instruments of violence. While it was admitted that resort to war in certain contingencies could not be excluded, the common assumption was that it should always be guided and restrained by political calculation (that it should, in Clausewitz's words, be "a continuation of state policy by other means"); that it should be terminated when its political objectives were achieved; and that it should never be allowed to assume its absolute form. These tacit assumptions were always, of course, at the mercy of ideological and economic factors. It was always easier to obey them when the members of the international community had common values and ideals, and the system was always more stable when there were a sufficient number of free territories and markets to allow for competition without excessive friction—as was true in the eighteenth century and in the first stage of nineteenth-century imperialism—than when scarcity of unoccupied and unexploited areas heightened the possibility of confrontation and conflict.

Finally, in all historical systems, the wishes of the larger and stronger states were given priority over those of the lesser, who were, indeed, often ignored and sometimes victimized by the Great Powers.

III

The system in which the characters of Orwell's *Nineteen Eighty-Four* live—or at least the one described in the book that Winston Smith is permitted to read—is one of triangularity carried to the extreme. The Nixon-Kissinger scheme was, after all, merely a way station intended in due course to be replaced by a more comprehensive system which would include Japan and Europe as equals of the other three Great Powers and would presumably recognize the legitimate interests of other states, or groups of states, in Latin America, Africa, the Middle East, and Southeast Asia. In the Goldsteinian world, there seem to be no lesser powers at all, for the principal actors have extended their frontiers to their natural limits and apparently abolished all local authorities and sovereignties within them. Eurasia now comprises all of Europe and the northern part of the Asiatic land mass; Eastasia embraces China, the lands south of it, the Japanese islands, and large parts of Mongolia, Manchuria, and Tibet; and Oceania unites the Americas, the British Isles, Australasia, and the southern part of Africa.

How this radical amalgamation was effected, the book that O'Brien plays into Winston's hands does not say, and Winston's own memory is incapable of supplying an answer. The Goldstein document suggests that the division of the world among three superstates was a logical development that could have been foreseen before the middle of the twentieth century, but this is a poor substitute for a historical explanation. How Russia, for example, was able to extend its dominion westward, not only to the Elbe, but to the English Channel, and how it managed to suppress the highly developed nationalism of the French and other Western peoples were questions that might have troubled Winston if he had known or remembered anything about countries other than his own. Did Russia's absorption of the continent and England's by the United States have any connection with "the time when the atomic bomb had fallen on Colchester"? Winston has no clear memory of that mysterious event and draws no cause-and-effect relationship from it. He simply accepts the picture given by the Goldstein book as an accurate description of the nature of the international system of his time.

There is no question that, as described, it is an efficient system, indeed that it has freed itself from those conditions that militated against efficiency

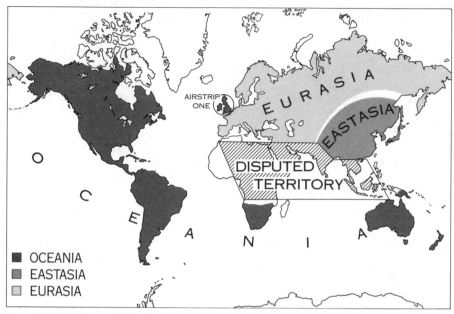

The world in *Nineteen Eighty-Four*.

in the international experiments in the first half of the twentieth century. In those years, and particularly after the end of the First World War, the possibility of establishing a smoothly functioning comity of nations was frustrated as a result of two factors: the rapid increase in the number of states that took an active and continuous interest in foreign affairs—a development that complicated the task of reaching agreement on any issue of importance—and the breakdown of the internal homogeneity of the diplomatic community as a result of the growth of ideological differences among the powers, which compounded the difficulty.

In Goldstein's description, it is clear that these disturbing tendencies have been checked and eliminated. A ruthless process of acquisition and centralization has reversed the proliferation of international players, and differences of political and economic philosophy have disappeared. What is left of the international community is entirely homogeneous. The three superpowers appear to have the same kind of political structure and system of social stratification and, in other respects too, they are mirror images of each other. What Hans Magnus Enzensberger has said of the superpowers of our own day can be applied, perhaps more accurately, to those of Winston Smith's: the destructiveness that Karl Marx maintained was inherent in capitalism is present in each of them in magnified form; the productive forces of society have become dissociated from human need and social progress; any proposed change in policy or in social or political structure is regarded as threatening and consequently as impermissible; and the salient feature of the regime in each superstate is its essential inhumanity, indeed, its contempt for the human beings whom it destroys in the process of sustaining itself. Because the superpowers are in every respect identical, their international system is never at the mercy of misunderstanding or miscalculation. Their needs and motivations are similar and are perceived as being so.

Although by Marxist standards the economic policies of the superpowers are irrational, their international collaboration does not suffer from that fact. On the contrary, a mad logic animates all aspects of their policy, and their external behavior is so rigorously determined and guided by their domestic needs that one is tempted to see in this circumstance the ultimate manifestation of that *ragione di stato* to which Renaissance theorists aspired—policy as the perfect expression of interest, unaffected by chance or extraneous factors. This facilitates the operations of the international system.

Finally, the world order described in Goldstein's book is free from the kind of danger that subverted the system of the years 1907 to 1914. At that time the diplomatic flexibility and amenability to compromise that are important in maintaining the viability of complicated political structures were lost because the instruments of war slipped out of the control of the policy makers. Planning for war assumed its own momentum, and the operational calculations of the soldiers tended increasingly to tie the hands of the heads of state and to deprive them of freedom of choice. Thus, in 1914, military expediency dominated the decision-making process, and war declared itself.

In Winston Smith's world, that possibility has disappeared. In contrast to all previous international systems, the one described by Goldstein has succeeded in achieving the age-old dream of controlling international violence, which it has done, not by eliminating it, but rather by taming and institutionalizing it and giving it a full-time occupation. It has assigned to warfare a vital function; it has supplied a mechanism for making it perpetual; and it has prescribed rigid limitations, both with respect to the permissible areas of military operations and the means at the disposal of those who command them.

The assigned purpose of warfare is to protect the established regimes and the social structures of the superpowers. This is, to be sure, a traditional function of military establishments, although the enemy to be defended against is usually a foreign antagonist. Here the threat comes not from abroad (although the citizens of Oceania are constantly bombarded by propaganda that is intended to make them believe that this is so) but from the productive potential of their own industrial economy. Their foe, in short, is the machine, which has the capacity, if left to its own devices, not only to create abundance, not only to feed and clothe the masses and improve their living conditions and education, but to raise their level of expectation and awaken their political sense, which has long been dulled by the desperate struggle for the bare means of subsistence. If this quickening of the critical faculties is allowed to take place, Oceania's hierarchical social structure and its totalitarian form of government cannot long survive. Their existence, and that of the comparable institutions in Eastasia and Eurasia, depend upon the poverty and ignorance of the masses, and to preserve these the natural operations of the productive system must be subverted and crippled.

This cannot be accomplished by decreeing that all machines be destroyed, for the regime depends for its efficient functioning upon some of their products, and in any case any such act of deliberate retrogression, unless done universally and simultaneously, would leave the power that took the initiative vulnerable to fatal attack by the machine-made weapons of the others. The wheels of industry must, therefore, continue to turn, without increasing the real wealth of the world and without creating threats of upheaval. This can be effected only by a systematic destruction or absorption of most of those goods and materials that could both benefit the masses and make them restive as soon as they are produced. One is reminded of Karl Marx's description in 1848 of the periodic orgies of waste with which capitalism overcame crises, and his prediction that this senseless profligacy would hasten the coming of the proletarian revolution. While using terror to make the threat of revolution infinitely remote, the superpowers described in Goldstein's book have elevated the principle of waste to a law of survival and made warfare its executor.

To provide and manage the wars against the threat of plenty is the chief, and perhaps the only, function of the international system, and it fulfills it in a dialectical, almost Hegelian way that assures the permanence of conflict. The system assigns to each of the superpowers a potential enemy and a potential ally. These are endlessly exchanged, each bilateral conflict eventuating in an alliance that automatically creates a new enemy and a reopening of hostilities *ad infinitum*. Exactly when the time has arrived, in a practical sense, for each successive conformation in the political process to produce its antithesis, and how this is recognized by the political elites of the three superpowers, is not apparent. There is no mention of diplomacy in Goldstein's book, and it is clear that the international system has no need for anything like the headquarters of the League of Nations in Geneva or the United Nations organization in New York; the multifarious diplomatic activities characteristic of historical systems have all but disappeared. It seems probable that forms of tacit negotiation are highly developed: the mutual decision to stop employing atomic weapons appears to have been achieved without formal interchanges between the powers. This does not explain how decisions to switch partners are communicated and agreed upon, but the Goldstein document does not exclude the possibility that this may take place according to some prearranged schedule or system of signals.

The important thing is that war should continue, and it does. But it is a kind of war that has lost any nobility that it may once have had; it no longer possesses the awful majesty that derived from its sporadic and eruptive nature; and it has been deprived of the glory that accrued to great triumphs and the tragic dignity attendant on defeat. For there is no victory or defeat in the endless campaigns conducted by the superpowers in the great belt of disputed territory that extends across the globe from the line between Tangiers and Brazzaville to that between Hong Kong and Darwin. In the deserts and rain forests of these forlorn lands, their armies—in a monstrous parody of Lenin's vision in *Imperialism, the Highest Stage of Capitalism*—seek to lay their hands, not upon the kinds of resources that will fuel the productive capacity of their countries, but rather upon the coolie labor necessary to produce more weapons for the wars that will consume the fruits of that productivity and upon the territories that can serve as battlefields for that purpose.

From attempts to pass beyond the perimeters of this shabby occupation, from dreams of military triumphs on a grand scale, of offensives against the heartland of their enemies, the military commanders of the three superpowers have been effectively discouraged. They are bound perpetually to the Malabar front or the sands of North Africa, where they engage in the localized forays that are as much as their miserable weapons are capable of supporting. It is all too apparent that the art of war has deteriorated markedly since the great conflicts of the first half of the century. The superpowers stockpile atomic weapons, apparently on the grounds that at some time in the indefinite future their use may become possible, but no progress has been made to develop delivery systems that could give actuality to that flimsy expectation. Bombing planes have been superseded by self-propelled projectiles, but these, if we can judge from Winston's experience of them, are no more destructive in their effects than the V-2s of the Second World War. Air power now means little more than helicopter forces—in short, the kind of aircraft suitable for jungle warfare. Most of the other weapons in use appear to be appropriate for the same kind of limited conflict, and it is perhaps significant that there is no mention of heavy artillery. As a power girded by the oceans, Oceania has a naval force, but it appears to be composed largely of submarines and a few stationary Floating Fortresses, purely defensive weapons designed to protect strategic approaches to the homeland. The nature of their armament is undisclosed, but no mention is made of aircraft or other offensive weapons, and the Fortresses do not appear to be highly mobile.

From all of this, it is apparent that weapons development has been at a standstill for years. This being so, there is no encouragement of strategical thinking, which has been inhibited also by the shrinking of the size of military forces and the denial of all targets that would challenge the imagination of military planners. For massive breakthroughs spearheaded by thousands of tanks, for *Kesselschlachten* that hold whole armies in their toils, the time is out of joint. The great *Feldherren*, the Napoleons and Schlieffens *in spe*, see their dreams fading away on the banks of the Mekong and the Congo. War has become a trivial and down-at-the-heels enterprise, not dissimilar in its objectives from that of the slavers of the eighteenth century. And, at the same time, it has lost all of its former capacity to arrogate to itself political functions and responsibilities, to intervene in the decision-making process, and to subvert the international balance by its own momentum.

Like Henry Kissinger's triangular system, the one described in the Goldstein document is not designed to provide for the collusion of two of the superpowers against the third, although this might seem to be true to the superficial observer. In reality, it is a grandiose conspiracy of the three superpowers against their own subjects, implemented by a form of war that has been rationalized to the point where it simultaneously protects the power and the territory of the governing elites by means of an imposed system of restraints. It keeps their peoples in bondage, through controlled violence designed to eliminate the wealth that might free them. From the inherent weaknesses that vitiated all of the historical models of international order, this one is free, and there is no logical reason why it shouldn't continue forever.

IV

That is, if it exists at all. When Winston Smith's brief career as a conspirator comes to its miserable end, he learns that the book that revealed the nature of his world to him was not the product of Goldstein's pen after all but, at least in part, of the Party intellectual O'Brien's. There is no reason to suppose, therefore, that its contents correspond to any reality except that which is convenient to the Party or that the world picture provided to appeal to Winston's active imagination has any connection with actual circumstances. Winston's lover, Julia, may have been entirely justified in refusing to share his enthusiasm when the document came into his hands and for drifting off to sleep while he read it to her. To her uncluttered mind, the world around her is the only real one and, to explain what happens in it, there is no need to look for answers in regions that her eyes cannot see. There is perhaps a deep wisdom in her casual remark that the war is not happening at all and that the rocket bombs that fall on London are probably fired by the government of Oceania itself "just to keep the people frightened." Was there really a world outside the British Isles? Had organized political life survived the atomic wars of the forties and fifties in Europe and Asia? Was the international system real or imaginary?

As Julia would have seen it, it didn't really matter. The ultimate purpose of international systems is to protect the interests of the governments of their member states. Real or imaginary, this one fulfilled that purpose admirably.

# 5 Sidney D. Drell

# Newspeak and Nukespeak

*All three powers merely continue to produce atomic bombs and store them up against the decisive opportunity which they all believe will come sooner or later.*

THE IMAGES THAT GEORGE ORWELL'S *Nineteen Eighty-Four* commonly brings to mind are "Big Brother," "doublethink," thought control, "Victory gin," and "two plus two equals five." I recalled them all upon rereading *Nineteen Eighty-Four*, but my great surprise was the essential accuracy of Orwell's predictions about nuclear weapons and nuclear conflict. I found it remarkable that Orwell wrote his scenario just three years after Hiroshima, in the dawn of the nuclear age. There were then none of the intercontinental missiles that today are poised many thousands of miles, but less than thirty-minutes' flight time, away from our homeland, their thousands of nuclear warheads threatening total devastation. There were no hydrogen, or fusion, bombs—for which the primitive atom, or fission, bombs of the type that obliterated Hiroshima and Nagasaki are mere triggers. Nevertheless, although he was incorrect in many details, Orwell's prophecy—or was it a warning?—accurately foresaw the basic elements of the world's present nuclear stalemate.

We learn of the nuclear politics of Orwell's world along with Winston Smith as he surreptitiously reads Chapter 3, "War Is Peace," of the banned book *The Theory and Practice of Oligarchical Collectivism* by that shadowy and subversive object of Hate Week, Emmanuel Goldstein:

> What is more remarkable is that all three powers already possess, in the atomic bomb, a weapon far more powerful than any that their present researches are likely to discover. Although the Party, according to its habit, claims the invention for itself, atomic bombs first appeared as early as the Nineteen-forties, and were first used

on a large scale about ten years later. At that time some hundreds of bombs were dropped on industrial centers, chiefly in European Russia, Western Europe, and North America. The effect was to convince the ruling groups of all countries that a few more atomic bombs would mean the end of organized society, and hence of their own power. Thereafter, although no formal agreement was ever made or hinted at, no more bombs were dropped. All three powers merely continue to produce atomic bombs and store them up against the decisive opportunity which they all believe will come sooner or later. . . . None of the three superstates ever attempts any maneuver which involves the risk of serious defeat.

Orwell erred in not foreseeing the great jump in destructive energy by factors of 100 to 1,000 that came with the development of hydrogen bombs. He also erred in anticipating that a major war would be waged between industrial powers in the middle of the nineteen-fifties, with atomic weapons dropping on their cities, and that "the ravages of the atomic war of the Nineteen-fifties have never been fully repaired." But Orwell is right on target in prophesying—or warning—that atomic war would become an incalcuable risk that "would mean the end of organized society"; or, as he also remarked, "no decisive victory is possible." That is an accurate description of our world today—our real-life 1984. We label the nuclear standoff anticipated by Orwell as nuclear deterrence. We recognize that any nation initiating a nuclear war may be literally committing suicide. The fact that U.S. and Soviet citizens are mutual hostages in a world heavily armed with nuclear weapons is a physical reality, whether we like it or not. There is simply no technology that can defend our society against nuclear annihilation. Today's nuclear standoff has no precedent in history; it is a consequence of the enormously destructive power of nuclear warheads. Furthermore, the standoff grows increasingly perilous as more and more countries develop the capability to build nuclear bombs.

Many find our present policy of deterrence morally repugnant, based as it is on the threat to annihilate hundreds of millions of innocent people in retaliation against nuclear aggression. Many more are confused by the logic of building and threatening to use weapons of suicide. However, it is generally recognized that, short of doing away with all or almost all of our present nuclear arsenals, we have no better alternative to deterrence. Our task is to make deterrence work and to avoid nuclear war, as Orwell's three great powers in *Nineteen Eighty-Four* managed to do by common consent.

The limited military utility of nuclear weapons has been recognized by our most senior, thoughtful, and battle-tested military leaders from the time of the first hydrogen bombs. As long ago as 1956 President Eisenhower took a leaf from *Nineteen Eighty-Four* when he recognized that there would be no winners in a nuclear war, and wrote, *"We are rapidly getting to the point that no war can be won."* Maintaining that with nuclear weapons war would be no longer a battle to exhaustion and surrender, Eisenhower noted that the outlook had now come close to *"destruction of the enemy and suicide."*

The military uselessness of nuclear weapons was expressed directly, convincingly, and simply by Lord Louis Mountbatten in his last writings before his tragic assassination in 1979:

> *As a military man who has given half a century of active service I say in all sincerity that the nuclear arms race has no military purpose. Wars cannot be fought with nuclear weapons. Their existence only adds to our perils because of the illusions which they have generated.*

The dangers and defects of a policy of nuclear deterrence have drawn increasing—and well-deserved—attention of late. Our predicament today is very well summarized in the remarkable pastoral letter on "The Challenge of Peace" adopted by the U.S. National Conference of Catholic Bishops on War and Peace early in 1983. The bishops commented that although

> *deterrence cannot be accepted as "an end in itself," . . . [it] may still be judged as morally acceptable provided it is used as a step toward progressive disarmament.*

The bishops came to this judgment because they were persuaded that deterrence offers the best promise of avoiding nuclear conflict while making the long, slow journey out from under the nuclear sword of Damocles. I concur.

In summary, our predicament today is not all that different from that foreseen by Orwell. He foresaw no more nuclear wars in *Nineteen Eighty-Four*—not even limited ones that are occasionally described to us today as survivable and winnable. Orwell suffered no such illusions. His continual state of war was waged with conventional weapons only. Our own pattern of conventional strife differs from the scenario painted by Orwell. He wrote of intermittent bombs dropping on major industrial cities causing but few casualties, together with combat on peripheral battlefields that "involves very small numbers of people, mostly highly trained specialists, and causes comparatively few casualties." In our combat the bombs have not rained on our cities; they have been confined to the battle areas where they have wrought vast civilian death and destruction. But as to the nuclear dimension, and war on the scale of megadeaths and megatons, a nuclear stalemate has lasted for thirty-eight years and Orwell's prophecy—or warning—has come true.

II

In *Nineteen Eighty-Four* Big Brother found it useful and convenient to falsify history in order to maintain the position of the Party. Our challenge in today's heavily armed nuclear world is quite different: it is to understand that we have lost history. History is no longer valid as a guide in matters of nuclear weapons and war. Security can no longer be found either in greater strength or in defense, as it could before nuclear weapons. Nuclear war can no longer be regarded as "a continuation of state policy with other means," in Karl von Clausewitz's frequently cited words. George Kennan eloquently expressed his concerns about the new weapons of mass destruction while counselor to Secretary of State Dean Acheson in 1949, the same year that *Nineteen Eighty-Four* was published:

> *The weapons of mass destruction . . . reach backward beyond the frontiers of western civilization, to the concepts of warfare which were once familiar to the Asiatic hordes. They cannot really be reconciled with a political purpose directed to shaping, rather than destroying, the lives of the adversary. They fail to take account of the ultimate responsibility of men for one another, and even for each other's errors and mistakes. They imply the admission that man not only can be but is his own worst and most terrible enemy.*

Since we have lost history we must give many words new meanings and change maxims derived from historical experience. Big Brother did this in *Nineteen Eighty-Four* as a cynical manipulation to consolidate power—writing in his Newspeak such famous slogans as "War is Peace," "Freedom is Slavery," and "Ignorance is Strength." At times it seems that we today have our own version of Newspeak (or Nukespeak), such as *New nuclear weapons are bargaining chips, A new missile* [MX, SS-24, or many others] *is arms control,* and *We must build up in order to build down.*

Nuclear weapons have also caused other basic changes in the meanings of words. These changes seem just as contradictory as the famous three maxims of Big Brother, but they are, in fact, central to our security. The lesson we learned in prenuclear times was that we must arm to defend our vital interests and to enhance our security. Today, however, we are, as President Eisenhower emphasized, dealing with weapons of suicide, weapons against which there is no defense. The old common sense based on history must, therefore, be replaced with a new common sense that recognizes as fact, rather than as a cynical manipulation of words, that we do *not* improve our security as we further increase the destructive power of our nuclear arsenals. On the contrary, as new weapons threaten deterrence our security decreases; and in this sense we must understand *More weapons mean less security.* In addition, we have come to understand *Defense is provocative,* a maxim that is at once the most challenging to our credulity, the most contentious to many, yet the most helpful for explaining the concept of deterrence.

The idea that defense is provocative is expressed in the preamble to the first formal strategic arms limitation treaty (SALT I), signed by the United States and the Soviet Union, which limits the deployment of defenses against ballistic missiles (i.e., of anti-ballistic missile—ABM—systems). Signed by Richard Nixon and Leonid Brezhnev on May 26, 1972, it is of unlimited duration and is in effect today. In its preamble we find this statement of common purpose:

- *Proceeding from the premise that nuclear war would have devastating consequences for all mankind,*
- *Considering that effective measures to limit anti-ballistic missile systems would be a substantial factor in curbing the race in strategic offensive arms and would lead to a decrease in the risk of outbreak of war involving nuclear weapons,*
- *Proceeding from the premise that the limitation of anti-ballistic missile systems, as well as certain agreed upon measures with respect to the limitation of strategic offensive arms, would contribute to the creation of more favorable conditions for further negotiations on limiting strategic arms. . . .*

This treaty recognizes the technical infeasibility of a nuclear defense of one's nation—the people, the cities, the industry—as well as the fact that a major undertaking to develop and construct such a defense will very likely stimulate further buildup of offensive nuclear weapons. This is precisely what occurred prior to the SALT I treaty limiting the ABM.

During the 1960s the U.S. observed initial construction of a rather primitive Soviet ABM system around Moscow, as well as similar activity at Leningrad. In response, we simply multiplied the size of our nuclear force. We did this by putting many warheads on each missile (the MIRVs, or multiple independently targetable reentry vehicles) in order to overpower and defeat whatever limited, partial effectiveness one could conceivably ascribe to the Soviet defenses. Furthermore, we went ahead with the development and deployment of thousands of MIRVs even after SALT I prohibited the deployment of the nationwide ABM defenses that were the original justification for the MIRV program. Predictably, the Soviets followed our course, four to five years later, with bigger, more menacing ICBMs and MIRVs.

The end result of the effort to develop nuclear defenses was simply to provoke a further major buildup in the offensive nuclear forces of both the U.S. and the Soviet Union. Offenses were enhanced in order to maintain a policy of deterrence based on a sure ability to retaliate effectively against nuclear aggression by an opponent. Defenses were at the same time negotiated away as technically ineffective.

The issue of defense against nuclear attack has been raised once again in 1983, but I believe offense predominates over defense just as strongly now as it did in 1972. This time the proposal is for a space-based "star wars" defense with exotic directed-energy weapons such as high-powered lasers, X-ray lasers driven by nuclear explosions, and particle beams. There have, indeed, been very impressive technological advances in recent years—but I think it is likely that the new systems will remain vulnerable, just as the ABM systems of a decade ago were, to relatively simple and inexpensive countermeasures by the offense.

The fundamental problem with defense in the nuclear age is simply that it must be very close to 100 percent perfect or it fails. The offense has a great advantage simply because nuclear bombs are so enormously destructive. Thus it takes but one medium-sized warhead of the more than 8,000 in the current strategic missile and bomber forces of the Soviet Union (the U.S. total exceeds 9,000) to obliterate a major metropolitan area the size of San Francisco, causing some one million immediate casualties. I know of no current or planned technology that will lead to a defensive system that can operate effectively amidst many nuclear explosions and that can react to technically available countermeasures by the opponent's offensive forces with anything approaching 100 percent success.

Even if a defense were 95 percent perfect—so that only 5 percent, or 400, of the existing Soviet strategic nuclear warheads exploded on the U.S., or vice versa—what good would it be? Immediate casualties would still be well above 100 million, and the devastation beyond comprehension! Orwell seems to have implicitly recognized this fact by his neglect of the possibility of defense against atomic attack. His fictional great powers, having learned their lesson from an "actual" atomic war in the 1950s, well understood the unacceptability of nuclear conflict and, by tacit agreement, avoided their use. They practiced nuclear deterrence.

There is, of course, no theorem that says it is impossible for us to do better than deterrence in the future. Perhaps with the help of new technologies—together with progress in arms control and even some evolution in human behavior and political structure—we can change the maxim from *Defense is provocative* to *Nuclear weapons are unnecessary.* It is my judgment, however, that we cannot escape the nuclear threat with technology alone. The U.S. maintains a strong research and development effort in many weapons-related areas, including defense, to guard against technological surprise, and this is as it ought to be. Fortunately, our overall scientific effort bears very little resemblance to Orwell's scenario: "The search for new weapons continues unceasingly, and is one of the very few remaining activities in which the inventive or speculative type of mind can find any outlet. In Oceania at the present day, Science, in the old sense, has almost ceased to exist."

That is not to say that there is no cause for concern that so large a fraction of our most advanced technology and our best young university trained minds are engaged in the military-industrial complex about which President Eisenhower cautioned in 1960. Weapons production and research do constitute a drain on the world's important resources, and we must ask how long it will be healthy or wise to divert those intellectual resources (not to mention the financial resources) from more productive pursuits. This problem is just one more important argument in support of arms control, a subject not even mentioned by Orwell. Beyond reducing the risks of nuclear war, the levels of destructive power in the nuclear arsenals, and the waste of material resources to the arms competition, effective arms control could also help in redirecting our most precious intellectual resources into more creative channels. General Omar Bradley, the great "American GIs' general" of World War II, addressed this very issue in 1957:

> The central problem of our time—as I view it—is how to employ human intelligence for the salvation of mankind. It is a problem we have put upon ourselves. For we have defiled our intellect by the creation of such scientific instruments of destruction that we are now in desperate danger of destroying ourselves. Our plight is critical and with each effort we have made to relieve it by further scientific advance, we have succeeded only in aggravating our peril.

> If I am sometimes discouraged, it is not by the magnitude of the problem, but by our colossal indifference to it. I am unable to understand why . . . we do not make greater, more diligent and more imaginative use of reason and human intelligence in seeking an accord and compromise which will make it possible for mankind to control the atom and banish it as an instrument of war.

With General Bradley, I believe that we must look to arms control if we are to work our way out from under the nuclear threat. Technology can contribute, but to imply that technology alone can lead the way, under the banner of "star wars" or by another name, is to retreat from physical realities. If we are to make serious progress, our record at arms control during the decade ahead will have to be better than it has been in the decade just ended—which saw a *tripling* of the number of nuclear warheads on the intercontinental missiles and bombers of the U.S. and Soviet Union despite all our negotiating efforts to reduce precisely these forces. Our record pretty much matches Orwell's account: "All three powers merely continue to produce atomic bombs and store them up against the decisive opportunity which they all believe will come sooner or later."

Although our nuclear arsenals are still growing, it is by no means a commonly held view today that a "decisive opportunity" for a nuclear war threatens us in the future. In Orwell's world of escalating nuclear forces, there were no formal agreements or arms negotiations, and it is very sobering to think that we have managed to show little, if any, advantage relative to Orwell's *Nineteen Eighty-Four* in spite of years of intense arms control negotiations with the Soviet Union and national effort at the highest levels of government.

*Man* by Juan Genovés, 1968, oil on canvas, 74¼″ × 59″. Estate of Joseph H. Hirshhorn.

For the present our major challenge is to make deterrence work and to avoid a nuclear holocaust. Should we fail, Orwell's most famous maxim, "War is Peace," will come true—in the literal sense first introduced nineteen centuries ago by Tacitus. Writing about the campaigns in Britain of the great Roman leader Agricola, Tacitus tells of how Calgacus, the leader of the beleaguered defenders, tried to rally his troops by describing the devastation caused by the Roman legions with the words:

*Ubi solitudinem faciunt, pacem appelant.*
("They create a desolation and call it a peace.")

The basic theme of *Nineteen Eighty-Four* is the perpetuation of power by a clique—the Party and Big Brother—by whatever means available. It is a tale of cynical use and abuse of power in which nuclear weapons are almost incidental. Having learned from their atomic devastation in the 1950s, Orwell's major powers simply withhold nuclear weapons from the wars they continuously wage with one another. There can be no independent voice or expression of concern among the people of Oceania about the moral issues raised by the possible or threatened use of nuclear weapons of mass destruction. Big Brother would of course not allow it.

Fortunately, that is not our circumstance. Indeed, as we enter our 1984, the moral issues are being discussed with increasing emphasis, and the moral power of people concerned about the nuclear danger is gaining importance as a factor to be reckoned with in the formulation of policy. In the West this development has been accompanied by the growth of a public constituency for arms control. In part, this growth has been spurred by the collapse of formal arms control negotiations between 1979 and 1982, which awakened many to the fact that it was unwise to abandon such a vitally important (if also complex) issue to the attention of professionals. In part, this awareness was triggered by disturbing rhetoric about "winnable" and "survivable" nuclear wars. In part, it stemmed from growing concern with the seemingly incessant deployments of new generations of nuclear missiles.

We now have for the first time a major arms control constituency in the West (if it exists in the East, it is necessarily stealthy), impatient for progress and demanding persuasive evidence of a strong commitment to nuclear arms control by our leaders. How enduring, how politically effective, how constructive this public movement will eventually prove is a subject for speculation, but it offers the prospect of one of the most significant differences between our 1984 and that of Orwell in the realm of weapons and arms control.

III

Our 1984 comes thirty-six years after Orwell wrote his classic. Let us look ahead another thirty-six years to 2020. What is our 2020 vision without the benefit of hindsight?

I think that what 2020 will be like depends on the further development of the two factors I have been discussing: the moral pressure of a concerned citizenry and the impact of new technologies on deterrence. If the newly created public arms control constituency continues to grow and if it restores the moral dimension to the formulation of nuclear policy, there is good cause for optimism.

As new technologies are developed, however, and as new weapons are designed and tested, the policy of deterrence will come increasingly under attack, particularly from the nuclear-war fighters, with their talk of limited and winnable nuclear wars. If we go to space with star wars, will we accomplish anything beyond the addition of yet another dimension to the arms competition as the race between technological countermeasures intensifies? What will this competition do to such existing arms control achievements as the SALT I treaty limiting ballistic missile defenses? SALT I stipulates that

> Each party undertakes not to develop, test, or deploy ABM systems or components which are sea-based, air-based, space-based, or mobile land-based.

Will this, our major arms control achievement to date, have to be weakened or sacrificed as we pursue a futile technological escape from deterrence?

My vision of 2020 is that of an optimist, based on my hope that the force of reason and arms control will prevail. I also suspect that after several years of serious effort we will come to the same conclusion with respect to star-wars defenses that we did in 1972 with respect to the last generation of defensive technologies; namely, that defense is an impossible challenge and that there is no technical alternative to deterrence. I think there is a finite chance that this time we will have learned a lesson and that, in contrast to the decade following the SALT I treaties, we will make serious progress in reducing nuclear armaments and in stabilizing deterrence at a lower level of weaponry.

The sooner this happens the better, for time in which the superpowers can make this progress is running out. In nuclear (as well as political) matters the world of 2020 can be expected to look very different from Orwell's model. We face the almost certain prospect of a world with many nuclear-armed nations in 2020, and as nuclear weapons proliferate around the world the dangers to peace and survival will multiply.

Shortly after the first atomic explosion Albert Einstein warned that *"The unleashed power of the atom has changed everything save our modes of thinking; we thus drift toward unparalleled catastrophe."* We are still drifting as the tides grow increasingly perilous. The year 2020 will require not just a clear vision—but a strong commitment, wisdom, and patience in charting a new course.

# 6 *Kenneth J. Arrow*

# The Economics of *Nineteen Eighty-Four*

*An all-round increase in wealth threatened the destruction—indeed, in some sense was the destruction—of a hierarchical society.*

IF THE PURPOSE OF AN ECONOMIC SYSTEM is to produce goods and services for the benefit of its members, the economy of *Nineteen Eighty-Four* is surely a miserable failure. From the viewpoint of a consumer, even a relatively privileged one like Winston Smith, the results are poor. Orwell, with his ability to depict reality through enumeration of specific, concrete details, makes us wallow in the failure. Unappetizing stews that resemble vomit, cramped living accommodations complete with bedbugs, decaying streets and buildings, severe rationing of chocolate, empty shelves in stores characterize the consumer economy as foreseen in 1948. There are evidently no personal automobiles except for the Inner Party; indeed, consumer durable goods in *Nineteen Eighty-Four* are virtually nonexistent—a far cry from real-life 1984. Even alcoholic beverages are not what they used to be; only an inferior gin is available to Winston Smith, though the proletarians still have their beer, and O'Brien his wine (we have no evidence of its quality; Smith's gin-trained taste buds were not very discriminating).

Still, perhaps there are other criteria. Even in our private-property, relatively individualistically oriented society, much consumption is collective. Close to one-quarter of our national income is spent on goods which are held and used collectively, not under the control of individuals: schools, police, defense, parks, streets, courts, flood control, and the like. Perhaps the economy of *Nineteen Eighty-Four* is efficient but has directed its productive capacities differently. Oceania does indeed maintain large armies and navies, engaged in perpetual conflict with fluctuating enemies. The Ministry of Love does seem to have a large staff and at least some technologically advanced equipment for torture (though a cage of rats does not require much in the way of resources). Two-way television in every home is something of an exception to the general poverty of consumer durables, but this is an instrument of thought control.

Yet even collective activities of these kinds do not seem efficiently provided. I do not know to what extent the book by "Goldstein" is to be regarded as an accurate account of Oceania and the workings of Ingsoc; O'Brien does tell Smith that it is accurate as far as it goes, but then he has told Smith lies; he assures Smith at one point that Goldstein exists and is the author of the book under his name and later identifies himself as one of its authors. But if it is accurate, there is a paucity of innovation in the military sphere. There is indeed much investment in military research and development, but the actual weapons remain pretty much unchanged. It appears to be true, however, that the volume of arms used and consumed in battle is quite large. In addition, arms of all kinds are evidently scrapped as obsolete even when there has been no significant technological progress.

Orwell's book does not provide the data for an estimate of gross national product. We are not even told the proportion of the working force devoted to arms production, the aggregate or per capita outputs of military and governmental goods, or anything else relevant except for the indications of the low level of per capita consumption. But we certainly have the overall impression of poor performance in every dimension.

Since it is suggested that the economy has retrogressed from its prewar levels, low as those were, its present failures cannot be explained by lack of technological knowledge, for it is not even using the knowledge that is available. How does the system operate to work so poorly? A laissez-faire economist would have no difficulty in arriving at an explanation: It is a socialist system, not using the price system to any great extent, and therefore lacking in incentives for efficiency. We are not told in any detail how the system functions, who decides how much of what to produce, and to whom it is to go. We do hear much talk of rations, which suggests that prices are not set at the level at which supply and demand are equal. If prices are relatively rigid, then production decisions are made at a political level, rather than by firms seeking to maximize profits and therefore responsive to market forces.

Workers such as Winston Smith receive salaries and can spend them on goods; but because many particular commodities are rationed, their expenditures are not at their discretion. Smith is indeed free to buy diaries and glass paperweights enclosing pieces of coral from antique stores, but these are hardly significant items in the national economy. Housing too is evidently allocated, not chosen freely in the market. Without price guides, it is hard to see how decisions on producing consumer goods can be made rationally.

We are not told if decisions on production are made rationally, that is, if the production of goods requires a technological minimum of inputs. The implications are certainly negative. Among Smith's tasks at the Ministry of Truth is the changing of the records of old economic plans, so that they always appear to be fulfilled or overfulfilled. He concludes that neither the plans nor the alleged actuality have any basis in reality. To be sure, his tasks relate to newspapers, to facts released to the public. But it is of the essence of the constant rewriting of history that no one, not even insiders, have any record or memory to conflict with the version of reality which holds in the present. This presumably means that there are not even any confidential records in which the truth appears. In that case, the possibility of rational planning and intentional economy, whether through the price mechanism or in any other way, appears to be negligible indeed.

Obviously, Orwell's idea of an economic system was powerfully shaped by the perceived reality of the Soviet system, no doubt augmented by the depressing state of Great Britain during and immediately after the war. Great Britain too had rationing and moved only slowly toward a free market economy. But it was the Soviet Union that had the frenzied drives for production, the Five-Year Plans, and the alleged successes and real failures (there were in fact real successes in production but none in consumption; the army was built up). Further, as we now know even better than Orwell could, production figures were falsified or even nonexistent. Students of the Soviet economy consider that our gaps in knowledge of the 1930s will never be made up; the Soviets never had the numbers we seek because it was too dangerous to the statistical analysts to record the unpleasant truth. The rewriting of economic history, as of all other history, may not have reached the high state of development that Orwell describes, but the Soviet Union of the 1930s certainly suggested the beginnings of that process.

Orwell is not an economist. He is not concerned, of course, with the particular reasons why the economy is inefficient and is diverting such a large fraction of its resources away from the well-being of its members. Rather, he gives an explanation of the function this economic failure serves. It is the one sketched in the epigraph to this chapter. Goldstein accepts a view that is quite common among social observers, including some economists: Modern technology, the "machine" in Goldstein's terms, permits abundance. There is no longer an economic problem in the sense of scarcity to be overcome. Hence, our failure to live in this feasible Eden needs an explanation. Keynes saw the problem as institutional, an excess of saving or deficiency of investment, which creates unemployment and therefore wastes resources. Orwell sees it rather as the result of an effort by the ruling class of the day to maintain its position. If everyone were living comfortably, then inequality of income and power would be perceived to be unnecessary, and the ruling class would be thrown out.

This factor, according to Orwell-Goldstein, was not absent under capitalism; the unemployment and stagnation of the period 1920-40 had the same purpose—the preservation of inequality—as did the destruction of goods through war in Oceania. (The period 1921-29 was highly prosperous in the United States, but Great Britain was indeed stagnant and had considerable unemployment throughout the interwar period.) The hypothesis is bold and imaginative, and what more could be asked of a literary work? But it does suffer from a certain unimaginative concept of scarcity and abundance. Certainly the United States, Japan, France, Sweden, and West Germany have reached consumption levels for the average citizen which would have been unimaginable even fifty years ago. Do people feel that there is nowhere to go, that there is no further progress to be made, and that therefore the need for inequality has vanished? Aspiration levels of human beings, at least in modern societies, seem to have no limit. At any moment, indeed, the human imagination is limited, and we see bliss at some not-too-distant level of satisfaction. When asked how much income is needed for a fully satisfying life, most people in most countries estimate about 20 percent above their present level, whatever it may be.

(I do not want to leave the impression that great inequality of power and income is necessary for economic growth. On the contrary, some forms of inequality, as of educational opportunity, clearly harm economic growth. Further, while some inequality is needed to supply incentives, very considerable steps toward income equality have only minimal impact on economic growth and efficiency, as has been demonstrated by the general postwar experience of Sweden and, to a lesser extent, our own and that of Japan. However, we digress from an examination of Orwell at this point.)

Nevertheless, Orwell's intuition that some forms of economic inefficiency are structural necessities in both capitalist and socialist countries is thoroughly compatible with the facts. As Orwell hints, the form of economic inefficiency may be different in the two systems—unemployment under capitalism and shortages under socialism—a thesis which has been advanced by that outstanding contemporary Hungarian economist János Kornai. The capitalist system has indeed been distinguished from all other economic systems by a recurrent tendency to underutilization of its resources, both of labor and of capital. Even under conditions of prosperity, there is rarely an excess demand for labor relative to its supply, while in a depression the amount of productive labor left idle can reach the enormous proportions of the Great Depression or the large figure of over 10 percent at the beginning of 1983. It is important to realize that the causes of this unemployment and wastage of productive resources are not accidents of nature, as they might have been in earlier economic systems. The causes are within the system itself. Economists have yet to arrive at a completely satisfactory explanation of the business cycle in capitalist societies. Clearly, an essential component is the decentralized nature of economic decision making. But it is very possible that another element in the explanation is the role of unemployment in increasing discipline over labor at work.

The Soviet Union and its satellite Socialist countries in Eastern Europe have typically avoided unemployment and business cycles, except as they are induced through their trade with the Western World. But on the other hand they are clearly inefficient and wasteful, at least relative to the West. As repeated statements by the socialist economists themselves make clear, the excessive concentration of economic decision making is a prime cause of the inefficiency. There are recurring demands for "liberalization," even by the highest authorities (Yuri Andropov, the effective head of the Soviet Union, being the latest example), but they are responded to only mildly or not at all. Clearly, a really major step toward decentralization of economic power, to the plant managers or the workers themselves, is perceived as a threat to the system.

Nevertheless, economic systems of any kind are not immutable. Goldstein's analysis of the essence of a system of pure power should not be taken and probably was not intended by Orwell to be taken as an inevitable tendency. Real social systems are always too complex to be reduced to a few simple principles. Multiple centers of power and reward have developed under capitalism. The labor union shares in authority at the workplace. Government regulation constrains the performance of businesses in selling and producing. The incomes of the members of the economy derive in part from transfer payments by the government—primarily social security but also welfare payments and subsidies to farmers. The consumption of education and of medical services has come to be paid for largely through collective agencies. The governments of all Western countries have taken a responsibility for managing the economy through monetary and fiscal policy, and the extraordinary prosperity of most of the postwar period was surely due in part to this change of function. Through all these changes, capitalism is still essentially the same system, modified in detail though it be.

It is too soon to tell whether socialism can similarly accommodate modifications in the direction of liberalization and still survive. Yugoslavia and to some extent Hungary have certainly taken steps in this direction. In view of the complexity of history and society, the possibility of a system essentially socialist in nature but with more decentralization of economic and other authority and therefore more freedom cannot be excluded.

Orwell was writing a novel, not a scientific treatise. He caught beautifully certain trends immanent in our world and exposed them without complications. But surely his own view was Winston Smith's reply to O'Brien: "You could not create such a world as you describe. It is a dream. It is impossible."

"Tell me again how it was back in 1977 before we ran out of everything"

Cartoon by Robert Graysmith. From *Best Editorial Cartoons of the Year*, 1978 edition. © 1978 Charles Brooks. By permission of Pelican Publishing Company.

# 7 Paul R. Ehrlich and Anne H. Ehrlich

# 1984: Population and Environment

*When you see how the people live, and still more how easily they die, it is always difficult to believe that you are walking among human beings. All colonial empires are in reality founded upon that fact. The people have brown faces—besides, there are so many of them!*

from "Marrakech," 1939

THE ANALYSIS OF THE ENVIRONMENTAL ASPECTS of *Nineteen Eighty-Four* that follows is in several respects unfair to George Orwell. Anyone who writes about the future knows that precise prediction is impossible. One can forecast the implications of current trends on the assumption that they will continue; but the forecaster is always aware that many trends are unlikely to continue. We would view *Nineteen Eighty-Four* as a *scenario*, a device used to stimulate thinking about the future implications of the present course of society. In that context it was an enormous success, for, whether it was intended as a forecast or a warning, *Nineteen Eighty-Four* alerted people to certain dehumanizing trends—some of which still seem very threatening today—flowing partly from technological advances.

What struck us most sharply, however, upon rereading *Nineteen Eighty-Four* for its treatment of environmental issues was not Orwell's prescience in this area, but his blindness. In this particular context he was completely a man of his times. But that the same blindness should still afflict many educated people today is frightening. These people have little excuse for their affliction; unlike George Orwell, they live in a society where information on environmental issues is widely available. Environmental blindness allows people to imagine humanity as abstracted from nature and affected only by social phenomena, answerable only to itself and to the gods of its invention. Partly because of this blindness, Orwell's fictional world, created just after

World War II, is a poor reflection of the real world of today.

A major theme in *Nineteen Eighty-Four* is the use of perpetual warfare by the Party, not just to generate a continuous war hysteria and thereby manipulate the citizenry more easily, but also to avoid the surpluses that would inevitably be created if peace were to reign. This policy is explicitly stated: "The primary aim of modern warfare . . . is to use up the products of the machine without raising the general standard of living. . . . If the machine were used deliberately for that end, hunger, overwork, illiteracy, and disease could be eliminated within a few generations."

Orwell here appears to have embedded a local partial truth in a global misperception. It is true that one function of military expenditure in either war or peace in real "steel-eating" societies is to accelerate the conversion of natural resources to rubbish—to boost the economy by speeding up throughout. But whether this function could legitimately be called primary, and whether it is ever consciously planned for the purpose of keeping the general standard of living low, are much more problematic.

The operative global misperception is that past triumphs of "the machine" indicate that it has a capacity, in essence, to solve permanently all problems for a human population of indefinite size. This misperception—based in ignorance of physics, chemistry, and biology—is widespread in society even today, as evidenced by the writings of cornucopian economists. Harold Barnett and Chandler Morse, the authors of *Scarcity and Growth*, got the second law of thermodynamics exactly backward and provided the classic statement of the cornucopian position: "Science, by making the resource base more homogeneous, erases the restrictions once thought to reside in the lack of homogeneity. In a neo-Ricardian world, it seems, the particular resources with which one starts increasingly become a matter of indifference." Yet another economist, Mogens Boserup, has chimed in with the opinion that "the entropy story . . . is irrelevant . . . for human action and policy." At the extreme, the cornucopian position is symbolized by the statement of a professor of advertising, Julian Simon, that the only limit to the amount of copper that could be made available to humanity is "the weight of the universe."

There are, of course, some economists who understand that there are limits on what the machine can accomplish. But this view is as yet accepted by only a minority of the profession and probably of society as a whole. Orwell's mid-century picture of humanity as virtually disconnected from the physical and biological worlds is still all too persistent among the most influential of social scientists.

For much of Orwell's adult life, demographers were concerned that populations in the industrialized world might *decline*. It is not surprising, then, that Orwell paid scant attention to the problems of overpopulation. The demographic history of the thirty-five-year period between 1949, the year

*Nineteen Eighty-Four* was published, and the approaching year 1984, has, of course, created conditions totally unlike those Orwell described. He indicated that the nation of Oceania—consisting of Britain, the Americas, Australasia (Australia and New Zealand, presumably), and southern Africa—have a 1984 population of about 300 million. This is actually well under the 1950 population of the Western Hemisphere alone, and far below the roughly 740 million people now living in that "nation."

Orwell's Oceania missed the post-World War II population explosion— arguably the most significant event of the era he was previewing. But there were good reasons why that explosion did not occur in Orwell's world. One was the decrease in reproduction achieved by the repression of sexual activity, as exemplified by the Junior Anti-Sex League. O'Brien states the goals of the Party: "Children will be taken from their mothers at birth, as one takes eggs from a hen. The sex instinct will be eradicated. Procreation will be an annual formality like the renewal of a ration card. We shall abolish the orgasm. . . . There will be no love, except the love of Big Brother."

Had Orwell been more scientifically oriented, he might have predicted that technological advances would make it possible, as indeed they have, to allow eggs to be taken from women and "hatched" elsewhere. Sex then could have been totally abolished in Oceania. The test-tube baby did not, however, originate in the societies (the Soviet Union and China) that most closely resemble that of *Nineteen Eighty-Four*. The process was first perfected in richer, less repressed nations, not as a step toward state control of reproduction, but as a method of restoring fertility and gaining reproductive freedom.

Over the past few decades, there has been a growing realization that sex has many important functions in human society beyond its reproductive role. The increasing separation of sex and reproduction has, as implied by Orwell, led to less childbearing. But the effect of this separation on human relationships, and especially on that between the citizen and the state, has varied from culture to culture.

Ironically, recognition of the seriousness of overpopulation has produced in the real world a situation that in some respects resembles the reproductive milieu of *Nineteen Eighty-Four*—the stringent "Birth Planning" program of the People's Republic of China. The Chinese policy focuses more on limiting births than on repressing sexual activity, yet one inevitably affects the other. Young people in China are virtually forbidden to marry before their mid-twenties, and social mixing of single young people is discouraged.

The other demographic clues to the absence of the population explosion in *Nineteen Eighty-Four* are Oceania's very high infant mortalities, constant political purges, and permanent state of war—all of which imply higher death rates than prevail today in all but the very poorest, war-ravaged countries. The Party *claimed* an infant mortality rate in Oceania of 160 per thousand (live births, presumably), down from 300 before the revolution. An infant mortality rate of 160 per thousand is nearly double the present world average rate and sixteen times that in most rich countries. It was exceeded in 1982 only in a handful of African nations and Democratic Kampuchea (the record holder with 212, much of it undoubtedly due to the war there).

Infant mortality rates above 100 per thousand are indicators of poor nutrition and appalling public health conditions; they are associated with high crude death rates (the number of people of *all* ages dying per thousand per year). Poor nutrition and less than adequate public health conditions (at least for proles) seem to be the norm in *Nineteen Eighty-Four*. But the mortality among adults such conditions would cause is augmented in *Nineteen Eighty-Four* to an unstated (but apparently large) extent by the regular purging of politically undesirable people—both proles and Party members—and by combat deaths.

Nations with high death rates today generally have extremely high birth rates and are growing rapidly. But there are few signs of rapid population growth in the Orwellian world—for example, no indication of a youth-heavy age composition of the population, which inevitably accompanies such growth. Oceania is afflicted with chronic food shortages, but they are due to bureaucratic inefficiency, a decline in science, and malevolence on the part of the Party, not to the population's outstripping its capacity to produce food. Families of Party members are small: never more than two children and often none. Proles are more prolific, though; Winston wonders how many children the woman singing below the window of the room over Mr. Charrington's shop had borne—and muses that it might easily be fifteen. And the sounds of children playing are mentioned several times.

There are, however, no indications of *declining* population size in Oceania. Although the government is said to have control over demographic changes, Big Brother is certainly not exhorting the population to greater reproductive efforts in order to maintain a supply of cannon fodder. Thus Oceania must be assumed to have either a slowly growing population or a stationary one in which the high death rate is balanced by a high birth rate. Or, most likely of all, Orwell never carefully considered the demographic situation in Oceania.

On the other hand, Orwell did visualize a population explosion in some parts of the world. "Whichever power controls equatorial Africa, or the countries of the Middle East or Southern India, or the Indonesian Archipelago, disposes also of the bodies of scores of hundreds of millions of ill-paid and hardworking coolies." That would put the population of those areas at a minimum of four billion people (two-score hundred million); on the order of three times their present population and six times their population when Orwell wrote. One wonders whether Orwell's upper-class English attitudes led him to pay little attention to the potential situation of nonwhite populations.

If Orwell was conscious of the implications of these demographic details, we could infer that he was projecting a rate of population increase that would double those populations every fourteen years or so—a growth rate of some 5 percent per annum. Such a rate is higher than any ever observed in a human population; the record holder, Kenya, is now growing at about 4 percent per annum. Again, it seems likely that Orwell made no attempt to rationalize his demographic projections.

Orwell's world view clearly was shaped by one of the great trends of the twentieth century—urbanization. In 1950 just slightly over a quarter of Earth's people lived in urban areas; by the year 2000 about one-half will. But the world with which he was familiar—Europe in the 1940s—was already thoroughly urbanized. *Nineteen Eighty-Four* is about city folk. The countryside plays a minor role—basically that of a park to which urbanites can escape briefly for hikes or illicit copulation. The states of natural and agricultural ecosystems are not explicitly discussed in Emmanuel Goldstein's "book" within *Nineteen Eighty-Four*, *The Theory and Practice of Oligarchical Collectivism*. We learn only that "The world . . . is a bare, hungry, dilapidated place compared with the world that existed before 1914," and that horse-drawn plows have replaced tractors.

Accordingly, when Orwell (through Goldstein) describes the world of 1984 as more bare, hungry, and dilapidated than that of 1914, he is undoubtedly describing an urban world. For the cities of the developed nations, this projection clearly was inaccurate. Urban dwellers today are better fed, housed, clothed, cared for medically, and entertained than they were before World War I. The peak in their quality of life may have come a decade or two *before* 1984, but in no sense could most of the cities of Europe and North America be considered bare, hungry, or dilapidated compared to 1914—or 1949. The principal adverse changes have been the increase of pollution, especially air pollution, and the collapse of some inner cities. Orwell never mentions pollution problems, although he clearly is describing a fully industrialized (if badly managed) society.

In many poor nations, by contrast, the urban situation today is much worse than that imagined by Orwell—largely because migration from the countryside has caused rates of urban population growth to outstrip even the high rates of natural increase (surplus of births over deaths) in those nations. Cities in most developing countries have been expanding at rates of 10 to 15 percent per year—doubling their populations in as little as five years. Huge slums and shantytowns, sky-high rates of unemployment, malnutrition, disease, and early death are the rule for all but a small elite in these cities. Sanitation is so poor in Mexico City, for example, that in the winter dried human wastes are swept up by the wind from where they were scattered and showered on the city as "fecal snow." Making such cities merely bare and dilapidated would be an improvement for many of their inhabitants.

The complete ignorance of the basic functioning of Earth's life support systems Orwell displayed in his most famous book is still widespread in the real world of 1984. The average American today is an urbanite who knows nothing of these systems and more or less believes that food materializes by magic overnight in supermarkets. It is quite possible to be educated at the finest of our universities and still remain uninformed about the basics of ecology, even agricultural ecology. (There is, for example, no requirement at Stanford that a graduate have even the vaguest grasp of what is involved in feeding society.)

In this sense, the world today is truly Orwellian. Even decision makers are largely unaware that society is supported by a series of essential "public services" supplied by natural ecological systems—ecosystems. These ecosystem services include regulation of the quality of the atmosphere, control of climate and weather, provision of fresh water, generation and preservation of soils, disposal of wastes, recycling of nutrients essential to agriculture, control of the vast majority of potential pests of crops and carriers of human disease, provision of food from the sea, and maintenance of a vast "genetic library" from which humanity has already withdrawn the very basis of civilization and whose potential has barely been tapped. Disruption of natural systems, including those that underpin agricultural systems, leads to losses of the essential services and an impoverishment of society—though the cause often goes unrecognized.

Any projections of a future world that do not carefully consider the basic status of these services is fundamentally flawed. It is like a description of future naval warfare that fails to consider the geography of the oceans or the physics of water, for it is upon the "sea" of ecosystem services that social, political, and economic systems must float. Their status is closely tied also to the exploitation of natural resources.

Rather than human habitations, it is natural ecosystems that are rapidly becoming bare, hungry, and dilapidated today. The planet is in the midst of an episode of ecosystem destruction unprecedented in the past 50 million years. Deserts and weeds are on the march everywhere, and the entire Earth is being assaulted with novel toxins manufactured by one dominant species, *Homo sapiens*. A major result of these environmental traumas is a growing epidemic of extinctions. Species are disappearing at a rate very roughly one hundred times that which has prevailed for most of this planet's history. More important, genetically distinct populations are going extinct at a rate that is at least one hundred times more rapid still. Earth's nonhuman organisms are working parts of the ecosystems that supply those essential services; their loss amounts to a continual deterioration of the planet's capacity to support human life.

The decline of ecosystem services contributes, along with related overpopulation and maldistribution of resources, to a world food problem that will not go away even in the absence of manipulations by a malicious party. It also plays a role in the continuing decline of the global economic system.

In essence, humanity is consuming and dispersing a one-time bonanza of capital, including fossil fuels, concentrated ores of other minerals, fertile soils, ice-age underground water, and biological diversity.

None of these resources is renewable on a time scale of interest to society. They are "stock" resources. As stock resources are depleted, humanity will increasingly be forced to rely on renewable, "flow," resources—primarily solar energy. This reversion to renewable resources will go on in all industrial nations regardless of political system, seemingly out of the control of "Parties." The process could be slowed significantly, but not halted, by technological cleverness. But technological cleverness is not an option available in Oceania. Following the principles of Ingsoc, "technological progress only happens when its products in some way can be used for the diminution of human liberty." There is no word for "science" in Newspeak. But ironically, in the real world of 1984, Science has become a secular religion that is looked to for the solutions to all problems. The side of science that defines and describes the constraints on human endeavor is conveniently ignored; rather, Science is endowed with the ability to make humanity omnipotent.

Orwell is still capable of alerting us to the potential dark side of the sociopolitical system. But his crystal ball did not show him any of the four other intertwined threats that cloud the future of the real world of 1984: the threat of nuclear annihilation, the steady deterioration of ecosystems, increasing difficulties of resource mobilization, and the ever widening gap between rich and poor nations.

Basically, *Nineteen Eighty-Four* was the vision, prophecy, or warning of an intelligent urban man, preoccupied with the social and political trends of his time, but unaware of the underlying resource/environmental conditions that often help to shape those trends. He could no more have had a realistic view of the environmental future than he could of the future of the female half of the human population—he was as cut off from ecology as he was from the strivings of women for equality (see Anne Mellor's essay in this volume). In these respects, most politicians today are frighteningly Orwellian.

That Orwell overlooked matters that are major concerns today may, however, in part be his own doing. Perhaps if he had not worried and written about doublethink, Newspeak, the Ministry of Love, and the like, our political and environmental situation might now be even bleaker. Society in Western Europe and the United States might be much more similar to that in the Soviet Union, where even less attention is paid to the more subtle and fundamental environmental threats faced by humanity.

# 8 Scott R. Pearson

# Economic Doublethink: Food and Politics

*In any time that he could accurately remember there had never been quite enough to eat.*

FOOD IS SCARCE IN *NINETEEN EIGHTY-FOUR*. The Ministry of Plenty promotes starvation, and rationing of food items is standard. The diet of most of the people in Oceania is grim. Inner Party members eat very well and sip wine; Outer Party members have dull meals and drink Victory gin, and proletarians are kept at the margin of subsistence and guzzle beer. Why does George Orwell's Oceania suffer extreme food scarcity and vastly uneven distribution of food in its industrialized urban centers?

Fat and happy workers and bureaucrats would too likely question or even oppose the hypocritical truths of Big Brother's party, truths continuously being remolded by the elite 2 percent who are Inner Party regulars. The desire of the Party for permanent authoritarian power can be realized only through contrived economic scarcity for the masses—the proles, who comprise 85 percent of Oceania's population, and the Outer Party members who make up another 13 percent of the total.

This economic strategy depends on constant warfare. War can be fought with or against either or both of the two other authoritarian superstates, Eurasia and Eastasia, but the battlefields inevitably are in parts of Africa and Asia that are not integral sections of any of the three superpowers. Oceania's persistent state of warfare achieves two objectives, one economic, the other psychological. The creation and destruction of military goods consumes vast resources that might otherwise be used to raise the standard of living of the Outer Party members and proles. Although the promise of growing and more evenly distributed incomes is central to the rhetoric of the Party, *economic doublethink* consists of gradually reducing actual living standards to maintain political power. Food consumption, generally considered the most basic human need, is closely controlled by diverting Oceanian resources to trumped-up military needs. Scientific research and technical changes in production are confined to military equipment (and to communication devices for strengthening domestic political control), thereby reversing two centuries of uneven but steady progress in improving dietary and living conditions for most of Oceania.

Constant warfare has psychological dimensions that buttress the internal economic objectives. Material deprivation of the largely illiterate and powerless proles does not require much external justification; occasional parades of prisoners of war can create circuslike entertainment and stir innate xenophobic instincts. More important, the Outer Party members, particularly the unquestioning, nationalistic ones, find it easier to rationalize their meager and incredibly boring diets of thin soup, dark bread, watery stew, foul cheese, and Victory coffee if they believe they are sacrificing for the preservation and eventual world supremacy of Oceania. Even the lower echelons of the Inner Party are whipped into wartime hysteria in an alleged effort to spread the Oceanian way of life.

Only party leaders at the very top are permitted to know that there is no realistic chance of Oceania's conquering either of the other superpowers; that the political, economic, and social structures of both Eurasia and Eastasia are already virtually identical to the "Oceanian way of life"; and that there is nothing to be gained strategically by controlling, even permanently, the unclaimed war zones in Africa and Asia. These areas contain untapped mineral resources and hordes of unskilled laborers, but Oceania is already having a difficult enough time managing its economy so as to waste its own resources and reduce domestic standards of living. If by some fluke Oceania were to gain peacetime hegemony over the hundreds of millions of proles in these war zones, political control would be cumbersome and economic management might be impossible. True, these areas could easily absorb the Oceanian resources not consumed in military ventures. Then, however, unless the "foreign aid" projects were totally unproductive, the transfers would raise the living standards of the new Asian and African proles, making political control even more difficult.

In Orwell's Oceania, therefore, food is scarce by design, not by the accident of mismanagement. High-quality foods—white bread, real coffee, good meat, tasty chocolate, fine wine—are made available only to the elite Inner Party members. Some redistribution of these quality foodstuffs takes place on the black market, but such supplies are expensive and illegal and thus dangerous to procure. It is not clear why the Party permits the black markets in food (or other consumer goods) to operate; given its effective information

## "Anything Left For Me?"

ROY JUSTUS
*Courtesy Minneapolis Star*

Cartoon by Roy Justus. From *Best Editorial Cartoons of the Year*, 1975 edition. © 1975 Charles
Brooks. By permission of Pelican Publishing Company.

network, the government would have little trouble in suppressing the illegal
food trade. One is left to presume that the government of this authoritarian
state, like most real totalitarian governments, finds it convenient to allow
free markets to smooth out the worst excesses of inefficient, centrally planned
rationing.

The central point, however, is that the government of Oceania fundamentally does not care about efficiency in the production of food crops and
distribution of foodstuffs to consumers. The state fights wars principally to
deprive its own citizens of food and other consumer goods. If economic
resources are also wasted because food is grown or marketed inefficiently,
so much the better. In light of Oceania's strategic food policy, Orwell does

not even need to concern himself with the vexing issue of whether the authoritarian state could feed its people better if it wanted to.

II

Orwell's *Nineteen Eighty-Four* has been variously interpreted as a prophecy, a warning, and a description of London in 1948; for example, Anthony Burgess in his book *Nineteen Eighty-Five* discusses all three interpretations, but focuses on the last one. Whatever Orwell intended, it is difficult to resist the temptation to contrast his description of food in Oceania in 1984, thirty-five years in the future at the time the book was published, with the actual trends of food production, distribution, consumption, and policy between 1949 and 1983.

As a prognosticator of political change (if that is what he meant to be), Orwell obviously missed the boat. Significant areas of all four of Orwell's geopolitical divisions are not run by authoritarian governments. Although three major power blocs have formed, the configuration is substantially different from the *Nineteen Eighty-Four* pattern and none of these blocs is a unified superstate. Moreover, economic doublethink has never developed as a guiding force for policy. No government, totalitarian or otherwise, has deliberately tried to reduce the standard of living, including food intake, of its country's people. Limited wars have broken out with depressing regularity (in contrast to Orwell's atomic warfare in the 1950s followed by revolution and continuous war in the sixties, seventies, and eighties), but governments have not waged war to deprive their own consumers of food and other necessities or luxuries. Some might interpret the arms race as being roughly equivalent economically to the Orwellian notion of reducing living standards by engaging in unremitting war, but few would argue that any contemporary government is spending militarily for the express purpose of starving its own populace.

Orwell foresaw most people in the world experiencing a declining standard of living and periodic starvation because of purposeful policy decisions taken by authoritarian governments. Asians and Africans residing in areas not contained in any of the three superstates are described in *Nineteen Eighty-Four* as remaining at a miserably low, bare subsistence income level through a combination of superpower wars fought in their homelands and Malthusian checks (whereby incomes temporarily higher than subsistence result in more rapid population growth, which in turn reduces incomes per head to a subsistence level).

Food issues since World War II have differed enormously from those portrayed in *Nineteen Eighty-Four*, but they nonetheless have great contemporary significance in national and international politics. As many as one-fourth of the world's people are undernourished; policy makers in many poor countries view setting the domestic price of food as perhaps their single most important annual political and economic decision; and diplomats from many of the world's richest countries argue heatedly with each other as they threaten to engage in agricultural trade wars.

### III

Orwell defined Oceania as much of the British Commonwealth (the United Kingdom, Canada, Australia, New Zealand, and southern Africa) and North and South America. Countries in this region have accounted for most of the world's supplies of cereal grain exports in the postwar period. The world's dependence on the United States for cereal supplies has increased to the point where this country alone furnished nearly half the world's grain exports (wheat, coarse grains, and rice) in 1982. If exports from the other breadbasket countries in Oceania—Canada, Australia, Argentina, and South Africa—are added to the American share, Oceania's control of world exports in 1983 rises to more than 80 percent. Oceania, if it existed, would thus be overwhelmingly the world's main exporter of starchy food staples. These commodities currently supply more than half the food calories for more than three-fourths of the world's people.

All of the cereal exporters in the Oceanian region are highly efficient; all use scientific, mechanized techniques to farm and market their crops. But most of these countries have adopted policies that support some very inefficient producers of certain commodities; for example—with the notable exception of New Zealand, the world's most competitive producer of dairy products—they produce many dairy products under protection at high cost. Undernutrition is rare in the richer countries of this region; the United States, for one, has largely solved its hunger problem through a controversial but effective food stamp program. In parts of Latin America, however, notably northeast Brazil and Central America, severe undernutrition is perpetuated by extreme poverty; in much of this area, questionable government policies that keep incentives to farmers slight and prevent meaningful land reforms have resulted in low levels and slow growth of food production. With these exceptions, however, Winston Smith and his friends and enemies would be hard pressed to find very many places in Oceania today where the quantity, quality, and variety of foodstuffs were as appallingly limited as they are in the London of Airstrip One.

### IV

Eurasia presents a mixed and quite different story. Orwell's Eurasia appears to be an extension of the Soviet Union westward to incorporate all of Europe except the United Kingdom. Actual food and agricultural policy in this region has roughly reflected the political split between West and East. All of the large and some of the small countries of Western Europe—France, West Germany, Italy, the United Kingdom (awkwardly for Orwell), the Netherlands, Belgium, Luxembourg, Denmark, Ireland, and Greece—have formed the European Community (EC) and created the Common Agricultural Policy (CAP).

The CAP is a cornerstone of Western European integration. It guarantees very high and stable prices to farmers, thereby inducing investment in better production techniques and generating surpluses of food commodities (such as the now fabled "mountains of butter" and "lakes of wine") that must either be stored or exported with large EC subsidies. These export subsidies and American efforts to counter them are at the heart of the agricultural trade war threatened between the EC and the United States. Despite the high food prices to consumers in the EC, hunger is almost nonexistent in Western Europe, largely because comfortable standards of living evolved in the very successful postwar economic recovery. If Winston and Julia could visit Paris today, they would find food expensive (especially in the restaurants) but in plentiful variety, and there would be no signs of rationing or of the consequent black markets.

A different situation prevails in the eastern part of Eurasia—Eastern Europe and the USSR. Tight rationing, long queues, poor quality, and occasional shortages—but very little hunger—typify the food situation in these countries. Agricultural policies in Eastern European countries have not been uniformly bad; Hungary, for example, has provided a reasonable set of incentives with good results. But the Soviet Union suffers from both dubious policies and weather-vulnerable crops, and Poland's agriculture has taken a great beating during the recent period of political and economic instability.

The agricultural policies of these governments, though authoritarian, do not fit the Orwellian mold. Orwell's characters would no doubt feel that Warsaw or Moscow in 1983 resembles their London of *Nineteen Eighty-Four* more closely than do other world capitals, but they would probably be impressed with the absence of extreme deprivation and undernutrition. They would see an agricultural sector of state farms struggling to meet unrealistic targets with inefficient management and shortages of production requisites, and alongside it a private farm sector geared to local markets and thriving on individual initiative. Is authoritarian socialism compatible with efficient agricultural production and distribution in Eastern Europe and the Soviet Union? There is evidence that farmers in Communist countries, as elsewhere, respond to positive agricultural incentives with greater output and productivity; the dismal record reflects inappropriate policies, not incompetent farmers.

The similarities, so far as they go, between food in *Nineteen Eighty-Four* and food in contemporary Communist Eastern Europe are therefore limited. Agricultural inefficiency and restricted food supplies are a desired focus of agricultural policy in the former, but are an unintended outcome of inappropriate Socialist policy in the latter. Moreover, food consumers are gaining increasing influence in Eastern Europe. During the past decade, for example, the Soviet Union has been offsetting domestic grain shortfalls by importing wheat and corn in order to avoid cutting consumption levels of bread and meat, and the diet of Soviet proles is improving.

V

The third major superstate in Orwell's imagined world is Eastasia, comprising China, Japan, and continental Southeast Asia. The contemporary countries that occupy this geographic region, like those in Eurasia, contain both authoritarian and democratic regimes. The Communist revolution in China was just completed as Orwell published *Nineteen Eighty-Four*. Since then—1949—China has made impressive strides in feeding its people. Through a combination of political stability, land reform, labor-intensive innovations, high-yielding seeds, population control, and effective decentralized bureaucracies, China under Communist policies has overcome many of the causes of famine, starvation, and malnutrition.

It is probably premature to claim that China has solved its food problem; some observers, though necessarily lacking hard evidence, report that as many as 10 percent of China's more than one billion people still suffer from undernutrition. Moreover, just as the problem of making adequate food calories available to most Chinese people is on the way to resolution, another type of food problem is emerging. Because of successful development policies, increasing numbers of people in China are earning incomes high enough to permit more meat in their diets. Consequently, China has begun to import increasing quantities of feed grain, mainly American corn, following the well-established pattern of the newly industrialized countries, such as Hong Kong, Singapore, Taiwan, and South Korea in East Asia, and of the oil-producing developing nations. This phenomenon, whereby growing incomes lead to changes in diet and consequent adjustments in international trade, is brutally finessed in *Nineteen Eighty-Four* by the Orwellian policy of economic double-think through which incomes of the masses are forced to decline.

The other large country in Eastasia is Japan. Japanese agricultural problems and policies are akin to those in Western Europe. The issue is how to wind down a politically resistant agricultural sector that has lost its international competitiveness—largely because rapid industrial growth has raised wages throughout the economy. Japanese officials, so adept at industrial policy, have been no more successful than their European counterparts in finding a sensible answer to the problem of agricultural adjustment. Instead, Japan has opted to protect one of the most inefficient agricultural sectors in the world. Rice prices in Japan are four or five times the world price level, and Japan's stock of rice is more than half the annual amount that moves internationally in the entire world rice market. American negotiators try continually, with fleeting success, to convince the Japanese government to permit greater entry of U.S. beef, citrus, and other heavily protected agricultural products. Hence, rather than the contrived food shortages depicted in *Nineteen Eighty-Four*, Japan has large surpluses of rice, high food prices—and no hunger problem.

VI

Orwell left two large regions of the world out of the direct hegemony of the three superstates. The northern ice cap has no agricultural interest (in spite of the professor who insists that, given large enough subsidies, tomatoes could be grown on the North Pole), and thus is ignored here. But the main war zone in *Nineteen Eighty-Four* is that vast reservoir of land, minerals, and "hard-working, unskilled laborers," described by Orwell as bounded by Tangier, Brazzaville, Darwin, and Hong Kong. (Orwell's geography is suspect here since continental Southeast Asia is supposed to be part of Eastasia.) Together with Latin America, which Orwell placed in Oceania, this huge area comprises what has come to be known as the Third World. Many countries in the Third World have not yet solved their food problems. Their hunger problem will not finally be overcome until economic growth and income distribution permit poverty to disappear.

Most of the several hundred million hungry people in the world live in Asia. Nevertheless, in the face of contrary odds, many poor countries in Asia have made impressive progress during the 1960s and 1970s in providing higher incomes and better diets for their people. India, following disastrous droughts and famine in the mid-1960s, has become self-sufficient in cereals (wheat and rice). Indonesia has increased output of rice, the primary staple, by more than one-half during the 1970s. These and other Asian countries introduced the Green Revolution: they employed high-yielding seed varieties, improved water control, chemical fertilizer, credit to purchase these improved inputs, and government extension programs to diffuse the innovations to small farms.

The Green Revolution has been largely an Asian phenomenon and limited to farmers with irrigated plots. Rain-fed agriculture, including that in most of Africa, has not benefited much from scientific innovations. Partly because appropriate new techniques are lacking—but more generally because of inappropriate policies that reduce the profitability of farming—sub-Saharan Africa experienced a decline in per capita food production during the past two decades and shows unhappy signs of being the main locus of food shortages during the coming decades.

Orwell was far too pessimistic in imagining that most Asians and Africans would exist at bare subsistence levels because of Malthusian checks and great power wars. Enormous barriers to sustained economic development remain, but progress is being made in most developing countries. Food policy decisions have proven to be especially difficult because they involve trading off politically convenient low food prices to consumers against economically desirable high commodity prices for farmers. Poor people (and middle-class urbanites with political power) clamor for cheap food, but producers, whether capitalist or socialist, small or large, require positive incentives to increase output and invest in better techniques of production. The food price dilemma is not ideological; all governments of low-income countries face it. Success in food policy is ensured neither by revolutions on the left or right nor by middle-of-the-road indecision. Poor countries with better-fed people, from China to the Ivory Coast, have found ways of making it profitable for their farmers to grow more, while ensuring food availability for the neediest consumers.

## VII

What would the Inner Party theoreticians—O'Brien and his colleagues—conclude if they were to take a world tour in 1983 for the purpose of gathering information on food and hunger? Following their initial shock at being allowed to leave Airstrip One for any reason other than a military one, they would be in for many surprises. The greatest disappointment would probably be the absence of any country, even those with totalitarian governments, practicing economic doublethink, that is, claiming to be offering more food and consumer goods for its citizens while actually carrying out policies, such as perpetual war, to provide less material comforts but more party control. Big Brother's acolytes would find numerous examples of inane food policies and poor management leading to hunger, shortages, rationing, and black markets, which might deceive them into believing that some contemporary governments were following their advice. But they would be observing the fruits of ineptness, not malevolence.

For the Inner Party ideologues, the world tour would present many apparent contradictions. They would probably expect to find the fewest surprises in authoritarian states. In Eastern Europe and the Soviet Union, they would indeed observe the familiar food queues, ration shops, black markets, and shoddy quality. But they would discover little hunger, even among the proles, and they would be amazed at the relatively high standard of living that the party permitted the proles to attain. In China, the Inner Party team would find both rationing and some hunger. There, however, they would marvel at the rapidity of change (just think of having to rewrite all that fast-moving history!) and at the efficient and decentralized decision making. In the Third World, the visitors would observe some widespread hunger, especially in the poorer areas of the countryside and the large cities. Yet they would also find farmers eating well and sporting bicycles, transistor radios, and other signs of improved living standards.

Most mind-boggling of all would be the visits to the Western, industrialized countries. There the party faithful would encounter an almost complete absence of hunger and a wide diversity of food; consumers willing to pay high prices for food in order to support incomes of farmers; an active research and development community promoting and profiting from increases in agricultural productivity; a series of complicated commodity exchanges on which large, privately owned multinational companies trade; and governments continually harassed by well-organized farm lobbies demanding more public support for agriculture. Having witnessed the world food economy in 1983, the Inner Party experts would have to exercise all their best powers of economic doublethink to rationalize their own food policy and to continue to love Big Brother.

*Computer Thinker* by Gary Viskupic. © 1983 *Discover Magazine*, Time, Inc.

# 9 *Robert E. McGinn*

# The Politics of Technology and the Technology of Politics

*The ideal set up by the Party was something huge, terrible, and glittering—a world of steel and concrete, of monstrous machines and terrifying weapons. . . . The reality was decaying, dingy cities.*

NINETEEN EIGHTY-FOUR is, among other things, a critical commentary on the relationship of technology to modern society. Orwell utilizes every aspect of material culture—from the physical landscape of the city to the mundane products of daily life to exotic technologies and technological systems—to enrich his indictment of the order of life in the world of Big Brother.

By far the most prominent features of the urban landscape in Big Brother's London are the government ministry buildings. The Ministry of Truth is "an enormous pyramidal structure of glittering white concrete, soaring up, terrace after terrace, three hundred meters into the air." The buildings housing the other three ministries are of "similar appearance and size." The immensity of these buildings, dwarfing all others in London, symbolizes the enormous political power of the government, while their shape, evoking the pyramids of ancient Egypt, suggests the government's immortality and stability. But, whereas the Egyptian pyramids were the burial places of the Pharaohs, the pyramidal Ministry of Love building is the scene of the spiritual death and burial of the individual, the person of independent thought and human affection. At the termination of his coercive "therapy" in the Ministry of Love, Winston has become one of those "corpses waiting to be sent back to the grave." That the Ministry of Love has "no windows in it at all" suggests both the unnaturalness of its inner environment and the immunity of the activities transpiring within from scrutiny in the natural light of reason. By contrast, Winston's apartment house, Victory Mansions, has glass doors, symbolizing the almost total lack of privacy created by the presence of tele-screens within and the swooping, prying Police Patrol helicopters without.

Except for the glittering white concrete ministry buildings, the labyrinthine city is grim in appearance. From the moderately high apartment buildings with their grimy exteriors, there are vistas of dilapidated housing papered with posters of Big Brother. The brown-colored, overcrowded proletarian area is a maze of narrow alleyways, battered doors, boarded windows, and dusty pubs. Winston recognizes the stark contrast between the Party's pro-fessed ideal for the physical side of Oceania ("something huge, terrible, and glittering—a world of steel and concrete, of monstrous machines and terri-fying weapons" as epitomized in the ministry buildings) and the prepon-derant reality of "decaying, dingy cities." It then dawns on him—a conclusion that his visit to O'Brien's home later forces him to qualify—that "the truly characteristic thing about modern life [is] not its cruelty and insecurity, but simply its bareness, its dinginess, its listlessness."

This contrast between the real and the ideal parallels that between the depressing areas of London where the proles and Outer Party members live and the exclusive quarter of town where the Inner Party stalwarts live. When Winston and Julia meet at O'Brien's house in the Inner Party quarter of town, they are astonished to the point of intimidation at "the whole atmosphere of the huge block of flats, the richness and spaciousness of everything."

Orwell also invidiously contrasts London and the surrounding countryside. The devitalizing, antisensuous, technological city is counterposed to the tonic, erotic effects of the lush natural environment beyond the city boundaries. With its springy turf, clear waters, and hideout in the natural clearing sur-rounded by a forest of tall saplings, the countryside is the "Golden Country" of Winston's dreams. At first glance the contrast between technological city and natural countryside seems vitiated by an apparent oasis within the city: the park where Winston and Julia meet after having been released from "therapy." However, through his use of symbols Orwell makes it clear that, spiritually speaking, the park is decidedly of the city. For when Winston and Julia meet there at the end of the novel, it is a frigid March day, "when the earth was like iron." Moreover, they sit down "on two iron chairs, side by side but not too close together." In the nontechnological countryside, however, they make love on the grass among the fallen bluebells. Thus Orwell uses a technological resource, iron, as a symbol of their lobotomized spiritual con-ditions. He projects a stark opposition between nature and technology, be-tween the organic and artificial, throughout the work. Without exception, every item of technology composed of human-made materials—concrete, glass, iron—has a negative connotation or association. Modern technology and its materials bear the bulk of the negative symbolic meaning in the work.

The limited inventory of products for everyday use, the gritty, dark brown soap, tinny saucepans, and pathetic food are, like the public physical environment, repellent. Other items, such as razor blades, buttons, and darning wool, are scarce. Still others, such as the regulation lunches and Outer Party costumes, symbolize the uniformity of thought which is an explicit element of Party ideology.

Personal possessions are in deplorable condition. Winston carries a "black, very shabby briefcase." Much of the food—chocolate, coffee, sugar, bread—is artificial, and the loathsome smelling Victory gin is scientifically formulated to induce a state of passive pleasure.

Beyond the paltry quality and apparent scarcity of individual necessities and useful goods, important communal facilities are in disrepair, notably the lift in Winston's apartment. All three of these aspects—quality, scarcity, upkeep—come into bold relief when Winston and Julia visit Inner Party member O'Brien. The latter, as it turns out, enjoys good food, good tobacco, and good wine; has "silent and incredibly rapid lifts" in his building; and owns high-quality possessions, from soundless, soft carpeting and stemmed wine glasses to a silver cigarette box. Thus is Winston's earlier conclusion about the universal paltriness of modern life shattered.

Orwell exploits the malfunctioning of another mundane technological item to symbolize subtly the decline of another perennial human value. When a neighbor, Mrs. Parsons, asks Winston to fix her blocked-up kitchen sink, it seems at first as if this episode is meant either to display the brutality of her children or to criticize bureaucratic inertia and insensitivity. ("Repairs, except what you could do for yourself, had to be sanctioned by remote committees which were liable to hold up even the mending of a window for two years.") But Orwell drops a clue regarding his real target: it was not food but a clot of human hair that had blocked up the pipe. The kitchen, in other words, serves also as a bathroom. In fact, there are no private bathrooms alluded to in the novel—and the public one at the Ministry of Truth is equipped with telescreens. Orwell thus utilizes even minor events to underscore the demise of privacy, a value whose status is intimately linked to the prospects for human individuality.

Privacy is also the appeal of the empty "young lady's keepsake album" that Winston purchases at Charrington's antique shop. This blank book offers him a medium in which to crystallize his subjective consciousness and retain a record of past events—which, he knows, is tantamount to a revolutionary deed. Books in general represent individual liberty, as implied by the fact that the only place in his flat where Winston is able to avoid the eye of the telescreen is in the alcove, which "had probably been intended to hold bookshelves." We subsequently learn that, with the exception of propagandistic textbooks and exercise books, works by autonomous authors have been systematically destroyed. Winston found the diary "peculiarly beautiful"—one of only six times this word appears in the text (twice in reference to the book's smooth, creamy paper).

To Winston the creamy paper deserves to be written on with a nibbed pen—"an archaic instrument" that had to be obtained furtively—rather than an "ink-pencil." The combination of private writing, creamy paper, nibbed pen, and ink pot serve to awaken Winston's critical faculty much as the communion with nature (and Julia) in the countryside had energized the dormant instinctual side of his being. The common denominator here is sensuousness, precisely that which is utterly lacking in the bookless, unnatural, technological environment in which most of the novel unfolds.

Even the room above the antique shop is maintained by the Party as a trap for those alienated from the present order. Its ingratiating artifacts could just as readily have been destroyed as real books and people were. Thus, despite its appearance, this room (like the city park) is of the tyrannical techno-political order. Nevertheless, its furnishings are seemingly devoid of intrusive modern technologies (the telescreen is hidden behind the engraving on the wall) and the room's attractiveness is intimately bound up with nature. Each item conveys a value-laden message about the past and present ways of life in Airstrip One. A small bookcase contained only "rubbish," for "the hunting-down and destruction of books had been done with the same thoroughness in the prole quarters as everywhere else." Then there is an enormous bed, unlike any seen nowadays "except in the houses of the proles." Its size and springiness surprise Winston and Julia. The link with nature is not just through the opportunity for sexual contact the bed affords, though. The frame is made of a natural material, mahogany, just as the frame of the engraving of St. Clement's Dane Church hanging on the wall is of rosewood. That the hideaway episode symbolizes the severed link between humans in the industrial society and nature is further suggested by the fact that, along with the clearing in the country, the room is the only place where Winston partakes of natural foods.

The deep armchair and gateleg table remind one of rooms that were once legitimately commodious and of the demise of ancient craft traditions which utilized natural materials. The dying notions of freedom, beauty, nature, craft, and love come together in the symbolic figure of the old, hemispherical glass paperweight that Winston cherishes. The "peculiar softness, as of rainwater, in both the color and texture of the glass" give the figure a remarkable depth, conveying a sense of extensive inner space in which Winston and Julia could move freely and safely. Besides the notebook, the paperweight is the only other beautiful thing Winston encounters in the novel. The coral piece embedded in the heart of the exquisitely crafted crystal seems to Winston to represent himself and Julia, together forever, free, and surrounded by beauty. The room and diary episodes are of a piece: the technological items associated with each afford Winston a sense of a past radically different from his suffocating present. They thus enable him temporarily to achieve a critical perspective on the present—something the Inner Party would not tolerate.

III

The most eye-catching technological products in the book are Orwell's futuristic devices and techniques—some of which now seem considerably less exotic than they must have in 1949. But his references, for example, to a human vaporizer—the Inner Party could afford neither physical nor informational residues of certain of its victims—and to "remoter possibilities," such as focusing the sun's rays through lenses suspended in outer space and weather-modification techniques, display an excellent technical imagination. More interestingly, Orwell is prescient in projecting a balance of terror among the superstates arising out of extensive scientific and technological research. Incidentally, in describing the locus of such research as "vast [government] laboratories," Orwell recognized the emergence of what has come to be called "big science" years before this trend was discussed by historians of science.

Complementing his interest in writing as a weapon in the cause of individual freedom, Orwell seems to have been disturbed by the possibility that new technologies might compromise the integrity and creativity of the writing process. I refer here to technologies like the *speakwrite*, the *versificator*, and the *novel-writing machines*. It is precisely the physical act of writing down and continuously scrutinizing one's words that the speakwrite machine eliminates. The cramp in Winston's hand after writing the first paragraph in his journal symbolizes the atrophy of both mind and body occasioned by the fact that, short notes aside, Winston dictated everything into the machine. The versificator composes the words to countless similar songs "without any human intervention whatsoever." The novel-writing machines, resembling big kaleidoscopes, are used to rough in the plots of novels following the general directives issued by the Party Planning Committee. These machines are part of a highly mechanized group process for the "production" of novels. Besides the demise of the role of the creative individual writer, what dismayed Orwell about such devices was that such facility as they might afford would be purchased only at the cost of diminished powers of individualized human expression and communication.

Of the medical technologies referred to in the work, the most noteworthy have to do with human sexuality and with the alteration of human thought and feeling. The Party-controlled Junior Anti-Sex League's advocacy of artificial insemination (*artsem*) and O'Brien's disclosure that Party neurologists were at work on research into how the orgasm might be abolished, project a future in which sexual activity is severed from both procreation and pleasure. By eradicating the sex instinct, the Party hopes to effect a state of affairs devoid of shared intimacies that could possibly come between person and Party. Medical science and technology are completely co-opted in the service of the Party. The private well-being of the individual is no longer the primary goal of medical practice and research. Rather, the power of the Party over the individual is to be increased by overcoming through medical science and technology any potential physiologically based source of resistance to that domination.

In the last fourth of the novel we learn that the Inner Party is able directly to alter a person's mind and feelings: to alter radically a person's perceptual judgments and memory bank, to demolish the ability to have certain feelings, and to focus a recalcitrant's specific feelings on selected targets. Winston and Julia had thought that even if the body of a rebel could be manipulated at will by the Party with its sophisticated technology and science—and even if the complete contents of a mind could be ascertained—nevertheless "the inner heart, whose workings were mysterious even to yourself, remained impregnable." Feelings, they thought, could not be changed by the Party. However, through a combination of physical deprivation, physical and psychological assault, drugs, electrocerebral technology, and fear, the Party succeeds in overcoming two of the few remaining limits on its power: private thoughts and feelings previously beyond its determination and control.

IV

The telescreen is the pivotal and most notorious element in the Party's total communications system. Although most proles do not have them in their homes, these sensitive, two-way, audiovisual devices are mandatory in the abodes of Outer Party members. There the receiver volume controls could be lowered but not turned off completely. (The versions in Inner Party members' residences could.) One effect of this systematic violation of privacy is to inhibit rebels like Julia and Winston even in the countryside where they arrange to meet. " 'I didn't want to say anything in the lane,' she went on, 'in case there's a mike hidden there. I don't suppose there is, but there could be. There's always a chance of one of those swine recognizing your voice.' " Winston's conditioning exacted a steeper toll: "He was facing her at several paces' distance. As yet he did not dare move nearer to her. . . . 'We're all right here,' [she said]. . . . 'We're all right here?' he repeated stupidly." Any spontaneity in his disposition had been crushed.

Curiously, the advanced communications system described in the novel does not include the telephone. This is understandable, however, for the telephone is part of a network of autonomous users who, to serve their own interests, periodically initiate private, two-way communications with immediate feedback. The telescreen system, on the other hand, disseminates the Party's information simultaneously to all network members for their involuntary consumption, and extracts information from them without their knowledge or consent. Unlike the Outer Party's intrusive telescreens, telephone communications can be terminated at will by either party, and the devices deactivated or disconnected to limit the options of would-be callers.

Since it is common knowledge in Oceania that all letters are opened in transit, few are sent. People rely on printed postcards with long lists of phrases, striking out the ones that are inapplicable. Thus the mail system reinforces the effect on communication that the Party dictionaries are intended to have: reduced richness, subtlety, and individuality in thought and expression.

In certain respects the novel's transportation system parallels its communications system. Winston travels most often by foot, occasionally by train or bus. Only Inner Party members have private autos and that traffic is apparently limited to the Inner Party quarter. Like the private telephone, the private automobile would place too much power in the hands of the average individual. The individual is limited to whatever is within walking distance of Party-authorized bus and train stops. This is why Outer Party members like Winston rarely "penetrate" the more congenial Inner Party quarter of the city and are astounded when they do.

Other technological systems, such as the electrical lighting and steam heating systems in multi-unit dwellings, are also centrally controlled. They thus serve to preclude autonomous use by the individual, reinforce the wartime mentality of scarcity, and offer another dimension of invidious contrast between the Highs and non-Highs. The precisely synchronized, centrally controlled time-telling system is another source of Inner Party power. The only person in the novel with a private timepiece—a wristwatch—is O'Brien. During his torture Winston is deprived of any conception of time or time passage. Knowledge of the time and the ability to control time signals is power.

V

Orwell seems to see modern technology as posing quite different kinds of dangers to different groups. First, technology in the form of machine production is inherently dangerous to the ruling elite's interest in preserving the status quo. If the capacity to create wealth for all were realized, the social distinction based on substantial differences in wealth which they enjoy would be eliminated. Orwell, assuming a perennial quasi-Nietzschean drive to enhance one's sense of power, suggests that modern ruling elites contrive and foster continuous war in order to expend what would otherwise be the surplus of wealth made possible by modern production technology. In this way they are able to maintain conditions of economic scarcity and the requisite psychology of emergency under which to continue to enjoy their superior socioeconomic status.

This rationale for war in the twentieth century is a striking alternative to the better-known Marxist account couched in terms of struggles to protect or expand markets. It is, however, a bit too neat. We can accept that extensive and continual war-related activities do have the effect of restricting the diffusion of wealth and limiting the upward social mobility of the disadvantaged without subscribing to the tidy conspiracy theory that such effects are the *purpose* of those activities.

The second danger Orwell sees in modern technology is that communications innovations do more than make government tyranny possible; by making behavior monitoring and opinion molding more efficacious, they actually *spur* tyrannies to intensify these pursuits. This claim is plausible only to the extent that government does control such communications systems in a given society, as in certain Eastern European countries. Nevertheless, Orwell seems to be touching on a point of more general application: as they trace their respective evolutionary paths, technologies which began as mere enabling or necessary conditions for some activity can become so efficacious that using them becomes irresistible to those who control them. Orwell thus noted quite early on a special case of the technological imperative of modern Western culture: if, technologically speaking, something can be done, it shall be done. There is a certain mystique about exotic technological achievement. The widespread interest in and research into *in vitro* fertilization and robotics, to take just two examples, are not explicable solely in terms of medical need and economic survival or advantage. Other basic factors are at work, among which may be Orwell's candidate: the intoxication of power. He is arguing that the modern craving for power—coupled with the ever increasing, seductive capabilities of our centrally controlled technological enterprises—does not augur well in the foreseeable future for the autonomous, humane individual.

VI

The fact that Orwell's dark vision has yet to materialize in the West is a tribute to both the resilience of democratic values and the balance of power among executive, legislative, and judicial institutions. However, this is scarcely grounds for smug self-congratulation. A more prudent response to the politico-technological horrors depicted in the work would be to reflect critically on the continuing degradation of our physical urban environment, on the mediocre quality of many technological items of everyday personal use, and on our fondness as a culture for embracing exotic new technologies in order to avoid coming to grips with vexing problems of equity, community, and the quality of life. The tendency to acquiesce in the creation of ever more powerful, centrally controlled technological systems is rationalized by pointing to the fact that such systems are essential to national military security and economic well-being. But this consideration in itself offers little cheer to the fragile values of political liberty and social justice. Given the virtual impossibility of turning back the technological clock, we must either develop alternatives to technologies currently under centralized control or limit strictly the ways and the conditions under which their controllers are entitled to use them. Awareness of Orwell's concerns about the technology-society relationship can help underscore the pivotal fact that, in the words of Harvard law professor Lawrence Tribe, "No task confronting civilization is more urgent than that of channeling technology to advance rather than destroy the fabric of life and the dignity of man."

# 10  *Raymond B. Clayton*

# The Biomedical Revolution and Totalitarian Control

*"They can't do that," she said finally, . . . "they can't get inside you."*
*"No," he said a little more hopefully, "no; that's quite true. They can't get inside you. If you can feel that staying human is worth while, even when it can't have any result whatever, you've beaten them."*

THROUGH THE PAST TWO DECADES medicine and biology have provided the arena for accelerating scientific and technological advance, and the trend promises to continue through the remainder of this century and on into the next. Organ transplantation and prostheses, immunological manipulation, psychobiological analysis and control, and genetic engineering—the transformation of the genetics (and hence the chemistry) of the living cell—these are all fields in which the tempo of progress shows every sign of increasing.

What will life be like in the biotechnological society ahead of us after 1984? Barring any of the obvious major catastrophes, life will be much better provided for and, medically speaking, it will be much more secure than ours. Genetic engineering will ultimately bring immense gains, not only to medicine but over a broad front, including agriculture and industry. To see today's genetic engineering in long-term perspective, we must compare it to organic chemistry in the 1860s, when the first synthetic dyestuffs presaged the rise of gigantic new industries with a wealth of products—pharmaceuticals, plastics, man-made fibres among them—that no one then could even imagine. In biomedical technology, many of the leads currently being followed in research in such fields as cancer, mental illness, and the degenerative diseases will yield therapeutic advances during the next thirty-five years that will make obsolete many of those that have taken place since *Nineteen Eighty-Four* was published.

Yet there is growing awareness that a price is being paid—and will continue to be paid—for these benefits, which is difficult to evaluate exactly but demands our concern and sober assessment. Still further proliferation of manipulative medical technologies (for example, in the field of human reproduction) will distance us ever farther from our biological nature. The new psychobiology will most probably lead to rational cure rather than mere "control" of the most destructive mental diseases such as the schizophrenias and depressive illness, but such advances will inevitably bring mounting confusion over questions of personal integrity and moral responsibility. Our descendants will differ from us in their attitude to such questions even more than we differ from our pre-Freudian forebears—and in the same direction of increasing moral relativism and depersonalization. As the grisly history of the twentieth century attests and as Orwell was at pains to point out, totalitarian regimes strive ruthlessly to attain precisely this result. Herein lies the danger.

As potential elements in a system of totalitarian control, the biomedical technologies could offer the "Inner Party" of a future Orwellian regime practical techniques for social control far more effective than the brutal methods described in *Nineteen Eighty-Four*. This possibility is suggested by the inherently political character of the new technologies: the definition of sickness or health and the indications for treatment are socially determined. Biomedical technologies are consequently peculiarly susceptible to Orwell's cardinal principle of *doublethink*. The notion of therapy for cure and therapy for social normalization of the patient, always subtly related, are readily confused. Psychiatry, as practiced in the USSR (and in the West, too, according to some critics) is especially liable to such confusion.

If the "patient" can be brought to share his controller's doublethink confusion of aims, the technology can be used most effectively for totalitarian control. In *Nineteen Eighty-Four* Orwell shows how O'Brien tortures Winston Smith into surrendering his powers of personal judgment:

> "How many fingers am I holding up, Winston?"
> "Four."
> "And if the Party says that it is not four but five—then how many?"
> "Four."
> The word ended in a gasp of pain. The needle of the dial had shot up to fifty-five. The sweat had sprung out all over Winston's body.

But an O'Brien of the biotechnological society of the future might behave more like a dentist working on a recalcitrant tooth:

"Hold on, Winston, old boy. One more go and I think I'll have these pesky neurons of yours fixed so you'll have no more trouble. Awkward little bastards, aren't they?" He cautiously adjusts the controls.

"Not hurting you am I? Good. You're lucky; this new machine they gave me is much more accurate than the old gear. Much faster, too. Should have you out of here in a jiffy. Now: how many fingers, Winston?"

"Five."

"Good! Excellent! You can go now. Just check back next week so that we can be sure it's permanent."

Here Winston shares O'Brien's view of himself as an object, a mechanism to be "fixed." He does not have to be bludgeoned into "unpersonhood" as Orwell envisaged, because the ethos of a society in which the biotechnologies have been fully assimilated has already attenuated his concept of his own personal integrity to an extent that makes resistance literally unthinkable.

It is not difficult to foresee technological developments that could lead the Winston Smiths of the future, step by step, to this compliance. In psychobiology, for example, non-invasive methods of brain scanning currently under development reveal the topography of chemical changes in relation to thinking and emotion. These techniques, now being used at Stanford for the analysis of schizophrenia, may well provide new insights into the mechanism of this disease that will be crucial for its ultimate cure. But what becomes of the autonomous "self" as thought and emotion are progressively reduced to their chemical and anatomical elements? Clearly, the implications of such technologies extend far beyond their immediate sphere of clinical application.

The nineteenth and twentieth centuries have amply documented man's insouciant betrayal of his own personhood in exchange for technological efficiency and expedience. Depersonalization in its many forms is indeed the central problem of our society, and its link to technology seems indissoluble, despite our best efforts to understand it. It is a sure sign of our concern that much of our humor revolves around the issue of depersonalization—the blurring of the line between man and machine: "No, Smithers, I'm afraid we're not replacing you with a computer—just a chip," or: "You have reached a live operator. All of our recorded messages are busy. If you will hold we will connect you with our first available recorded message." Clearly, the joke is on us. We embrace our new technologies enthusiastically, and with ample justification, as a great boon, only to find that there is a price to be paid that was not in the original contract. Invariably some part of that price is a further diminution of our sense of personal autonomy. In the revolution in biology and medicine, technological depersonalization has the most far-reaching implications. Biomedical technologies have an impact far more direct and profound than that of any other technology because they are applied to man himself. The person has become the machine, to be repaired or even modified, like any other—a chemical machine, to be sure, but a machine nonetheless.

II

It was, of course, not George Orwell but Aldous Huxley who grasped the three-way relationship between biomedical science, depersonalization, and totalitarian control. In *Brave New World*, published in 1932, Huxley showed how society might be far more easily controlled by the application of biological knowledge and the exploitation of man's innate hedonism than by the crude, punitive methods described by Orwell. But in the austere and biologically unsophisticated days of 1949, Huxley's world of human "hatcheries," "alphas," "betas," etc. was still seen as an outrageously funny, mildly pornographic fantasy. It carried none of the foreboding of *Nineteen Eighty-Four*.

There had in fact been amazingly accurate predictions of the biomedical revolution in which we now find ourselves, many of them made by scientists of the highest repute. For example, in 1881, Aldous Huxley's own grandfather, the biologist Thomas Henry Huxley, indefatigable agitator for scientific and technical education in complacent Victorian England, regaled the International Congress of Medicine in London with a vision of the future of medicine: The pharmacologist, he said, should soon be able to produce "a molecular mechanism which, like a very cunningly contrived torpedo, shall find its way to some particular group of living elements, and cause an explosion among them, leaving the rest untouched." Though medicine still lacked a specific cure for any disease, Huxley had every reason to express such confidence. Chemistry had recently entered a new phase of dazzling creativity and the medical world was humming with Pasteur's dramatic (though then still contested) findings on the nature of infectious disease.

Huxley's optimism was indeed justified by later developments, to such an extent that several leading scientists of the early twentieth century foresaw the possibility of fundamental chemical modification of life processes. One such prophet was Emil Fischer, winner of the second Nobel Prize in Chemistry in 1902. In his address at the opening of the Kaiser Wilhelm Institute in Berlin in 1915, he shared an extraordinarily perspicacious "dream" with his distinguished and, no doubt, incredulous audience:

> I see therefore, as if half in a dream, the rise of a purely synthetic chemical biology which will manipulate the living world just as chemistry, physics and technology have for so long manipulated the nonliving world.

Through the unflagging pursuit of these visions the great advances of medical science and technology of the twentieth century have been achieved and, concurrently, the concept of human personality has been undermined as never before in our history. How has this prodigious effort led to two such disparate results, the one so prized, the other so ominous?

Historically our notion of the rights of the individual to freedom and dignity and, conversely, the concept of his moral responsibility, derive from the picture of man as a divinely ordained, free-willed entity. In the traditional view, neither the body nor the mind of man is reducible to a mere mechanism; chemistry alone will never explain the marvelous and mysterious complexities of the human being. The very concept of humanity, indeed, implies irreducibility. These ideas about the nature of man are held with various degrees of conviction and intellectual confusion by the majority of people in our society. But they stand in flat contradiction to all the evidence of modern biological and medical science and its associated technologies.

Huxley's metaphor of the "cunningly contrived torpedo" has held the imagination of medical researchers for the past century. Paul Ehrlich, discoverer of the first synthetic drug to cure an infectious disease (syphilis), called it the "magic bullet"; the *Wall Street Journal*, reporting recently on the promising new technology of monoclonal antibodies, dubbed them "guided missiles" which found their target in cancer cells, etc. The essence of this concept is that the therapeutic "missile" must be able to distinguish between the vast population of "friendly" cells and those of the far less numerous "enemy"—the spreading cancer, the bacterial infection, or the aberrant cells of the depressed or schizophrenic brain. The missile can only be rationally designed to recognize its target in terms of the specific chemical structures that characterize various types of cells. No therapeutic strategy that is currently conceivable can be more effective than this, but it calls for the painstaking analysis of the structures and mechanisms of the body, down to their most intricate molecular details. As this analysis has been carried on with increasing efficiency and subtlety most of the functions of the body have been brought under some degree of therapeutic control. This approach now offers hope that the dysfunctions of the mind—the psychoses, anxiety, and depression for which psychopharmacological agents already offer some relief—will eventually be curable. But as the physician's therapeutic armamentarium expands, it is evident that this approach strikes at the heart of the concept of the "irreducibility" of man.

Fischer's dream of chemical manipulation of living things is even more momentous in its implications. The key to such manipulation is to understand the cellular mechanisms of genetic regulation. In the early 1950s, the deoxyribonucleic acid (DNA) of the cell was shown to be the carrier of genetic information, and its now familiar double helical structure was elucidated. Following this breakthrough, biology has moved with astonishing speed toward the realization of Fischer's dream and toward a still more mechanistic conception of man. In 1963, Joshua Lederberg, Nobel Prize winner and, at the time, Chairman of Stanford's Department of Genetics, wrote:

Now we can define man. Genotypically at least, he is six feet of a particular molecular sequence of carbon, hydrogen, oxygen, nitrogen and phosphorus atoms—the length of DNA tightly coiled in the nucleus of his provenient egg and in the nucleus of every adult cell, 5 thousand million paired nucleotides long.

Genetic engineering has followed swiftly. In 1980, Paul Berg of Stanford's Department of Biochemistry was awarded the Nobel Prize in Chemistry for his pioneering work in the genetic modification of bacterial cells—a technique which allows them to produce proteins that are quite foreign to the bacteria in their natural state. In the same year the Supreme Court approved the patenting of new life forms, and the technology is now well established industrially as a means of producing rare proteins of great medical significance: hormones, blood-clotting and anticlotting factors, antiviral agents, and other materials.

Insects, frogs, and mice have now been genetically "engineered" and though genetic engineering in man is still unrealized, its ethics are already being vigorously (and often irrationally) debated. A number of religious groups recently condemned it out of hand, but a presidential commission, in a report issued in 1982, saw nothing objectionable in using genetic engineering to cure genetically caused diseases. The commission cautioned against making attempts at genetic "enhancement," but they acknowledged the difficulty, once the techniques were established, in drawing the line between "enhancement" and "cure." They condemned in advance any attempts to hybridize the genetic characteristics of man with those of subhuman species, since this could only lead to increasing confusion about the nature of man and, in the long run, to a decline in the concept of human dignity.

The new biological knowledge, then, makes it unambiguously clear that, contrary to our traditional preconceptions, there is no reason to seek an explanation for the phenomenon of life, including that of man himself, elsewhere than in the ordinary laws of physics and chemistry. Advances in medical technology follow each other with bewildering speed to reinforce this mechanistic view of man—of his mind (his "soul") no less than of his body.

The new technologies of human reproduction provide some of the most startling illustrations of the trend. Once so private and mysterious, human reproduction is now under almost complete chemical control. Artificial insemination, oral contraception, prenatal screening for genetic disease (and hence abortion) are routine. Test-tube babies no longer make headlines, embryos can be transplanted from womb to womb, sex selection is a reality. The technologies in this field point toward the possibility of total *in vitro* reproduction—much as Aldous Huxley envisioned it in *Brave New World*. As reproduction is transferred from the bedroom to the laboratory it becomes more readily accessible to manipulative techniques of either the pharmaco-logical or the genetic engineering variety. In the meantime the concept of the integrity of the human body becomes increasingly strained as the technologies of organ transplants and prostheses become ever more sophisticated, and as life support systems protract "life" well beyond the normal physiological limits imposed by disease. Equally with the body, the mind loses its autonomy as all aspects of experience and emotion are dissected through the chemical and anatomical analysis of the brain by ingenious new techniques.

The depersonalization that results from these extraordinary biomedical advances is subtle and pervasive. There is scant resemblance between our traditional view of man and the "molecular man" of modern medical science. It is a great irony that our traditional concept of man, with his "right" to the dignity of good physical and mental health, is leading us toward a medical millennium in which the person, as once understood, will disappear—as if by the operation of some form of indeterminacy principle. The problem, not surprisingly, greatly perplexes theologians, one of whom, according to a recent *New York Times* report, asks plaintively: "Might we do things in genetic engineering that muck about in the soul?"

III

As a student at Manchester University, I read *Nineteen Eighty-Four* a short time after it appeared in 1949. The book carried immense conviction at the time. The world it described was one we had lived with for almost as long as we could remember—with war or the threat of it always in evidence and the totalitarian enemy (Nazism) the embodiment of unspeakable evil. It was a world of grim, half-destroyed cities, of irksome government regulations generally accepted as facts of life, and of maddening shortages of everyday necessities. The still unassimilated anxieties of the bomb and the cold war were forcing us, young and left-leaning idealists that we were, to a painful reevaluation of our naive views of Soviet Communism. The heroism and suffering of the Russian people during the war had been etched into our minds. Many of us harbored a deep conviction that their almost superhuman resistance had been the critical factor in bringing victory. The war, we were inclined to feel, had really been won at Stalingrad. If the Soviet system was as oppressive as it now appeared, how had it inspired such sacrifice by the people? We did not know—or did not care to know—that behind the Russian lines "inspiration" had taken the form of summary shootings of retreating officers and men or their mass deportation to Siberian death camps.

Orwell's book came along to give us a much needed helping hand, as we strove to make our mental readjustments. That same year, in *The God That Failed*, we were given further help by a half-dozen well-known former com-munist writers who told us of their disillusionment with the aims and meth-ods of the Party. The two books were, in a sense, complementary. Orwell told us with stark realism of the mechanics of oppression and showed, above all, the central importance of depersonalization for effective totalitarian control. The authors of *The God That Failed* revealed, on the other hand, how intelligent people can be misled into deliberately inviting such depersonalization and consequent loss of freedom. The most important message of that book was conveyed in Richard Crossman's introduction, in which he analyzed the seductive power of dogma:

> The attraction of the ordinary political party is what it offers to its members: the attraction of Communism was that it offered nothing and demanded everything, including surrender of spiritual freedom. . . . The communist novice, subjecting his soul to the canon law of the Kremlin, felt something of the release which Catholicism brings to the intellectual, wearied and worried by the privilege of freedom.

Whether a dogma is accepted or not depends not only upon the force and subtlety of its arguments—there is also the question of the individual's vulnerability: How robust is his sense of personal integrity, of that moral responsibility that lies at the very heart of the concept of freedom? When we look at our society today with this question in mind it is hard to avoid a disquieting conclusion: Our sense of moral responsibility is being steadily eroded by depersonalizing forces that are far beyond our control. Most potent among these forces are our technologies, and in particular those that are being developed in the context of medicine.

In the long run, this century's great biomedical achievements may well increase the vulnerability of our descendants to totalitarian control. Developing biomedical technologies, for all their benefits, could be perverted to control people whose very familiarity with them had enfeebled their will to resist. Our descendants might find that they had fallen heir to a Faustian bargain in the most literal sense.

Faust ultimately achieved salvation through reconciliation with God. The challenge that confronts us and those who will inherit the new biomedical knowledge calls for something of the same kind of reconciliation. For us, however, the need is for reconciliation with ourselves. We must find a way of redefining and reintegrating our secular concept of man so that his value as an autonomous individual is salvaged from the vast storage files of analytical data. We need, in short, a new definition of humanness that will accommodate the problems that surround reproductive manipulation (including abortion), life-sustaining measures, and techniques—of whatever kind—for modification of the person. It is impossible that debate on this issue will quickly bring any generally accepted conclusion. The problem in the U.S. is particularly confusing because of the extraordinary diversity of religious, cultural, and ethnic backgrounds, not to mention the great economic disparities, represented in our population. It is crucial, however, that we should take the issue seriously and keep it open to lively debate within the context of strong democratic institutions. We must on no account forget what can happen when Big Brother tells us who is "human" and who is not.

*New Man II* by Alex Grey, 1982. Courtesy of Ronald Feldman Fine Arts, New York.

# III
# IGNORANCE IS STRENGTH

# 11 Barbara Allen Babcock

# Lawspeak and Doublethink

*To know and not to know, to be conscious of complete truthfulness while tell-
ing carefully constructed lies, to hold simultaneously two opinions which
canceled out, knowing them to be contradictory and believing in both of them,
to use logic against logic. . . . Even to understand the word "doublethink"
involved the use of doublethink.*

I FIRST READ *NINETEEN EIGHTY-FOUR* more than twenty-five years ago. On
rereading it recently, I was struck again by the image of Room 101 toward
which the book moves so inexorably. Having long carried the humbling knowledge that I would sell out my loved ones, and certainly my country, under
the threat of a dentist's drill without novocaine, I realized that facing for
themselves what is in Room 101 has been part of the education of a multitude
of literate people since the book was published.

Room 101 is only one of the constructs presented as the inevitable ex-
crescences of totalitarianism. We can all apprehend some of the others—the
omnipresence of the two-way telescreen and Big Brother, for instance—as
appropriate symbols of the worst that can happen. But because *Nineteen
Eighty-Four* apparently is intended to have a bludgeoning effect, some of what
Orwell tells us about terrible things is splattered. At times, it is difficult to
sort out from confused and contradictory accounts precisely why a particular
aspect of Oceanic society is bad. From a lawyer's viewpoint, I will do this
sorting out of four of Orwell's constructs about life in Oceania: the absence
of laws, *thoughtcrime*, Newspeak, and *doublethink*. In the end, I will argue
that, in fact, doublethink has its benign uses, especially in the law, and that
it has its place even in a utopian society and surely in the year 1984.

There are two contradictions in Orwell's discussion of laws in Oceania.
First, he presents the fact, as part of the bleak and forbidding landscape,

that Oceania has "no laws." But then he also offers a positive reference to a society without laws. Winston Smith reads in a passage from the book by the (probably Party-invented) counterrevolutionary Goldstein of a dream of an "earthly paradise in which men should live together in a state of brotherhood, *without laws* and without brute labor. . . ." Thus, we are left to wonder whether and why a society without laws is terrible. Then, it turns out, as the second inconsistency, that Oceania is not such a society. We learn of all sorts of specific interdictions and the likely punishments for violations. There are laws against consorting with prostitutes, engaging in unsanctioned sex with a fellow party member, missing meetings, having an inappropriate expression (*facecrime*).

What Orwell means when he says that there are no laws—even though there are—is that the laws have been drastically misdirected from their traditional liberal purpose: to mark the boundaries where an individual's conduct impinges on the state or others, and to leave as large a zone as possible for individual liberty within those boundaries. The minimalist view of the place of laws steps back (or forward) from the utopian vision of a society where there is no need for laws because its people are in perfect accord.

But in Oceania the laws are neither the outgrowth of brotherhood and mutual understanding nor are they minimal. They are pervasive and their purpose is the destruction of human individuality. Even worse, the state is not actually concerned with punishing the violation of the specific laws that exist. As the inquisitor O'Brien tells Winston: "We are not interested in those stupid crimes that you have committed. The Party is not interested in the overt act: the thought is all we care about." Thoughtcrime as the ultimate offense corrupts the meaning of the rule of law—even to the point where one might say that there are "no laws." (This is a new kind of perversion for secular government, though its antecedent and analogue is the crime of heresy in the religious state.)

The equation of the existence of thoughtcrime with "no laws" at all does not mean party members in Oceania are unadvised as to forbidden acts. Although the particulars of thoughtcrime are nowhere written down, the Party members understand exactly what is permissible. Winston Smith *knows* that he should not fall in love, covet a beautiful paperweight, write a diary, inquire about the verses of an old nursery rhyme. The horror of thoughtcrime is not vagueness or lack of definition—which would violate traditional values of the rule of law—but rather the entire abrogation of substantive human freedom. Instead of creating a zone in which each person is free to act, the laws in Oceania eliminate individuality. Manifestation of personality itself leads to, or perhaps is, thoughtcrime.

And for the ultimate crime, there is the ultimate punishment: "Never again will you be capable of love or friendship, or joy of living or laughter, or curiosity, or courage, or integrity. You will be hollow. We shall squeeze you empty, and then we shall fill you with ourselves."

Of course, this is what the Party intends for all of the citizens of Oceania, but for those less recalcitrant than Winston Smith, Newspeak rather than torture is planned as the way to erase thoughtcrime. Orwell explains in an appendix devoted to the principles of Newspeak that it will be the official language of Oceania, intended to replace standard English by the year 2050. "Its vocabulary was so constructed as to give exact and often very subtle expression to every meaning that a Party member could properly wish to express, while excluding all other meanings and also the possibility of arriving at them by indirect methods. This was done partly by the invention of new words, but chiefly by eliminating undesirable words and by stripping such words as remained of unorthodox meanings, and so far as possible of all secondary meanings whatsoever." One of Winston's colleagues in the Ministry of Truth tells him that the explicit purpose of Newspeak is "To narrow the range of thought. . . . In the end we shall make thoughtcrime literally impossible, because there will be no words in which to express it. . . ."

A second way in which Newspeak would operate to eliminate thoughtcrime is by obscuring the meaning of the few words that were left in the language so that they could no longer stir emotions such as despair or revulsion. Orwell saw this trend already occurring. In 1946, in a now famous essay, "Politics and the English Language," he wrote, "Defenseless villages are bombarded from the air, the inhabitants driven out into the countryside, the cattle machine-gunned, the huts set on fire with incendiary bullets; this is called *pacification*. Millions of peasants are robbed of their farms and sent trudging along the roads with no more than they can carry; this is called *transfer of population* or *rectification of frontiers*."

Newspeak is one of the major horrors of *Nineteen Eighty-Four*, right down there with thoughtcrime. Yet there is a subtle contradiction between Orwell's hatred of Newspeak and his repeated denunciation of Oceania as a society without laws. Newspeak is a fantastically rule-bound language. In fact, it is a legal code-maker's dream. There is absolute clarity, no room for ambiguity, misunderstanding, or conflicting interpretations. Newspeak is quite the opposite of the English about which Orwell wrote: "To write or even to speak English is not a science but an art. There are no reliable rules. . . . Mere correctness is no guarantee whatever of good writing. A sentence like 'an enjoyable time was had by all present' is perfectly correct English. . . . Whoever writes English is involved in a struggle that never lets up even for a sentence. He is struggling against vagueness, against obscurity, against the lure of the decorative adjective, against the encroachment of Latin and Greek, and, above all, against the worn-out phrases and dead metaphors with which the language is cluttered up . . ." (from "The English People," an essay written in 1944).

It is not the abstract idea of language reform to which Orwell objects (he

Ceci n'est pas une pipe (*This is Not a Pipe*) by Magritte. © ADAGP, Paris 1983.

himself once suggested an effort in that direction) but the use and purpose of Newspeak to prevent thoughtcrime. Newspeak will be the end of the struggle for original and forceful ways of saying things, and therefore, ineluctably, the end of individually conceived thought and action. The language of Newspeak, like the society of Oceania, is not lawless—far from it—but its laws are designed to eradicate rather than to preserve a zone for the expression of personality.

In the interim, before Newspeak becomes the official language, thought-crime is controlled in *Nineteen Eighty-Four* by doublethink. "Doublethink means the power of holding two contradictory beliefs in one's mind simultaneously and accepting both of them. . . . To tell deliberate lies while genuinely believing them, to forget any fact that has become inconvenient, and then, when it becomes necessary again, to draw it back from oblivion for just so long as it is needed, to deny the existence of objective reality and all the while to take account of the reality which one denies." Orwell presents the pervasiveness of doublethink in *Nineteen Eighty-Four* as unrelievedly awful. Winston Smith is a hero who is finally destroyed because he can't do it.

Orwell wrote to an American journalist that he intended *Nineteen Eighty-Four* as "a show-up of the perversions to which a centralized economy is liable and which have already been partly realized in communism and fascism." The realization of doublethink that Orwell identified was the Party line, which may change from day to day, be entirely contradictory, yet must be uncritically accepted. But there is a conceptual difference between the Party line as Orwell saw it in postwar communism and fascism and doublethink as he describes it. The acceptance of the Party line is actually *singlethink* carried to extremes—replacing completely one idea with another. The only doublethink involved is the knowledge that this replacement may be for a limited time only.

Doublethink is a more sophisticated phenomenon than the willed acceptance of the crude manipulations of party propagandists. In a sense, it is accommodation to contradiction, close to Keats's "negative capability," a state of mind described by Keats as "when man is capable of being in uncertainties, mysteries, doubts, without any irritable reaching after fact and reason." Some doublethink is necessary to ease all aspects of life in society: in politics—the arms race is against my principles but my constituents need jobs in a missile factory; in family life—my heart is filled with love for this deeply irritating person.

Most striking in light of Orwell's flat denunciation of doublethink is how necessary it is to literature—where the writer tells us, "This is true and it is a fabrication." The linguist Roman Jakobson refers to the "double-sensed message" in writing "as it is cogently exposed in the preambles to fairy tales of various peoples, for instance, in the usual exordium of the Majorca storytellers: *Aixo era y no era* (it was and it was not)." Similarly, metaphor, the most powerful instrument of the writer, involves saying that something is what it is not. Furthermore, the possibility of doublethink is enhanced by the open texture and quirkiness of the English language, which Orwell so much loved.

In law, as in politics, family life, and literature, doublethink is also often a valuable instrument. A good example is the presumption of innocence for the criminally accused. The law enjoins fact finders to treat the defendant as "clothed" in this presumption when he is brought to trial. One of the oldest, and best, defense lawyer's stratagems is to ask prospective jurors whether they have formed an opinion about the defendant's guilt. When a juror says "no," the lawyer responds: "Well, you should have an opinion; your opinion should be that according to the law this is an innocent person." In fact, the presumption of innocence is a "carefully constructed lie" which must be entertained together with the statistical and common-sense knowledge that in the vast majority of cases the accused is guilty and that he is on trial as a result of an intensive investigative process that has produced evidence to that effect. The two beliefs—that the accused is innocent and that he is probably guilty—must be held simultaneously and both accepted.

Another example of doublethink in the legal system is that of the trial judge's role in the face of jury nullification. Deeply embedded in our law is the right of the jury to disregard the law: the classic example is that the jury may decide to acquit the person who steals bread (or even steaks) to feed his starving family. That the jury may do this and do it without any possible appeal or reversal of their decision is well known to the judge. But, in all sincerity, he tells the jury the opposite; that they must follow his instructions on the law in deciding whether to acquit.

In the legal world, doublethink serves not only to ease and effect dealings among people but also serves the cause of fairness. We have erected the presumption of innocence and accepted jury nullification in order to mitigate the power of the state when it seeks to deprive a person of all liberty. Through doublethink we enlarge the power of the individual to prevent his being overwhelmed by the superior resources of the state in an adversary trial. George Orwell might willingly acknowledge that doublethink for the purpose of enhancing individual human personality is also *goodthink*.

# 12 *Elizabeth Closs Traugott*

# Newspeak: Could It Really Work?

*"It's a beautiful thing, the destruction of words."*

LIKE OTHER ANTI-UTOPIAS, *Nineteen Eighty-Four* poses the question: Can human beings be made to forget that they are human? Of all attributes of humanity, language is the most central—language as a system of communication and, above all, as a system underlying our ability to think rationally and creatively. If language were destroyed by somehow making "articulate speech issue from the larynx without involving brain centers at all" (a phenomenon known as *duckspeak*), then humanity as we understand it would be destroyed too. To further the principles of Ingsoc, the totalitarian government of Oceania has established just this goal, to be achieved by the year 2050 through development of a new language, Newspeak. In the novel itself, Orwell allows us only a few glimpses of Newspeak, since the language is still being worked out and in *Nineteen Eighty-Four* is used almost exclusively in political mouthpieces such as the *Times*. However, the portrait of Syme, the compiler of the Newspeak dictionary, captures very well the fanaticism of the project and its projectors:

> It's a beautiful thing, the destruction of words. . . . Every year fewer and fewer words, and the range of consciousness always a little smaller. . . . The Revolution will be complete when the language is perfect. . . . The whole climate of thought will be different. In fact there will be *no* thought as we understand it now. Orthodoxy means not thinking—not needing to think. Orthodoxy is unconsciousness.

The ideology behind Newspeak and the structures of language it permits are treated at greater length in the appendix entitled "Principles of Newspeak," but conceptually little is added. The overriding message is that Ingsoc envisions a world in which the language can be perfected and fixed, with the result that the political system will be fixed; all links with the past will have been severed, because the language of the past will have been translated into Newspeak or will have become incomprehensible; and all links with the future will have been forged for eternity since the political system and language are immutable: "Newspeak is Ingsoc and Ingsoc is Newspeak." Could such destruction of language and hence of human consciousness occur? Did Orwell believe it could? Or was he creating a nightmare world in which all that horrified him about language and language use was rolled into one, with only the briefest of glimpses at the factors that make the survival of language possible?

Can a language be fixed in a "final, perfected version"? No. Because language does not exist as an organism, or in dictionaries, or in computer programs. Crucially, it must be learned anew by each generation, and each generation interprets sounds, sentence structures, and meanings in different ways. Crucially, too, metaphorical use of language is almost inescapable. We have few ways of talking literally about anything abstract, and even some of the most everyday terms derive historically from metaphorical extensions of words with more concrete meanings. When I say Orwell attacks totalitarianism, I do not mean that he attacks it literally, but rather that he talks about totalitarianism as if he were in a physical battle with it. In fact, a great many of our words for different types of discourse are metaphorical at least in origin, as for example *express* (press out), *put ideas into words, open up the discussion, put an end to the argument*, and *put/pose the question*. Even prepositions like *before* and *after*, when used to express time, as in *before Winston met Julia*, are metaphorical extensions of spatial terms (cf. *before* in the sense of "in front of," an expression which itself is now becoming quite common, as in *two minutes in front of the hour*). Language without metaphor is almost inconceivable; new metaphors constantly replace old, dying ones, and inevitably lead to flux.

II

Another reason why language cannot be fixed is that different groups use language for different purposes. Whether a language is written or not has an effect on its structure, and so do the particular purposes to which it is put. The linguistic repertoire of groups who engage actively in riddling (as in the Old English period) or in ritual insults such as playing the dozens (as in ghetto black culture) is obviously different from that of groups who do not. Equally obvious, the range of a person's linguistic repertoire affects the range of inferences which that person is likely to make in any linguistic situation, since language designed for one situation can always be used in another, whether metaphorically, ironically, or otherwise. For example, Southern Baptist preaching has some specific linguistic characteristics that may be imitated or used for special effect outside of the church. So one speech style may readily change under the influence of another.

Orwell envisions three distinct linguistic functions for Newspeak, and three different vocabularies. One vocabulary consists of concrete words for everyday life, such as *hit, run, dog*, with all ambiguities and shades of meaning purged out (presumably one could not address someone metaphorically as *You dog!*), and totally unsuitable for literary, philosophical, or political use. The second vocabulary is designed specifically for political purposes. Many of these words are blanket terms covering a wide number of current abstract concepts such as *honor, justice, democracy*, all subsumed under *crimethink*. All words in this political vocabulary are ideologically biased, and most have "highly subtilized meanings." The third type of vocabulary is designed for scientific and technical purposes, and is largely reserved for specialists; naturally, it has no ambiguities.

In actual practice, since people do not confine their use of language to exclusively scientific, political, and everyday purposes, it would be impossible for the three vocabularies to be kept entirely distinct. The political vocabulary of Newspeak is full of ambiguity and overtones of approval or contempt. Syme says of *duckspeak*: "Applied to an opponent, it is abuse; applied to someone you agree with, it is praise." On the other hand, the scientific and everyday vocabularies admit of no ambiguity. How does language-processing of one kind of vocabulary not carry over and affect the other, especially when the referents of the concrete words of everyday life are themselves not always unambiguous—what are the boundaries between slow running and fast walking, between shrubs and trees? How can we stop the tendency for speakers to extend technical terms such as *hysteria* into the general domain?

The desire to fix language is age-old. It reflects our insecurity and desire to immortalize ourselves and the system (or sometimes a slightly earlier one; Swift, for example, writing in the eighteenth century, claimed that the language was at its peak in Shakespeare's time and the first half of the seventeenth century). It reflects our drive for power—after all, *whose* language is to be preserved? Surely one that we already master. And thus it serves our desire to legislate over the humanity of others. And it also serves the more humanistic wish to minimize change over time and therefore make the literature and philosophy of every period available to every other—this was one of Swift's prime motives in proposing in 1712 that an academy should be established for "correcting, improving, and ascertaining ['fixing'] the English tongue." Swift recognized that language could not be absolutely fixed, but he hoped to foster greater sensitivity to language, and especially to promote a simpler language, stripped of florid, cliché-ridden phrases, and newfangled shortenings (for example, he inveighs against the loss of the unstressed vowel in the past tense of verbs like *disturb'd*). Similarly Dr.

Johnson, in his preface to his famous *Dictionary* (1755), discusses his urge to "fix" the language in order to prevent "corruptions" through ignorance, poor judgment, careless speech habits, and faddish influences such as excessive borrowings from French. He fears

> the licence of translatours, whose idleness and ignorance, if it be suffered to proceed, will reduce us to babble a dialect of France.

But he, too, understands that no dictionary maker can "embalm his language," since the development of the sciences, changes in literary styles, new social mores, contact with other languages, and a myriad of other factors will inevitably continue to make language mutable.

Swift and Dr. Johnson were, of course, thinking of a world in which the intellectual life is all-important, and ties with the past are crucial for the maintenance and development of that world. In the world of Ingsoc, however, the past is to be severed for fear it might encourage dangerous thoughts, and all intellectual life is to be destroyed. Winston perceives that even Syme, the dictionary maker, will be vaporized; however orthodox he is, he does not have the requisite "sort of saving stupidity." In such a world, the causes for change that arise out of language usage itself—processes of acquisition, the tendency to metaphorize, and so forth—cannot be expunged.

### III

Newspeak is a language that is meant not only to be fixed, but also to be highly simplified. The equation of good language with simple language has long been made by those who deplore flowery style and excessive use of jargon or borrowed words. Battles between the proponents of elaborate and simple language were particularly rife in the sixteenth century, when English was being used for the first time instead of Latin as the vehicle not only of literature but also of philosophy and science, and the search for new vocabularies was a major concern among writers and grammarians. Shakespeare frequently mocks the "fantastical," Euphuistic style, which can at times be a veritable nonpolitical duckspeak in its formulaic meaninglessness (though not, of course, in its Latinate diction). For example, in response to the "waterfly" Osric, who has just attempted to extol Laertes in flowery language, Hamlet outdoes him with:

> But, in the verity of extolment, I take him to be a soul of great article, and his infusion of such dearth and rareness as, to make true diction of him, his semblable is his mirror, and who else would trace him, his umbrage, nothing more.

In a literal translation this means, roughly:

> But, in the truth of praise, I take him to be a soul of great im-

portance, and his essence of such scarcity and rareness as, to speak truly of him, his only real likeness is his mirror, and anyone who would try to follow him is his shadow, nothing more.

And, simply put:

No one can equal him.

Concern with similar issues is as vocal today as it was in Shakespeare's time. It is heard in the protests against the obfuscation of legal language, in the legislation promoting plain English in insurance policies, and in reactions to the proliferation of vocabulary drawn from science, computers, or psychology. In the latter part of the seventies, "psycho-babble" was the target of much amusement (among those who did not use it), as in this brief excerpt from Cyra McFadden's *The Serial*:

> Bill said on the phone that he had something heavy to lay on him and thought they ought to get together in a nurturing environment. Ethel's did a mind-blowing trout. Minted trout was nurturing. . . .

To correct or halt the inappropriate use of *nurturing* and *mind-blowing* one will want either to eradicate the words or constrain their meanings drastically. The problem is that the more words are eradicated, the larger the meanings of the remaining words become. If a word has no obvious referent (trout obviously has, mind-blowing and nurturing do not), the possible connotations become so numerous as to make the word almost meaningless. One need not think only of Orwellian terms like *Trotzkyism, democracy,* or *socialism*; more recently, words like *relevant, sexist* (as opposed to sex-biased), *ironic, human rights* have similarly come to mean more or less whatever the speaker wants them to mean. What is relevant is whatever one thinks important at the time; male behavior that a woman does not like she is apt to label sexist, whatever its motives; anything slightly unexpected is ironic; and human rights are supposedly observed in this country, despite gross inequities in the treatment of defendants of different ethnic backgrounds in the courts. It is only a small step ideologically from wanting to purge the language of such gobbledygook to the drastic simplification and reduction that Orwell predicts.

In normal language situations, old meanings are always being changed and replaced. This is partly because words come to be reinterpreted in their most frequent contexts, but also partly because there is a very close, somewhat spiral-like relation between language and thought. Language makes certain thoughts possible; for example, it gives a name and therefore a reality to things that don't exist (cf. Lear's "Nothing will come of nothing"). But thought itself can motivate the search for a word or the best way of saying something. The theoretical concept of black holes presumably preceded the restriction of that phrase within the domain of physics to an intense gravitational field thought to be formed by a collapsed star; it was not the existence of the phrase *black hole* that led to the concept. The promoters of Newspeak, however, believe firmly in the primacy of language over thought:

> The purpose of Newspeak was not only to provide a medium of expression for the world view and mental habits proper to the devotees of Ingsoc, but to make all other modes of thought impossible. . . . Newspeak was designed not to extend but to *diminish* the range of thought, and this purpose was indirectly assisted by cutting the choice of words down to a minimum.

IV

The possibilities of fixing the language or of simplifying it have fascinated and puzzled thinkers for a very long time. So has the relation of language to thought. Until this century, the general view was that language was a representation (or "dress") of thought, albeit not always a very accurate one. But in the earlier part of this century, the opposite view came to predominate, partly as a result of the "structuralist" theory of language associated with the Swiss linguist Ferdinand de Saussure. In this theory every part of a system gets its meaning from its relation to the other parts, not from some preconceived view of the world. De Saussure argued, for example, that the words for colors were dependent on each other for their meaning, not on some external reality; so *red* has its meaning by virtue of not being *orange*, *green*, *blue*, and so forth. To support this view de Saussure claimed that

> Psychologically our thought—apart from its expression in words— is only a shapeless and indistinct mass. . . . Without language, thought is a vague, uncharted nebula. There are no preexisting ideas, and nothing is distinct before the appearance of language.

(It is interesting to note that subsequent research has shown that the meaning of color terms is related, not to thought as such, but nevertheless to the conic structure of the eye, and therefore has a neurological, not an entirely linguistic, basis.)

Later, in a paper entitled "Science and Linguistics" (1940), Benjamin Lee Whorf articulated a belief similar to de Saussure's. His dictum, "We dissect nature along lines laid down by our language," has for some become the slogan for the view that language influences thought. Whorf hypothesized, for example, that since Hopi (the language of the Pueblo Indians) does not express the same space-time correlations as Indo-European languages like English or Russian (cf. spatio-temporal *before, after, be going to, up* as in *finish up*), Hopi physics, were it to be developed, would be very different from ours; specifically, it would not use Time or Velocity as basic principles, but

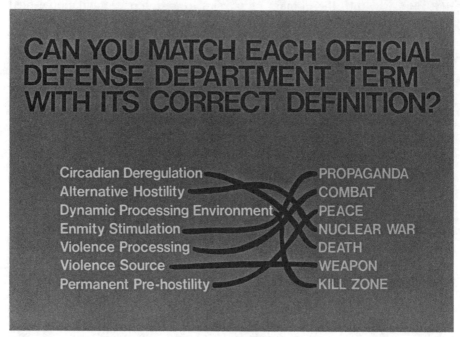

# CAN YOU MATCH EACH OFFICIAL DEFENSE DEPARTMENT TERM WITH ITS CORRECT DEFINITION?

Circadian Deregulation                PROPAGANDA
Alternative Hostility                  COMBAT
Dynamic Processing Environment    PEACE
Enmity Stimulation                  NUCLEAR WAR
Violence Processing               DEATH
Violence Source                   WEAPON
Permanent Pre-hostility             KILL ZONE

*Defense Dictionary* by Erika Rothenberg, 1982. Courtesy of the artist and Ronald Feldman Fine Arts, New York.

rather Intensity.

The view that language influences thought has had both bad and good effects. The negative effects have nearly all resulted from an extremist approach particularly favored among some practitioners of behaviorist psychology who hold that the primary learning mechanism is stimulus-response. Since language is overt and accessible, it is considered to be the stimulus, while thought, being covert, and only indirectly accessible through language, is the response. It naturally follows from this view of learning that language must influence thought, and not the other way round. There are potentially dangerous consequences of taking too literally the idea that language influences thought, and that language is expressed in words rather than sentence structures or sound patterns. An example can be found in some programs adopted in the sixties for teaching "disadvantaged children" (what an example of doublethink!) not only to speak "book" English but also to think in it. It was argued that if a ghetto child did not use a word such as the conjunction *if*, he or she could not conceptualize hypothetical situations; teaching the word *if* would teach the concept. This totally overlooked the fact that children, whether from ghettos or not, use rising tones on the first clause in a sentence like "You go, I'll go too," and that there are many ways of expressing conditionality in language. By focusing on what they thought was a deprivation, teachers belittled the knowledge the children had, and confused them by presenting as new what was already known but expressed in a different way.

On the other hand, recognition of the extraordinary influence that language can have on thought has been invaluable in alerting people to its potential for mind control: to the ways in which politicians can influence voters, doctors can influence patients, lawyers can put ideas into eye-witnesses' mouths, advertisers can dupe the public into buying what it does not want; to the fact that the use of generic *man*, as in "the history of man," or of *he* (instead of *he and she* or, where appropriate, *they*) can serve to silently exclude, and so devalue, half the world's population. In a well-known case in the early seventies, a doctor was convicted for performing an abortion; the defense spoke of a *fetus*, but the prosecution chose to speak of a *baby*, a loaded term that apparently made clear thought impossible for the jury (the conviction was subsequently overturned). The lesson of the power of language choice has been well learned by those who, especially since that court case, call themselves defenders of the right to life rather than antiabortionists. Equally thought-provoking are studies of the ways in which witnesses' testimony can be skewed by the questions asked. In one test fifty subjects were shown a movie of a car accident. One group was asked how fast the cars were going when they *hit*, another how fast they were going when they *smashed*; the *hit* subjects estimated a slower speed than the *smash* subjects. Then the subjects were asked whether they saw any broken glass. Seven of the *hit* subjects said they did, while sixteen of the *smash* subjects claimed to have done so. In fact there was no broken glass in the movie. The positive responses were a function of the suggestion that some glass was broken and the associations triggered by *hit* versus *smash*.

Orwell left the question of the relation of language to thought as an unexplored claim in *Nineteen Eighty-Four*. What position should we take as readers of the book? There can be no doubt that language influences thought. On the other hand, this does not appear to be the whole story. Whorf himself believed that language is "in some sense a superficial embroidery upon deeper processes of consciousness" and would presumably have rejected as unrealistic the assumptions behind the program for disadvantaged children mentioned above, or Ingsoc's program for destroying consciousness. Whorf's chief concern, however, was that, in focusing on language as the dress of thought, people had overlooked the extent to which language actually shapes thought. In recent years the focus has been not so much on whether language or thought is primary but on the close connection between the two, and on the nature of human beings' mental (including linguistic) capacities to act and to interpret experience.

Since the early sixties cognitive psychology has slowly replaced behavioral psychology, partly under the influence of the linguist Noam Chomsky. Chomsky argues that humans are "hard-wired" with certain linguistic principles which biologically determine the range of possible sounds, meanings, sentence types, and semantic interpretations of sentences in a language. A key factor in Chomsky's argument is that the language children hear (as stimulus) and process (in response) is inadequate by itself to explain how they acquire a linguistic system. However, there is much debate about how inadequate what children listen to really is—child-minders appear to tailor the language they address to children quite carefully, and to choose vocabulary and sentence structures only slightly more complex than the child's, at whatever stage of development, so providing the child with fairly well-selected examples of linguistic structures. However, it is clear that what children hear will not in itself account for language acquisition. Whether we are born with a set of strictly linguistic factors as Chomsky suggests, or more general systems of perception and production, of which the linguistic system is only one, we must clearly postulate some kind of rational "thought system" that is partially independent of the actual language used by any one speaker or community of speakers. If what children hear underdetermines language acquisition in any way, then language cannot determine thought entirely, and the principle on which Newspeak is built is, fortunately for humanity, invalid in its strict sense.

Orwell is actually not fully consistent in his presentation of the theory that language influences thought and not vice versa. He hedges when he says a thought for which there was not a word would be impossible by adding, "at least in as far as thought is dependent on words." And when he discusses how *free* could be used only in the sense found in "This dog is free from lice," but not in the sense "politically free," he says the latter meaning did not exist "since political and intellectual freedom no longer existed even as concepts, and were therefore of necessity nameless." As part of his prophecy of the destruction of language by the totalitarian state, the admission that thought might possibly influence language is a source of confusion. However, as a clue to the reader that there may be hope after all, it has its place.

V

In some of his other writings Orwell clearly shows that he had faith in people's ultimate ability to use language well, and to overcome the destructive effect of language on thought. In "Politics and the English Language" he points out that there is a reciprocal relation between language and thought. The English language, he says, "becomes ugly and inaccurate because our thoughts are foolish, but the slovenliness of our language makes it easier for us to have foolish thoughts." Getting rid of slovenly language will help get rid of slovenly thought, and will be the first step in political regeneration, he claims.

In his essay Orwell proposes getting rid of dying metaphors such as *play into the hands of* or *hotbed*; of phrasal verbs like *give grounds for, exhibit a tendency to*; of pretentious, often Latinate diction like *liquidate, ameliorate, epoch-making* (the more recent *world-class* would surely meet his opprobrium); and of words which have become largely meaningless, like *romantic, freedom, justice*. He seeks words with unambiguous meanings and demands that one should use "the fewest and shortest words that will cover one's meaning." In other words, he approves of manipulating language. He expresses a similar view in "New Words," where he outlines a program for developing new words to lift English out of its Stone Age lumpishness and inability to express ideas explicitly. It is, of course, not easy to determine exactly what the fewest and shortest words are, and Orwell himself seems to have been uncertain about how to solve this problem. For instance, he dislikes "the inexpressive name *bug*" for the many different kinds of insect (one among many Americanisms he abhors). In several of his writings he appears to be uncomfortable with the fact that English, and American English in particular, allows verbs to be derived from nouns, e.g., *blitz*. Yet he also approves, in principle, the development of Basic English, an auxiliary language designed by C.K. Ogden and I.A. Richards in the forties for international use. It consisted of 850 words designed to cover the essential minimum of what anyone might want to say. His approval rests not on the smallness of the vocabulary, but on the fact that it is, he understands, impossible to say anything meaningless in this language.

What Orwell does in portraying the horror of dehumanization through control of language is to envisage a world in which the manipulation has bad rather than noble ends, and the debasement of thought through language is combined with a break from the healing wisdom of the past. Debasement of thought is promoted largely through political vocabulary: *doublethinking* is a virtue, and all unorthodoxy is thrown into the pit called *crimethink*—an exaggerated view of political language perhaps, but grounded in a reality that all thinking people repudiate. What makes the debasement of language so seemingly absolute is that the leaders of Ingsoc promote it through a program which, in moderation and in the right context, could be curative. The simplification of language being enforced is so extreme that, rather than fostering plain, meaningful language, it is meant to prevent language from being used with any nuances, metaphoric extensions, or ironies. Such a language would in the end be totally literal and indeed useless not only for higher thought but also for most communication.

Fortunately, as we have seen, language cannot be fixed; nor can it be used without some metaphoric extensions which, even if dangerous because they can lead to sloppy thinking, can also open up new paths of thought. The language-using mind is such that too much repetition leads not only to numbness but also to mocking quotation, irony, and therefore awareness. Advertisers know this; so do politicians; and therefore they seek to change their slogans. How often can one repeat terms like *New Deal* or *Camelot* without in the end subjecting oneself to ridicule?

Even so, Orwell's ultimate message is an important one. Even if a linguistic nightmare like Newspeak could not really work, what humans do with their capacities as language users will ultimately determine whether they remain human. The potential good that can come from the fact that to some extent thought influences language will be vitiated if the thought is evil. And the potential good that can come from simple language will be vitiated if the language is too minimal. With his usual ruthless honesty, Orwell saw that the principles he himself espoused so vehemently and tried to practice in his writing could become distorted and turn into monsters. The definition of a human being may be "language user," but of all the creatures in the universe, only humans seem to be able to threaten their very nature. Whether they threaten it with thermonuclear warfare or with mind control of the type Orwell envisions, they can do so only because they are language users. The survival of humanity must depend on responsible use of language.

# 13  Ian Watt

# Winston Smith: The Last Humanist

*Either the future would resemble the present in which case it would not listen to him, or it would be different from it, and his predicament would be meaningless.*

AT THE BEGINNING OF *NINETEEN EIGHTY-FOUR*, we are given a few facts about Winston Smith. He's thirty-nine and has "a varicose ulcer above his right ankle"; on the next page we're told he's a small, frail figure with fair hair, and afraid of the Thought Police; and on the next page we learn that he works for the Ministry of Truth in London, the chief city of Airstrip One, the third most populous province of Oceania. The rest of what we are told about him is fairly consistent with this, and makes it clear that there is nothing at all remarkable about Winston Smith except for his unique inner life.

The first thing we learn about it comes when he tries "to squeeze out some childhood memory that should tell him whether London had always been quite like this." The urgency of the word "squeeze" suggests that Winston Smith's interior consciousness is genuinely tormented by what is essentially a historical question. Winston's first significant act tells us a good deal more. He has left his job at thirteen hours, downed a teacupful of nauseating Victory gin, and moved to the alcove which, quite exceptionally, is out of sight of the telescreen, having probably been intended originally "to hold bookshelves." Once there he takes out a "peculiarly beautiful book," fits a nib onto an archaic penholder, and begins a diary. Winston Smith's secret life, then, is not merely puzzled by history; it is in love with the products of the past.

Until he started the diary, Winston Smith had imagined that "the actual writing would be easy. All he had to do was to transfer to paper the interminable restless monologue that had been running inside his head, literally for years." But it turns out not to be easy, and the reason for the difficulty is peculiar: "How could you communicate with the future? . . . Either the future would resemble the present in which case it would not listen to him, or it would be different from it, and his predicament would be meaningless." This surely shows that Winston's consciousness in general is dominated by two different kinds of persistent concern: the historical, with its tripartite division of future, present, and past; and the literary, which is more instinctive —he can think of no conceivable reader for his diary but he still writes it.

What first comes out on the page is the date: it is April 4th, 1984, though we've been told he can't be sure that "this *was* 1984." Next, there is a paragraph giving an account of his previous evening at the flicks: the crass patriotic hysteria of the audience and its amusement at the cruel bombing of a shipload of enemy war refugees, an amusement which is interrupted by the protests of an indignant prole woman. Winston's mind then goes back to the Two Minutes Hate ceremony earlier that morning; but when he turns his attention to the diary again he finds that he has written, no longer in his usual "small but childish handwriting" but in large and voluptuous printed capitals, half a page of "DOWN WITH BIG BROTHER."

When he sees what he has written Winston is tempted to tear the page out of the book in terror; but then he reflects that "the Thought Police would get him just the same," whatever he wrote in the diary, or, indeed, whether he wrote in it or not. Next he writes down, in "a hurried untidy scrawl," the words: "theyll shoot me i dont care theyll shoot me in the back of the neck i dont care down with big brother they always shoot you in the back of the neck i dont care down with big brother." What dooms him, he believes, is that, whether he writes down his thoughts or not, he has in any case committed "the essential crime that contained all others in itself. Thought-crime they called it."

The essence of Winston's thoughtcrime can be described by saying that he finds nothing in the life of the present that he can bear, and so his sensibility is dominated by the great question: Were things really better now? Some time later he thinks he may get some help on this from a very old man in a pub for the proles, but finds himself defeated by the random but invincible concreteness of what the old man remembers. Yes, the old man says, beer was cheaper in the old days, and it came in pints. Winston attempts to get him to say more; he lists all the alleged horrors of life in the old days, but he gets no reaction until he mentions the top hats worn by the capitalists, and then the old man recalls the last time he himself had worn a rented top hat, for his sister-in-law's funeral some fifty years ago. Winston goes on with his leading questions until he realizes that "the old man's memory was nothing but a rubbish heap of details," and that he can therefore expect no outside help in his quest to discover whether life was or was not "better

*Burden* by Paul Klee. © ADAGP, Paris 1983. Courtesy of Cosmo Press, Geneva, Switzerland.

before the Revolution than it is now."

He realizes, too, that there is a real urgency in his question, for, in "twenty years, at the most . . . the huge and simple question . . . would have ceased once and for all to be answerable" because all the evidence would by then have been altered or suppressed. Winston himself works at the Ministry of Truth doctoring the records whenever there has been a change in policy, or some individual has been disgraced or become an "unperson." For instance, we see him having to remove all mention of a formerly prominent member of the Inner Party, Comrade Withers; and in his place he creates, out of whole cloth, a heroic Comrade Ogilvy in "a few lines of print and a couple of photographs." How can there be history when everything inconsistent with the political needs of the Party today has been sent down the "memory hole," and no book exists in Oceania older than 1960? Even worse, something else is disappearing—the sense that merely knowing the true answer is important. For instance, there is the question of the truth or falsehood of the fact that only four years before Oceania had been at war not with its present enemy, Eurasia, but with its present ally, Eastasia; but this question did not seem important even to his love, Julia. Winston does not feel any temptation to tell lies to Julia, but her love for him is based not on her sense of truth, but on her partisan sense that "I knew you were against them"— the Party. Truth itself is already a casualty as far as other people are concerned; and so Winston is forced to accept the terrible conclusion, "History has stopped. Nothing exists except an endless present in which the Party is always right."

As he listens on the canteen television to the statistics of endless claims of increased productivity, Winston compares their picture of how "year by year and minute by minute, everybody and everything was whizzing rapidly upwards" with the disgusting and degrading realities of actual existence. Could he be *alone* in the possession of a memory?" he wonders. On the other hand, he cannot see how he should feel the present to be so intolerable "unless one had some kind of ancestral memory that things had once been different."

That mute conviction that he is right is one reason for Winston's love of Oldspeak. Newspeak, he senses, in effect creates a conspiracy of silence about all the horrors of the life that he sees going on around him; it epitomizes, to quote Emmanuel Goldstein's book, *The Theory and Practice of Oligarchical Collectivism*, that "denial of reality which is the special feature of Ingsoc and its rival systems of thought." The denial is not accidental but systematic. For instance, "The empirical method of thought, on which all the scientific achievements of the past were founded," is totally opposed, Goldstein writes, to the most fundamental principles of Ingsoc. As a result, he notes, "in Newspeak there is no word for 'Science'."

Winston's friend Syme, who is working in the research department of the ministry on the eleventh edition of the Newspeak dictionary, sees that Winston lacks a real appreciation of Newspeak, "whose whole aim," he says, is to "narrow the range of thought" that the language permits. When the process has been completed, and "Newspeak is Ingsoc and Ingsoc is Newspeak," thoughtcrime will become "literally impossible." Indeed, in the final revision of Newspeak its vocabulary will have been so drastically controlled and reduced in size that "there will *be* no thought, as we understand it now. Orthodoxy means not thinking—not needing to think. Orthodoxy is unconsciousness."

Syme, Winston realizes, will be "vaporized" because he "sees too clearly and speaks too plainly." Winston is soon proved right in his unspoken prediction; but Syme is also right when he says that Winston Smith in his heart would "prefer to stick to Oldspeak, with all its vagueness and its useless shades of meaning." Winston, of course, here exhibits the preference of the writer to that of the politician: and that opposition is fundamental. For, as Syme says, with the final triumph of Newspeak, "the whole literature of the past will have been destroyed. Chaucer, Shakespeare, Milton, Byron—they'll exist only in Newspeak versions, not merely changed into something different, but actually changed into something contradictory of what they used to be."

The novel does not give us much evidence of Winston's tastes in reading—if only because books of literature, as opposed to pornography and the like turned out collectively by the Fiction Department of the Ministry of Truth, do not seem to exist in the world of *Nineteen Eighty-Four*. Even Goldstein's book, it transpires, was apparently produced collectively. But we are given a good many indications of Winston's literary sensibility. Thus, when Winston dreams of his mother, thirty years missing and probably dead, he sets her and her passionate love for him in a setting of time and place that is very different from the present. It was, he reflects, a time when tragedy was still possible, a time when "there were still privacy, love, and friendship... dignity of emotion [and] deep or complex sorrows." Winston also imagines a perfect love encounter, which is set in what he thinks of as "the Golden Country"; it is a symbol of the ancient world of pastoral, and when he suddenly wakes up from the promise of the dream, it is "with the word 'Shakespeare' on his lips." Later he sees the lovely rural setting of his first tryst with Julia as "the Golden Country—almost." Winston's literary sensibility, then, contains the notions both of the tragic and the pastoral genres, and also of Shakespeare; and all three are associated with his notions of death and love.

There are other, and perhaps even more significant, details of Winston's literary tastes in *Nineteen Eighty-Four*. First, there is the diary itself. It is a literary *acte gratuit* of a heroic kind, since endangering his life merely to give an objective testimony to his view of the truth about himself and his time surely bespeaks Winston's deep need for self-expression. Secondly, there is another and almost opposite feature of Winston's sensibility—his characteristic obsession with the folk memories of the past; the most important one is the rhyme "Oranges and lemons, say the bells of St. Clement's,/You owe me three farthings, say the bells of St. Martin's,/When will you pay me? say the bells of Old Bailey,/When I grow rich, say the bells of Shoreditch." Here one attraction is the idea that the genre represents the literature of the proles; another is that this particular rhyme is a clue to an imaginative reconstitution of the old churches and customs of London as it had once been.

Lastly, there is the way that Winston's love of the past makes him give a symbolic value to the literature, and even to other more physical mementos of history: there is the physical diary itself, a book with cream-laid paper, such as is no longer made; there is the presumably eighteenth-century print of St. Clement's Dane; there is the vast old mahogany bed in which he and Julia make love; and there is the glass paperweight which he buys from old Mr. Charrington and which, Winston imagines, "was the room he was in, and the coral was Julia's life and his own, fixed in a sort of eternity at the heart of the crystal."

Winston Smith's sensibility, then, can be seen as representing a constellation of special intellectual, aesthetic, and literary values. There is the love of what Newspeak calls *oldthink*, that is, the ideas grouped round the equally outmoded concepts of "objectivity and rationalism" and of old folk rhymes. There is, further, his love of the particular and the detailed in other things. It is this love of the particular that makes Winston remember drawing his wife's attention long ago to the "tufts of loose-strife growing in the cracks of the cliff beneath them" in which "one tuft was of two colors, magenta and brick red, apparently growing on the same root." It is also this love of the particular that causes Winston, just before the Thought Police make their strike, to fall asleep "murmuring 'Sanity is not statistical,' with the feeling that his remark contained in it a profound wisdom."

Behind these aspects of Winston's inner sense of values is the larger idea that individual feeling is the most essential and desirable reality available. It is this idea that leads Winston, at his first and only real meeting with O'Brien until his arrest, to propose his toast, "To the past." The Party has persuaded people that "mere impulses, mere feeling, were of no account"; on the other hand, Winston is loyal to the values of an earlier generation—like his mother, who had assumed that "what mattered were individual relationships, and a completely helpless gesture, an embrace, a tear, a word spoken to a dying man, could have value in itself." It is also the rights of individual feeling which cause Winston to conclude that he must continue on his present course to the end; as he put it, if your "object was not to stay alive but to stay human, what difference did it ultimately make?" After all, he reflects, "They could not alter your feelings; for that matter you could not alter them yourself, even if you wanted to."

II

One term to describe this constellation of private thoughts and feelings in Winston Smith would be Humanism. The term has many diverse and not wholly clear meanings; but in the inner life of Winston Smith Orwell certainly describes both some main characteristic features of the earliest manifestations of Humanism in the history of the West, and some of the essential meanings the term has acquired more recently.

Among the Greeks and the Romans the central doctrine of Humanism was certainly rhetorical, and its first exponents were orators.

The nearest Greek equivalent to the Latin *humanitas* was *anthropismos*; and the early development of the notion, like that of its analogue *philanthropia*, had its basis in the close practical relationship in the life of fourth-century Athens between four forces which we would now call freedom of speech, the rule of law, the political freedom of the city, and the individual's right to make his own moral and political decisions. Humanism, then, arose in a society which was radically opposite to that of *Nineteen Eighty-Four*. For Isocrates (436-338 B.C.), who is commonly regarded as the chief precursor of Humanism, persuasion through speech was the key instrument of a free society; as he argued in his long essay, "On the Antidosis," it was the power of speech which made man superior to other living creatures: "Because there has been implanted in us the power to persuade each other and the power to make clear to each other whatever we desire, not only have we escaped the life of wild beasts, but we have come together and founded cities and made laws and invented arts; and, generally speaking, there is no institution devised by man which the power of speech has not helped us to establish."

Isocrates, we must remember, held that discourse, or *logos*, is not confined merely to rhetorical arrangement of the words; there is, or there should be, no essential break between form and content, and that content includes the inward qualities of feeling, understanding, and imagination, which can in part be learned from works of literature, history, politics, and philosophy. Still, for Isocrates the master art remains rhetoric; as he wrote in the "Antidosis," "Persuasion is one of the Gods."

It was left to the Romans to develop the idea of humanitas in education and to give it a more systematic development. In the second century A.D. the grammarian Aulus Gellius, in his *Attic Nights*, gave a famous description of its aims: "Those who have spoken Latin and have used the language correctly [notably Varro and Cicero] do not give the word *humanitas* the meaning which it is commonly thought to have, namely, what the Greeks call *philanthropia*, signifying a kind of friendly spirit and good feeling toward all men without distinction; but they gave to *humanitas* about the force of the Greek *paideia*; that is, what we call *eruditionem institutionemque in bonas artes* [education and training in the good arts]."

The word humanitas itself was apparently first used, in the sense of good feeling, in an anonymous treatise on rhetoric addressed to one C. Herennius in 81 B.C., a work formerly attributed to Cicero (106-43 B.C.). Cicero, however, certainly has the credit for the first extant use of the phrase "the liberal arts." He used it in his first book, *De Inventione*, and the idea, of course, denotes all the arts which the free men of the society ought to study, as opposed to the mechanical or practical arts learned by slaves and people who work with their hands. Cicero, an admirer of Isocrates, urged that rhetorical skill was valueless unless it was combined with true learning. In his *De Oratore* Cicero stresses the need not only for writing, paraphrase, translation, and imitation, but for the reading of works of oratory, poetry, history, law, and politics. This broader curriculum, or *encyclos paideia*, was worked out in more detail by Quintilian, whose *De Institutione Oratoria* (A.D. 95) supplied the basis of the school curriculum of the West throughout the Middle Ages. The liberal arts were eventually construed as seven, of which the first three, the *trivium*, were Grammar (including literature and criticism), Logic (or dialectic), and Rhetoric. Then there were the more advanced topics of the *quadrivium*— Arithmetic, Geometry, Astronomy, and Music.

In Renaissance Europe, the term Humanism took on a rather new meaning. It is specifically applied, in the *Oxford Dictionary*'s definition, for instance, to the study of "the language, literature, and antiquities of Rome, and afterwards of Greece." Renaissance Humanism began as the educational spearhead of the revival of learning in the fifteenth century, but eventually it acquired the general sense of the classical, and mainly secular, education which was established in high schools and colleges during the sixteenth, seventeenth, and eighteenth centuries. The "good art" became defined as the *litterae humaniores* (more humane letters) of Oxford and other universities on the grounds that the great authors of Latin and Greek literature were more worthy of study than those of other languages.

The final stages in the development of the concept of Humanism came to the fore in the twentieth century. On the one hand, the classical tradition lost much of its power; and on the other, Humanism was colored by the scientific, secular, and empirical attitudes of the period. The idea that man should limit his knowledge to the enquiries, objectives, and limitations of the individual human mind was developed as a specific school of thought by F.C.S. Schiller and William James. The scientific and experimental attitude which they systematized under the name of Humanism no longer survives as a movement, but it has supplied some of the term's secular connotations in its present use.

III

Winston Smith cannot be considered a humanist in any of its earlier senses, if only because he makes no mention of Greek or Latin, and we are told nothing about his schooling. On the other hand, his hostility to Newspeak, his obsession with language, and his need for a free exchange of ideas show him as beginning at exactly the point where the founders of Humanism began. Winston Smith holds fast both to the value of Oldspeak and to the ultimate rationale of the early humanist position—the achievement of individual freedom. This freedom, threatened in the days both of Isocrates and of Cicero, no longer exists at all in the society of *Nineteen Eighty-Four*; but it remains Winston's basic need, and it is essentially that need for free intellectual interchange that explains his obsession with meeting O'Brien, and that had led him to start his diary.

There is a little more to say about the relation of Winston Smith's ideas to Humanism, but first we should, perhaps, consider the question of whether his author, George Orwell, could have had any specifically humanist intention for *Nineteen Eighty-Four*. He would not willingly have affixed any ideological label to himself; but on the other hand it is an important part of his distinction as a writer that he took nothing for granted, and as a result he was often both well behind the times and well ahead of them.

One example of this concerns his religious position. He had lost his faith in his days at Eton, but in the period when he had returned from Burma and was starting to be a serious writer, Orwell was briefly on fairly intimate terms with a High Anglican curate, Parker, and his wife. He helped Parker in his clerical duties, went to services regularly, and even thought of taking communion. Still, Orwell mocks his "hypocrisy" about this in his letters to an old friend, Eleanor Jaques; and his biographer, Bernard Crick, is no doubt right in saying that it was an accidental and brief religious aberration, and concluding that "George Orwell was to be a clear Humanist, even a rationalist." Nevertheless, Orwell retained "an ironic attachment" to the Church of England and was buried, by his own wish, in a country churchyard.

More directly relevant is how very old-fashioned Orwell was in his attitude to language, and it wasn't just a question of his advocacy of the plain style. It was a lifelong passion. As he revealed in his essay "Why I Write," Orwell, at the age of "about sixteen . . . suddenly discovered the joy of mere words, i.e., the sounds and associations of words," and gave an illustration from *Paradise Lost*. A classmate, Steven Runciman, remembered that at about this time, when Aldous Huxley was for a year supposed to teach a class of Etonians French, he left one very definite positive impression: "Above all it was his use of words that entranced us. Eric Blair . . . would in particular make us note Aldous's phraseology. 'That is a word we must remember,' we used to say to each other. . . . The taste for words and their accurate and significant use remained." And when Eric Blair eventually came to do a little school teaching himself, the "joy of mere words" remained with him. One of his pupils remembered that he "once offered sixpence from his own pocket as a prize for anyone who could spot a ludicrous misspelling in a local laundry window." In his "Why I Write" essay Orwell wrote that he did not wish "completely to abandon the world view that I acquired in childhood"; and the first feature of it that he mentioned was to "continue to feel strongly about prose style."

This attitude to language is old-fashioned because neither the capacity to remember the "accurate and significant" use of words, nor how they are spelled, nor even a genuine concern with "prose style," were much more common then than they are today. For Orwell, however, they remained central;

and this was not wholly for literary and stylistic reasons, but because he was also alive, as few other writers have ever been, to the moral and political importance of the notion that, in Keats's words, "English ought to be kept up." In such essays as "Politics vs. Literature: An Examination of *Gulliver's Travels*," "Politics and the English Language," and "Inside the Whale," Orwell demonstrated the necessary connections between literature, language, and the collective life with a fine intensity; and there, as in many other essays, he makes us realize that relatively simple things such as the use of truthful or untruthful language are connected with the greatest issues of social value, political decency, and—ultimately—with the existence of human freedom or of its opposite.

These simple meanings—not unlike the basic views of Isocrates or Cicero—Orwell certainly intended, and indeed consciously and persistently pursued, throughout his life. Especially in *Nineteen Eighty-Four*. One reason for the clarity of this theme in the novel may be that, whatever conflicts may have existed between Orwell the radical and Orwell the traditionalist in his treatment of political problems, there was no conflict in regard to language.

Nor did Orwell's education stop short with his capacity to write. At school, Orwell was something of a social rebel and a political radical, but he was certainly a traditionalist in his studies. At his prep school, and later at Eton, Orwell was a student of the classics, of what amounts to a school version of the *litterae humaniores*; and later he chose Greek, Latin, and Drawing as his three optional subjects for the Civil Service examination that sent him to Burma as a policeman. He paid tribute, later, to the fact that Eton, despite its many faults, had "one great virtue . . . a tolerant and civilized atmosphere which gives each boy a fair chance of developing his own individuality." One wouldn't claim Orwell as a man who read the classics consistently throughout his life; and one must admit that he was bitterly contemptuous of St. Cyprian's, his prep school, and unenthusiastic about many aspects of Eton; nevertheless it was there that he received an education based on the old humanistic classical tradition, a tradition which he never attacked.

It is, therefore, just possible that Orwell, having some conception of the humanist tradition, deliberately used some of its values to inform the positive aspects of Winston's sensibility. This tendency, it must be conceded, goes only as far as is plausible, given the kind of the society depicted in the novel and Winston's own lack of educational opportunity; in any case, Winston Smith is not a conscious nor a heroic protagonist of moral and intellectual convictions. One remembers, for instance, his betrayals. They began with his earliest guilty memory of the last moment in which he saw his mother before she disappeared, when, overpowered by desperate childish greed, he had stolen the last quarter of the family's rare and precious two-ounce ration of chocolate from his helpless little sister, and with it fled from his home. At the end Winston betrays Julia—"Do it to Julia," he says, when faced by the rats; and he betrays himself when the novel finishes with Winston's succumbing to the overpowering pressures of the collective ideological machine, and discovering that "He loved Big Brother."

O'Brien affirms that "We"—the Party—"create human nature," and it is, of course, part of Orwell's warning in *Nineteen Eighty-Four* to show that "they" cannot be beaten. Winston learns that he and Julia were wrong when they thought that "They can't get inside you." They can, and, therefore, Winston does not even have the consolation of being able to say, as he once did, "if you can *feel* that staying human is worthwhile, even when it can't have any result whatever, you've beaten them." Orwell's picture of the future defines the villain as the general tendency of modern bureaucratic control to lead to a cripplingly anti-humanist monolithic collectivism; and so Winston Smith must be ignominiously defeated.

Not much, I believe, has been written about Winston's character; and there is obviously some truth in Irving Howe's concession that "there are no credible or 'three-dimensional' characters in the book." But, as Howe says, Orwell was trying to portray a society in which "the leviathan has swallowed man" and so "the human relationships" that are normally "taken for granted in the novel are here suppressed." Nevertheless, Winston Smith is worth our attention as a crucial test example, and he is in some respects a worthy one. His worth is suggested by his given name, Winston, and perhaps by his sharing Shakespeare's initials of W.S. In any case, Winston Smith has a legitimate love of the traditions of the past, and that love is combined with a genuine concern for the language and literature of Oldspeak, and for the right to independent thought. The critics have not made much of this side of the novel, but Winston Smith is, in the hated jargon of Newspeak, a martyr to the *ownlife*, meaning "individualism and eccentricity." He is even obsessed, in the typical humanist way, with unanswerable questions, and particularly the question of "Why?" As he writes in his diary, "I understand *HOW*: I do not understand *WHY*." That he eventually succumbs to the police and O'Brien doesn't weaken the truths of what he thinks and does in the first two parts of the novel. "Truisms are true, hold on to that!" Winston reflects, and writes down in his diary as a credo: "Freedom is the freedom to say that two plus two make four. If that is granted, all else follows."

That is not granted, but we can still say that, however grim his end, Winston Smith is the only person in the novel who makes any sort of stand for the simple intellectual and moral values which, for over two millenia, have had the majority of the literate and the decent on their side. O'Brien three times calls Winston "the last man," with increasing irony at this professed "guardian of the human spirit"; and this is reflected in the original title for the book, "The Last Man in Europe." Considering how little there is about Europe in the book, "The Last Humanist Man" might have been a more accurate title, although *Nineteen Eighty-Four* is no doubt better for other reasons.

*The Kiss* by Edvard Munch, woodcut. Courtesy of The Chicago Institute of Art.

# 14 *Anne Mellor*

# "You're Only a Rebel from the Waist Downwards": Orwell's View of Women

*"All this marching up and down and cheering and waving flags is simply sex gone sour."*

ORWELL'S *NINETEEN EIGHTY-FOUR* IS A POWERFUL WARNING against the dangers of totalitarian thinking and political control as well as an urgent prophecy of what the future may hold. I use "prophecy" in the sense advocated by the revolutionary poet-prophet William Blake:

> Every honest man is a Prophet. He utters his opinion both of private and public matters Thus If you go on So the result is So He never says such a thing Shall happen let you do what you will A Prophet is a Seer not an Arbitrary Dictator.

What does Orwell's *Nineteen Eighty-Four* prophesy about the nature and function of women in a totalitarian regime? And what does it tell us about Orwell's own conception of femininity and the social roles of women?

Oceania in 1984 is a fascist state controlled by an authoritarian ideology that is abstractly personified as that Stalin-like leader, Big Brother. Why Big Brother? Why not Big Mother or Big Father? The implications of Orwell's elevation of the eldest male sibling to this position of total power are fascinating. Readers who argue that *Nineteen Eighty-Four* is in fact a generalization of Orwell's experiences at a British preparatory school, as recorded in his vitriolic essay "Such, Such Were the Joys," lead us to expect a Big Mother as the ultimate authority in Orwell's totalitarian state. At Crossgates, Orwell's pseudonym for his own preparatory school, St. Cyprian's, the dominant figure is Mum, also known as Mrs. Simpson or Bingo. She is the source of the child's greatest terrors and his sense of guilt and shame. She is the one who exposes his crime of bed-wetting, his poverty and dependence on scholarship money, his lack of intelligence and motivation, his inherent sinfulness. She is the one toward whom the child feels nothing but fear and hatred. Her chubby-faced husband is but a minor threat (despite the fact that he beats the child with a riding whip until it breaks) in comparison to that all-powerful female monster, Bingo, who can inspire the horrors of sexual guilt and mental failure.

Why did Orwell, after giving us an image of Mum as terrifying as Philip Wylie's "American Mom" of the 1950s, not create a female leader for Oceania? In large part, of course, he was responding to political realities: the fascist leaders of the twentieth century—Franco, Stalin, Mussolini, Hitler—were all men. And as we shall see, Orwell thought it neither likely nor proper that women would play an active leadership role in politics in the future. But Orwell's masculine Big Brother draws our attention to a specific aspect of totalitarian ideology: its inability to respond affectionately to an individual. At Crossgates, Bingo had her favorites, however arbitrarily chosen and even more arbitrarily rejected; at St. Cyprian's, the boys spoke of themselves as "in favour" or "out of favour" with Mrs. Wilkes or Flip. Mum was thus capable of showing personal affection, however fleeting and irrational. But Big Brother is totally without love, without concern for the health and mental welfare of the individual. He is a logical abstraction, not a person. And for Orwell, who consistently associates the greatest capacity for rational thought with men, he is necessarily male.

Why not Big Father then? Assigning the role of political leader to a Big Father would arouse the expectation that the father would grow old, weaken, and eventually turn over his authority to his younger, stronger male heir. By elevating the oldest brother to the position of ultimate strength, Oceania effectively claims that there is no possibility of changing the status quo. Your older brother will live as long as you will, especially since he has always been bigger and stronger than you.

Even more important, Big Brother's absolute control of every aspect of personal as well as public life eliminates the possibility of sustained or pleasurable sexual experience. This is true not only at a pragmatic level (as we can see in Winston Smith's and Julia's affair); it is true at an even more significant symbolic level. For, as Freud has taught us, domination by the father inspires a powerful family romance: the young boy dreams of making love to his mother, the young girl fantasizes her father as her lover. But Big Brother has no wife whom a man can desire; and his relationship to his female comrades is entirely chaste, protective, and "brotherly." The domination of the brother over the father destroys the younger man's fantasies both of political power and of sexual virility. Every man is forever emasculated by his older and more powerful brother.

What Orwell has portrayed in Oceania is the complete triumph of a patriarchal culture, a fascist society in which the man with the most machismo, the older and stronger brother, reigns forever. In such a society, women are consistently assigned to limited, gender-differentiated roles. The female characters in *Nineteen Eighty-Four* fall into the traditional stereotypes constructed by a patriarchal, Judeo-Christian civilization: good women are virgins or mothers, bad women are whores.

In *Nineteen Eighty-Four* the mother is idealized as an entirely self-sacrificing woman. She devotes her entire life to her family, giving willingly of all her time, energy, and even food rations to her demanding husband and children. And when she no longer has any material possessions to give, she continues to give her love. We first encounter this loving mother in Winston Smith's diary, as he describes a war film he saw the night before:

> then you saw a lifeboat full of children with a helicopter hovering over it. there was a middleaged woman might have been a jewess sitting up in the bow with a little boy about three years old in her arms. little boy screaming with fright and hiding his head between her breasts as if he was trying to burrow right into her and the woman putting her arms round him and comforting him although she was blue with fright herself. all the time covering him up as much as possible as if she thought her arms could keep the bullets off him. then the helicopter planted a 20 kilo bomb in among them terrific flash and the boat went all to matchwood.

Even though the mother is totally helpless and unable to save her child, her futile gesture remains with Winston Smith as the epitome of the finest love of which human beings are capable.

It is this capacity for entirely selfless love that Winston Smith reveres in his own mother. He dreams of her drowning, his baby sister in her arms. Looking down on them as they sink into the green waters, he knows that they have died to save his life.

> He knew it and they knew it, and he could see the knowledge in their faces. There was no reproach either in their faces or in their hearts, only the knowledge that they must die in order that he might remain alive, and that this was part of the unavoidable order of things.

Later he remembers his mother spending her last few pennies to buy him a game of snakes and ladders; doing all the housework (his father had already disappeared by the time he was ten); nursing his sickly, dying baby sister; and giving him every morsel of food she could, taking it for granted that he, "the boy," should have more than his share, even starving herself and her daughter so that he might live. Guilty though he feels that he stole his sister's chocolate as well as taking his mother's share, Winston finally recognizes that he did not murder his mother. Rather, she gave herself willingly, lovingly, to the care and protection of her children, however feeble her help.

> He did not suppose, from what he could remember of her, that she had been an unusual woman, still less an intelligent one; and yet she had possessed a kind of nobility, a kind of purity, simply because the standards that she obeyed were private ones. Her feelings were her own, and could not be altered from outside. It would not have occurred to her that an action which is ineffectual thereby becomes meaningless. If you loved someone, you loved him, and when you had nothing else to give, you still gave him love. When the last of the chocolate was gone, his mother had clasped the child in her arms. It was no use, it changed nothing, it did not produce more chocolate, it did not avert the child's death or her own; but it seemed natural to her to do it.

However, such pure, altruistic, maternal love cannot survive in the world of Oceania. Winston's mother disappears, and even the dusty, dilapidated but still caring Mrs. Parsons is denounced by her own children to the Thought Police. There is no room for the life-nurturing, pacifistic love of a mother in the sadistic, militaristic society of *Nineteen Eighty-Four*.

In this patriarchal, sexist world, Julia embodies every man's most potent sexual fantasy: the seeming virgin who is in fact sexually available, a whore. Winston Smith (whose commonplace name, echoing Winston Churchill, indicates that he represents the British everyman) responds to the appearance of the attractive, vital, yet virginally belted Julia with a sadistic desire:

> Vivid, beautiful hallucinations flashed through his mind. He would flog her to death with a rubber truncheon. He would tie her naked to a stake and shoot her full of arrows like Saint Sebastian. He would ravish her and cut her throat at the moment of climax. Better than before, moreover, he realized why he hated her. He hated her because he wanted to go to bed with her and would never do so, because round her sweet supple waist, which seemed to ask you to encircle it with your arm, there was only the odious scarlet sash, aggressive symbol of chastity.

But Julia is not a virgin; instead, she has had affairs with Party members "hundreds of times—well, scores of times, anyway." She is thus what Winston most desires in a woman: she is sexually liberated, healthy, a creature of instinct and emotion but not intellect, a man-identified woman. She is in fact the stereotype of the ideal woman in a patriarchal culture: physically attractive, resourceful, resilient, courageous, loyal to her man—and anti-intellectual.

Despite her membership in the Junior Anti-Sex League, or perhaps because of it, Julia has rebelled "from the waist downwards." Far more than Winston, she has recognized that sexual repression is essential to the maintenance of the Party's power. Winston does not understand why "the Party was trying to kill the sex instinct" but Julia later explains to him:

> When you make love you're using up energy; and afterwards you feel happy and don't give a damn for anything. They can't bear you to feel like that. They want you to be bursting with energy all the time. All this marching up and down and cheering and waving flags is simply sex gone sour. If you're happy inside yourself, why should you get excited about Big Brother and the Three-Year Plans and the Two Minutes Hate and all the rest of their bloody rot?

Julia intuitively grasps that in the puritanical realm of the sexually unavailable Big Brother sexual intercourse as such is a political act. Sexual desire and consummation affirm nature over culture, human instinct over rational or technological control. Winston perceives this in his early dream of Julia:

> The girl with dark hair was coming toward him across the field. With what seemed a single movement she tore off her clothes and flung them disdainfully aside. Her body was white and smooth, but it aroused no desire in him; indeed, he barely looked at it. What overwhelmed him in that instant was admiration for the gesture with which she had thrown her clothes aside. With its grace and carelessness it seemed to annihilate a whole culture, a whole system of thought, as though Big Brother and the Party and the Thought Police could all be swept into nothingness by a single splendid movement of the arm.

Julia's celebration of her own body, of sexual desire, of the primal animal instinct of human beings, is thus a denial of all forms of mind control, a powerful political rebellion.

Julia's healthy animality is thus posed against the sexual repression of Katharine, Winston Smith's wife, who recognized the necessity of procreation but had been brainwashed by the Junior Anti-Sex League into regarding all sexual feeling as disgusting. Winston recalls his relationship with Katharine with horror:

> As soon as he touched her she seemed to wince and stiffen. To embrace her was like embracing a jointed wooden image. And what was strange was that even when she was clasping him

against her he had the feeling that she was simultaneously pushing him away with all her strength. The rigidity of her muscles managed to convey that impression. She would lie there with shut eyes, neither resisting nor co-operating, but *submitting*. It was extraordinarily embarrassing and, after a while, horrible.

Significantly, it was Katharine who refused to end their sexual relationship. Instead she insisted on making love once a week, with clockwork regularity, calling it "our duty to the Party." Katharine thus embodies what the Party wishes sex to become: an entirely unpleasurable and enforced activity, an obligation to an abstraction rather than a natural act. Such unnatural procreation or reproduction of life is as monstrous as that envisioned in Mary Shelley's *Frankenstein*, where the life-force is similarly perverted by technology. Like Frankenstein, Party leader O'Brien hopes to control absolutely the human reproductive process. As O'Brien tells Winston Smith,

> We have cut the links between child and parent, and between man and man, and between man and woman. No one dares trust a wife or a child or a friend any longer. Children will be taken from their mothers at birth, as one takes eggs from a hen. The sex instinct will be eradicated. Procreation will be an annual formality like the renewal of a ration card. We shall abolish the orgasm.

In the face of such mental and physical control, Julia's ardent pursuit of sexual pleasure is perhaps the most profound rebellion against which the Party must act.

Julia recognizes that her sexuality threatens more than the Party's efforts to control the reproductive process. By giving immediate pleasure to the individual, sexuality also paves the way toward an experience of personal commitment, of a pair-bonding that is felt as a love for an individual and not for a system. Julia seizes upon the primary importance of love as a revolutionary act when she initiates contact with Winston by passing him a note containing only three words, "I love you." And without hesitation Julia places love above resistance to the Party. When O'Brien asks Winston and Julia if they are prepared, in order to fight the Party, "to separate and never see one another again," it is Julia who responds immediately with an emphatic "No!" while Winston hesitates. And it is this love, this commitment to another person, that Julia and Winston cling to longest. Only after the ultimate terror and self-annihilation of Room 101 do they betray each other; only then are they entirely conquered by the Party and capable of "loving" that abstraction Big Brother.

But Julia, however courageous her refusal to submit to the Party's sexual puritanism, is "only a rebel from the waist downwards." Orwell insists on

her inability to comprehend intellectually the significance of the Party's ideology and techniques of mind control. She is "not clever," and even though
she works in the Fiction Department, she is not interested in reading or
writing, not even in the mechanical arrangements and rearrangements of the
six plot lines routinely assigned to the rewrite squad. As she tells Winston,
"I'm not literary, dear." She has no sense of the past, no awareness of the
significance of history, and "no memories of anything before the early Sixties."
She has not noticed that the enemies of Oceania have changed over the past
four years, nor does she care about this fact when Winston points it out to
her. And when Winston tries to read her Goldstein's book, the theoretical
basis of the revolutionary goals betrayed by the Party, she falls asleep. Nor
is Julia able to articulate the thoughts she does have with precision or complexity; Winston is surprised by the coarseness of her language and her
tendency to swear, which, on reflection, seemed to him "natural and healthy,
like the sneeze of a horse that smells bad hay."

Instead of a mind, Julia is credited with an innate cunning, a pragmatic
instinct for survival. In the Fiction Department, she works with her hands,
running and servicing a powerful but tricky engine. She can track her way
through the countryside like an experienced scout, memorizing landmarks
and drawing detailed maps. And she has the ingenuity necessary to arrange
their secret meetings. Julia embodies what we might call feminine wiles: she
can be deceptive and duplicitous when the occasion demands, yet can find
as though by instinct her way through the forest. She thus lives out that
special empathy with nature which has been traditionally assigned to the
female. She can lead Winston Smith to the Golden Country, the earthly
paradise of his dreams, ever present in the warm sun and singing thrush
of a springtime afternoon. And Julia is nurturing as well: like a mother, she
brings food to Winston, real chocolate and coffee and bread and milk. Even
without a mind, Julia is a survivor, a healthy creature guided by love and
intuition.

I began by saying that *Nineteen Eighty-Four* is both a warning and a prophecy. We have seen that the roles assigned to women in Oceania and in Winston
Smith's mind fall into very limited stereotypes: the pure self-sacrificing
mother, the frigid wife, the sexually aggressive and emotionally supportive
mate. We must now ask whether there is a "hidden agenda" for women in
this anti-utopian book. Does George Orwell in any way imply that women
in an ideal world should be different? The answer I fear is No. From the
perspective of a feminist living in 1984, Orwell's attitude toward women and
the family is discouragingly conservative and repressive. However brilliantly
Orwell foretold the horrors of totalitarian thinking and political control, he
failed to see that embedded in his own attitudes toward women was an
ideology almost as oppressive to the female as the Party is to Smith.

Desperately seeking an escape from the Party, Winston wrote that "if there is to be hope, it lies in the proles." To find Orwell's vision of the ideal woman, then, we too must look to the proles. And what do we find there? A cheerfully singing mother endlessly hanging up diapers to dry, whom Winston gazes upon with almost religious adoration:

> The woman down there had no mind, she had only strong arms, a warm heart, and a fertile belly. He wondered how many children she had given birth to. It might easily be fifteen. She had had her momentary flowering, a year, perhaps, of wildrose beauty, and then she had suddenly swollen like a fertilized fruit and grown hard and red and coarse, and then her life had been laundering, scrubbing, darning, cooking, sweeping, polishing, mending, scrubbing, laundering, first for children, then for grandchildren, over thirty unbroken years. At the end of it she was still singing. The mystical reverence that he felt for her was somehow mixed up with the aspect of the pale, cloudless sky, stretching away behind the chimney pots into interminable distances.

This mother, endlessly slaving for her family, endlessly singing mindless songs, is Winston Smith's taste of eternity.

And George Orwell's too, alas. For when we look back over Orwell's earlier books and glance at a few salient biographical facts, we find that Orwell had very little sympathy for the feminist movement in England. Orwell believed fervently that women should devote themselves to pleasing their husbands and raising a large family, because only a strong, stable, cohesive family can provide its members with a sense of personal identity, with a sense of the past, and with a commitment to the virtues of loyalty, self-discipline, and responsibility. As Orwell put it, the family is both the backbone of the political state and "the sole refuge from the state." The feminist movement in England in the 1930s and 1940s seemed to threaten the primary dedication of the woman to the family, and Orwell, while nominally supporting the equality and rights of women, feared the growth of the movement and subtly opposed it in his writings. We recall that Julia intensely disliked living in a hostel with thirty other girls: "'Always in the stink of women! How I hate women!' she said parenthetically." And in an entry in his notebook written while he was working on *Nineteen Eighty-Four*, Orwell tellingly reveals his own anxieties:

> The conversations he overheard as a small boy, between his Mother, his aunt, his elder sister, and their feminist friends. The way in which, without ever hearing any direct statement to that effect, and without having more than a very dim idea of the relationship between the sexes, he derived a firm impression that women *did not like* men, that they looked upon them as a sort of

large, ugly, smelly, and ridiculous animal, who maltreated women in every way, above all by forcing their attentions upon them. It was pressed deep into his consciousness, to remain there until he was about twenty, that sexual intercourse gives pleasure only to the man, not to the woman. He knew that sexual intercourse had something to do with the man getting on top of the woman, and the picture in his mind was of a man pursuing a woman, forcing her down and jumping on top of her, as he had often seen a cock do to a hen. All this was derived, not from any remark having direct sexual reference—or what he recognized as a sexual reference—but from such overheard remarks as "it just shows what beasts men are." "My dear, she's behaving like a perfect fool, the way she gives in to him." "Of course, she's far too good for him." And the like. Somehow, by the mere tone of these conversations—the hatefulness—above all physical unattractiveness—of men in women's eyes seemed to be established.

As George Orwell's biographer, Bernard Crick, acknowledges, this passage may reflect some of Orwell's own resentment toward his mother, whom Crick describes as a bit of a gadabout and a *femme libre*, who often left the children to go to parties and social outings with her female friends, although she was extremely fond of her children and especially kind to her only son. Orwell's hostility to feminist women is more openly reflected in his portrait of Elizabeth Lackersteen's mother in *Burmese Days*:

Elizabeth's mother had been an incapable, half-baked, vapouring, self-pitying woman who shirked all the normal duties of life on the strength of sensibilities which she did not possess. After messing about for years with such things as Women's Suffrage and Higher Thought, and making many abortive attempts at literature, she had finally taken up with painting. Painting is the only art that can be practiced without either talent or hard work.

Orwell seems to think that any attempt by an educated woman to find intellectual growth, political purpose, or even personal self-fulfillment outside of the home is pure self-indulgence and even stupidity.

Orwell's insensitivity to the intellectual, psychological, and even physical needs of women is reflected in his treatment of his wife, Eileen O'Shaughnessy. A bright, independent businesswoman who was getting a master's degree in psychology when she met Eric Blair, Eileen gave up her degree and career when she married. Thereafter, she worked full-time to support the impoverished author, doing a double day as both secretary and housewife. She did all the cleaning, cooking, laundry, shopping, and worked eight hours a day, while Orwell wrote at home. When he went to Spain to fight in the

International Brigade, Eileen accompanied him and worked full-time on the Republican side for the British Independent Labour party office in Barcelona.

Eileen's friend Lettice Cooper drew on Eileen for the character of Ann in her wartime novel *Black Bethlehem* (1947):

> When you speak to her she generally looks at you for a minute before answering, and then answers very slowly, as though anything you said to her needed careful consideration and was of the greatest importance. At first we thought her affected, and were impatient of waiting for her comments. Later we realised that everything was important to her because her sense of life was so intense that she got the full impact of any thing that turned up and saw it not isolated but with all its connections. I find it very difficult to put down what I mean about this, but I think that most people skim over most things. They only really get the impact of certain things that are specially interesting to them. Perhaps they have to be like that to get through the day in this crowded world. Certainly Ann finds it hard to get through the day. She does her work very well, but she almost always stays late to finish it. She goes home at night without meat or vegetables which she meant to buy in her lunch hour, but had not bought because she had not finished what she was saying at lunch. In the flat when she cooks and cleans for her brilliant, erratic husband and their friends, she is generally washing up at midnight . . .

Eileen Blair dedicated her life to supporting Orwell, even though she recognized that he cared more for his writing than for her. As Eileen told her friend Lydia Jackson in her grief over her brother's death, "If we were at opposite ends of the world and I sent [my brother] a telegram saying 'come at once' he would come, George would not do that. For him his work comes before anybody."

Orwell was also insensitive to Eileen's emotional needs. When her beloved brother died, Orwell made no comment in his diary. And he seemed indifferent to how she might respond to his occasional sexual infidelities. Worse, he seemed unaware that her health was failing. Even after she knew she had growths on her uterus that might be cancerous, he insisted despite her reluctance that they adopt a child. She died within the year, on the operating table, at the age of forty.

Orwell's obsession with starting a family, even though he and Eileen were unable to have children, only underlines his conviction that marriage and the family are the fabric of a good society. His own marriage was entirely conventional: despite his socialist principles and religious agnosticism, he insisted on being married in the Church of England. And in his writings, Orwell again and again envisions a gender-differentiated society in which men work in the public arena and women stay at home, cheerfully fulfilling their domestic responsibilities. In *The Road to Wigan Pier*, Orwell paints his perfect family picture:

> I would say that a manual worker, if he is in steady work and drawing good wages—an "if" which gets bigger and bigger—has a better chance of being happy than an "educated" man. His home life seems to fall more naturally into a sane and comely shape. I have often been struck by the peculiar easy completeness, the perfect symmetry, as it were, of a working-class interior at its best. Especially on winter evenings after tea, when the fire glows in the open range and dances mirrored in the steel fender, when Father, in shirt-sleeves, sits in the rocking chair at one side of the fire reading the racing finals, and Mother sits on the other with her sewing, and the children are happy with a pennorth of mint humbugs, and the dog lolls roasting himself on the rag mat—it is a good place to be in . . .

There is no suggestion in Orwell's work that women might be capable—as many women living in 1984 clearly are—of becoming successful mothers and independent thinkers; of being, in the best sense of the term, the comrades of men; of enjoying both domestic fulfillment and intellectual activity; of combining the roles of parent and worker and wife with the active and full cooperation of husbands who are also parents and workers. Orwell's vision of a permanently gender-differentiated society remains a powerful warning, but I hope not a prophecy for the role of women in the future. Despite Julia, despite Winston's "not intelligent" mother, despite Katharine, who "had without exception the most stupid, vulgar, empty mind that [Winston] had ever encountered," despite almost all of Orwell's female characters—women in 1984 can write books as well as read them.

# 15 *Martin Esslin*

# Television and Telescreen

*With the development of television, and the technical advance which made it possible to receive and transmit simultaneously on the same instrument, private life came to an end.*

ORWELL'S *NINETEEN EIGHTY-FOUR* IS DOMINATED by the mass media, and so is the actual, real life 1984 that has now dawned. To that extent, Orwell was right.

But the mass media—the cheap mass-circulation press, mechanically produced romantic novels and pop songs, war films, radio, and television—are not a mere fictional element in Orwell's negative utopia. It can be—and has frequently been—asserted, with some force, that the whole book was engendered by Orwell's own experience within one of the most powerful media organizations of his time—the wartime BBC.

I happen to have shared some of that experience with George Orwell and I can testify to the truth of this assertion from firsthand experience. I entered the German section of the BBC's wartime propaganda effort in April 1941: Orwell became a "temporary talks producer" in the Indian section of the Empire Service in the autumn of the same year and worked in that capacity till November 24, 1943. It is surely significant that the first outline of *Nineteen Eighty-Four*, entitled "The Last Man in Europe" (which Bernard Crick has published as an appendix to his biography of Orwell), can be dated close to the end of 1943, about the time Orwell left the BBC.

The Empire Service (later tactfully renamed the Overseas Service) was at that time housed in what had been, until the government requisitioned it for the BBC, the Peter Robinson department store at 200 Oxford Street. This building, a few blocks away from Oxford Circus and thus conveniently near the BBC's headquarters, Broadcasting House in Langham Place, had been converted by subdividing the open-plan sales floors into a honeycomb of small cubicles, separated from each other by flimsy hardboard partitions. In the basement were studios and the canteen. The large plate-glass shop windows toward the street on the ground floor were bricked up, those on the upper floors covered with dingy blackout curtains. A drearier, more dismal environment could hardly be imagined.

There can be no doubt that Winston Smith's cubicle in the Ministry of Truth is closely modeled on this setting:

> In the long, windowless hall, with its double rows of cubicles and its endless rustle of papers and hum of voices murmuring into speakwrites [in 1942 this murmur was produced by editors dictating to their secretaries], there were quite a dozen people whom Winston did not even know by name, though he daily saw them hurrying to and fro. . . . And this hall, with its fifty workers or thereabouts, was only one subsection, a single cell, as it were, in the huge complexity of the Records Department. Beyond, above, below were other swarms of workers engaged in an unimaginable multitude of jobs. There were the huge printing shops with their sub-editors, their typography experts, and their elaborately equipped studios for the faking of photographs. There was the teleprograms section with its engineers, its producers, and its teams of actors specially chosen for their skill in imitating voices. There were the vast repositories where the corrected documents were stored, and the hidden furnaces where the original copies were destroyed. And somehow or other, quite anonymous, there were the directing brains who coordinated the whole effort and laid down the lines of policy.

There were no printing shops in 200 Oxford Street, but otherwise this is exactly what it felt like to be working in that hive of propaganda activity: the vast anonymous hum of voices, the constantly changing personnel, the drabness. The only place where one could meet colleagues was the canteen—and that was the drabbest and dreariest environment of all:

> In the low-ceilinged canteen, deep under ground, the lunch queue jerked slowly forward. The room was already full and deafeningly noisy. From the grille at the counter the steam of stew came pouring forth with a sour metallic smell . . . walls grimy from the contact of innumerable bodies; battered metal tables and chairs, placed so close together that you sat with elbows touching; bent spoons, dented trays, coarse white mugs; all surfaces greasy, grime in every crack. . . . He looked round . . . nearly everyone was ugly, and would still have been ugly even if dressed otherwise than in the uniform blue overalls.

There were no uniforms in the canteen at 200 Oxford Street, but the impression of drabness and ugliness it exuded certainly was exactly as Orwell has so graphically captured it. The cups were chipped, the food was foul. The younger people had been called up for military service, so the average age of those left behind was high and they were anything but attractive; the elderly secretaries might well have been members of an anti-sex league. There was also a shortage of canteen and cleaning staff, so the table that one finally found empty was invariably covered with dirty dishes and pools of slops, exactly as in Orwell's description. This wartime canteen served as more than just the model for the canteen of the Ministry of Truth in *Nineteen Eighty-Four*. Its dreariness, its slovenly, run-down state was the source and model for the atmosphere that pervades the whole of Orwell's vision of the future.

During the day and evening the canteen was crowded, but work in the Empire Service went on throughout the night, as broadcasts were being beamed to parts of the world in widely different time zones. At two or three o'clock in the morning the badly cleaned, stuffy, blacked-out, windowless building was at its most depressing: an atmosphere of hopelessness and futility oozed from the dimly lit corridors and the empty, echoing canteen. Anyone who has experienced these night shifts instantly recognizes their mood in the pages of Orwell's novel.

II

It is no coincidence that Winston Smith in *Nineteen Eighty-Four*, exactly like George Orwell in 1943, should be working in a propaganda organization dedicated to manipulating public opinion and faking the image of history. Orwell based his description of this process mainly on what had already happened in the Soviet Union. Smith's job consists in rewriting history in the light of current—and constantly changing—political circumstances. This systematic eradication of the past was a feature of Stalinism. Fervently idealistic supporters of the Soviet revolution in the West had been deeply dismayed when they saw how, after the great purges, the formerly revered leaders of the revolution—men like Trotsky, Bukharin, Kamenev, Zinoviev, Radek—had been expunged from the history books, their features obliterated even on historical photographs. The articles devoted to them were deleted from the official encyclopedia and new pages supplied to replace those that subscribers were ordered to cut out.

But there are indications that Orwell had found similar tendencies nearer home as well—in the British propaganda effort. The work Orwell had to do as an editor in the Indian section of the Empire Service of the BBC was not quite as drastic as the Soviet obliteration of past history. But to a man of his political sensibility and anticolonialist views (which stemmed from his first job with the British police in Burma), many of the directives that reached him from the higher regions of the policy makers in the British government and the BBC must have been hard to swallow and execute. Being in charge of the English-language talks to India, a service largely aimed at the educated section of the population, Orwell was happiest in initiating literary programs, such as poetry readings by T.S. Eliot or William Empson (who, incidentally was a close colleague, being in charge of political commentaries that had to follow the official line).

The abrupt reversals that followed changes in the war situation were all too similar to the sudden remodelings of the shape of the past described in *Nineteen Eighty-Four*: from 1939 to 1941 Stalin had been a villain who had made a pact with Hitler and carved up Poland, our ally. But on the evening of the day Hitler invaded the Soviet Union, Winston Churchill was on the air offering Britain's hand of friendship to Stalin. Suddenly the BBC's propaganda stressed the sturdiness of the Russian people, the heroism of the Red Army, and Stalin's genius as a war leader. And then, when the war was over, the cold war started and Stalin was reconstituted as a sinister villain.

Much of the role of the mass media in *Nineteen Eighty-Four* also derives from Orwell's familiarity with the propaganda technique of Goebbels, the mastermind behind the German psychological warfare offensive. The German radio broadcasts of special announcements of victories were preceded by lengthy bursts of martial music and fanfares, in exactly the same manner as described in *Nineteen Eighty Four*. There was a special unit in 200 Oxford Street devoted to the daily analysis of German propaganda, its lies and methods. George Weidenfeld (later a well-known publisher), who worked in this unit, was the coauthor of a book, *The Goebbels Experiment*, which stressed, among the methods Goebbels used in his ministry—cynically labeled "Ministry for Popular Enlightenment and Propaganda"—his practice of *Sprachregelung*, i.e., "language manipulation." For example, Churchill was never to be mentioned otherwise than as "that brandy-sodden alcoholic Winston Churchill," or Roosevelt otherwise than as "that syphilitic degenerate Roosevelt." The principles of Newspeak in *Nineteen Eighty-Four* certainly owe much to the study of German propaganda that formed part of the daily routine of those working in the British propaganda effort. The manipulation of the masses by the media in *Nineteen Eighty-Four* thus is clearly an amalgam of the practices Orwell had encountered in Soviet and Nazi propaganda before and during the war, and his own experience as a propagandist in the BBC's English-language service to India.

As a politically minded writer Orwell was aware of the contrasts between the totalitarian propaganda methods of the Nazis and Stalinists and those followed by Britain; he later praised the BBC's scrupulous adherence to truthfulness in its news broadcasts. But even inside Britain wartime propaganda sometimes indulged in deception. Orwell's wife, Eileen, was at that time working in the Ministry of Food (the Ministry of Plenty in *Nineteen Eighty-Four*). Her job was to prepare recipes for foods the ministry wanted to push onto the public. When potatoes were among the few items in good supply Eileen had to write recipes, to be broadcast on the BBC, for potato dishes proclaimed to be wholesome and full of vitamins. When this publicity worked too well and potatoes became short, Eileen had to compose material about the fattening effect of potatoes and their relatively poor nutritional value. When the British government wanted to conceal that the RAF possessed radar, a Ministry of Food propaganda campaign stressed the value of carrots in improving night vision in the blackout. This, it was hoped, might explain to the Germans why the British pilots could see the German planes so well during night raids. The work of both the Ministry of Truth and the Ministry of Plenty thus reflect what the Orwells experienced at first hand during the war while working with the BBC.

III

If Orwell's forecast for the Britain of 1984 has proved off the mark, his vision of what the Communist world would be like on the other hand appears astonishingly accurate.

The drabness of daily life in the countries of Eastern Europe may not be quite as depressing as that in *Nineteen Eighty-Four*, but drab and colorless it certainly is. The division of the population into party members and "proles" is as marked as Orwell foresaw it. So also is the dullness and uniformity of the output of the mass media, whether newspapers, television, or radio. The incessant stream of predictable propaganda produces in members of the lower levels of the party the same indifference expressed in *Nineteen Eighty-Four* by Julia, "who knew it was all rubbish, so why let one be worried about it?" Even the hate sessions of *Nineteen Eighty-Four* have their parallel in the party meetings in present-day Eastern European countries at which attendance is compulsory, and members must display at least the outward signs of anti-American and anticapitalist feelings.

Orwell proved far too pessimistic, however, in anticipating that the boredom and indifference provoked by this incessant bombardment with predictable political slogans would lead to a total acquiescence of the population with the regime. The risings of "proles" and nonparty as well as party intellectuals in East Germany (1953), Hungary (1956), Czechoslovakia (1968), and Poland (at various times, but most notably in 1980-81) and the continuing dissidence among intellectuals in the Soviet Union itself prove that the totalitarian manipulation of popular feelings and ideas by the mass media is far less effective than Orwell had imagined.

Perhaps in 1984 we can see with greater clarity that the annihilation of the past can never be as effective as Orwell imagined it. In a society with the remnants of an educational system the total eradication of the literature of the past, as envisaged by Orwell, would be well-nigh impossible. There are in Orwell's book youth organizations modeled on the Hitler Youth and the Soviet Young Pioneers, but schools and universities barely get a mention. And yet, in a society as highly industrialized and geared to armaments production as that of Orwell's Oceania, there must have been institutions designed to train these specialists, not to speak of subliterary technicians such as Winston Smith himself. The continued availability of the classics in the Soviet Union, for example, to this day acts as a powerful antidote to the totalitarian manipulation of culture. A critical and humanistic tradition remains active and is the inspiration behind the major works of art produced by dissident writers, painters, and composers. It also inspires those who, while remaining within the establishment, continue to say a great deal between the lines in works that pass through the official censorship. Even if a total eradication of the literature of the past were possible, Orwell underestimated the time it would take. What Orwell imagined fully accomplished within some thirty years after the Ingsoc revolution in Britain has not as yet even begun to happen in the Soviet Union a full sixty-five years after the Bolshevik revolution.

IV

In the developed Western world, Orwell's pessimism about the demise of parliamentary democracy and the disappearance of any laissez-faire economy has, up to now at least, not been vindicated by events; and the general atmosphere of life in the industrialized countries of the Western world looks very different in 1984 from what Orwell imagined. Yet even here Orwell, while seemingly wrong at the surface, may, in may ways, have been right at a deeper level.

Britain and America—the hub of Orwell's Oceania—have reached an unprecedented degree of affluence in 1984; in spite of high unemployment and large budget deficits, the standard of living has reached levels that were unimaginable in 1949. There is still parliamentary government. Nevertheless, here too the trend toward mass apathy and mass manipulation Orwell foresaw certainly is present and subtly, if gradually, transforming society.

There is, after all, not that much difference between a society that floods the masses with cheap, novelettish romance, raucous and sentimental pop music, and pornography to keep them amused and politically inert and one that does the same thing for commercial gain—but with the identical ultimate political result: apathy, ignorance of real issues, and acquiescence in whatever the politicians are doing. And does not commercial television do just that?

In other words, the division of society into the manipulators and the manipulated which Orwell rightly diagnosed as the sinister side of Stalinist and Nazi totalitarianism, and thus as a primarily political phenomenon, might be in the process of coming to pass in the "free," nontotalitarian societies of the developed world simply by the operation of the mass media—through the incessant advertising of products in a manner all too suggestive of the blandishments and threats of Big Brother. (We love you if you buy our product! But woe to you if you do not buy it: your wife will hate you, you will have itching hemorrhoids, bad breath, slipping dentures, and a host of other terrible misfortunes!) It might be argued also that the media is well on the way toward transforming politics too into a mere appendage of the hard-sell advertising industry. This, ultimately, would result in a state of affairs very similar to that in the totalitarian countries: a population brainwashed into almost total apathy toward the political process, blindly following the slogans emanating from the mass media, above all television.

V

Orwell, so preeminently a literary man of the thirties, saw the process of the vulgarization of the masses almost entirely in terms of the printed word. It is odd, considering that he had worked in radio, that he did not rate the impact of that medium more highly. More astonishing, however, is his failure to foresee the nature and impact of television. At the time he was writing *Nineteen Eighty-Four*, television had already been a feature of British life; the BBC opened the world's first regular television service in 1936. True, at the outbreak of war this service was interrupted; the transmitters might serve as radio beacons for attacking German aircraft. But after the war the BBC resumed its television service. Admittedly, it did not make its real breakthrough as a mass medium until the coronation of Queen Elizabeth II in June 1953, but the portents were clearly there.

And Orwell was aware of television. What fascinated him, however, was not its potential for providing entertainment to be watched, but its possible use as an instrument for watching people unawares in their homes. The telescreens in *Nineteen Eighty-Four* are cameras that transmit the picture of the room they are surveying to a center where policemen watch individual citizens. The telescreens are omnipresent in the homes of members of the Party in *Nineteen Eighty-Four*, but with the exception of an early morning gymnastics broadcast there is scarcely a mention of visual programming. Repeatedly Orwell refers to the sound of statistics being read out and propaganda speeches being heard from the telescreens. In other words, Orwell saw the telescreens largely in terms of radio receivers with the capacity to transmit pictures to secret police watchers, but not as what they have actually become, the omnipresent, constant providers of highly colorful visual entertainment for the broad masses.

In spite of Orwell's awareness of the need for cheap entertainment to keep the proles happy, it is particularly remarkable that he should have failed to recognize in television the ideal provider of such shoddy hypnotic amusement. His interest in the new medium is fixed on its capacity to transmit from the individual home to the center, not on its capacity to provide the most powerful psychological stimuli through visual programming. "The great majority of

Ral/O Pasquim/Rio de Janeiro

Cartoon by Ral. From *O Pasquim*, Rio de Janeiro. By permission of World Press Review.

the proles did not even have telescreens in their homes." The analysis of the state of society in Ingsoc Britain in Goldstein's secret book does refer to the fact that "the invention of print . . . made it easier to manipulate public opinion and the film and the radio carried the process further. With the development of television, and the technical advance which made it possible to receive and transmit simultaneously and on the same instrument, private life came to an end."

And as the proles do not have television, the proles are, in fact, allowed to have a private life. They are not worth watching. Behind this elitist view that only the members of the Party—i.e., the intellectuals—are significant enough to be watched and to be deprived of a private life, there lurks a residue of the Old Etonian's contempt for the lower classes.

## VI

Many critical observers maintain that in the developed industrial societies of the Western world, television, principally in its commercial form, has come to play the part that thought control, Newspeak, and the whole manipulative apparatus in the hands of the Party perform in *Nineteen Eighty-Four*. Commercial television in the United States has become a multi-billion-dollar enterprise which in effect is making the population progressively more stupid, incapable of sustained thought and concentration, and politically more apathetic. And all this with the expressed purpose and explicit justification that it is advertising through the mass media which keeps the economy of mass-production going. In other words: it is the television industry that operates under the implicit assumption that "ignorance is strength."

It might even be argued that the two other slogans of Oceania—"freedom is slavery" and "war is peace"—also express some of the basic principles and practices of a society dominated by the television medium: after all, the obfuscation of the masses' minds by television and the political apathy it seems to produce might well be seen as a form of slavery—an abdication of the exercise of genuine democratic decision making by the masses; and it might also be argued that the way the international situation is handled by the media creates the illusion of peace while bloody and destructive wars are being waged around the globe.

This may seem an extreme way of putting the matter. But, on reflection, it should become clear that our situation in 1984 contains at least the germs of a development in this direction. The image of Big Brother is absent from the affluent West, yet it remains a fact that politicians here too are now sold by image through television advertising, the intellectual level of which certainly is no higher than the slogans that advertise Big Brother in *Nineteen Eighty-Four*. Nor is the image of the hated adversary, Goldstein, absent from our screens, where he assumes the multifarious shape of the terrorist, the spy, the subversive element, or, indeed, that eternal adversary, the rival superpower whose position as the perpetual enemy has become accepted as unquestionable and axiomatic.

It is moreover possible to assert that reasoned argument has been severely reduced in political discussion and debate, that the level of political knowledge among the masses is deplorably low, and that in many democratic countries the percentages of votes cast in elections are decreasing at an alarming rate. It can thus be argued that, albeit over a somewhat longer time span than Orwell envisaged, the masses might well decline to the status of disenfranchised and politically castrated proles.

This danger seems particularly acute in the United States, where commercial and advertising interests dominate television and radio, leading to the elimination of most "cultural" subjects from broadcasting. In those countries where television and radio are partly or wholly run as public services, there is considerable evidence that, in fact, the electronic media can be used to bring about a gradual improvement in the levels of taste in fields like drama and music, and that they may even be able to raise the political awareness of the population. But it is equally evident that this process is extremely slow and might, at best, merely increase what will always remain a small minority of highly educated and politically conscious individuals. This consideration is moot in the United States, where the deplorable state of television tends to be accepted as an immutable fact of life, almost a law of nature. The provincialism of this attitude, which ignores the evidence even of such a close neighbor as Canada, whose strong, publicly run broadcasting service has been able to a certain extent to maintain the presence of culture on the air in radio and television, is one of the sinister symptoms for the drift of the United States toward *Nineteen Eighty-Four*. On the other hand, the example of the use of the mass media in some European countries—Scandinavia, Holland, West Germany, Britain—provides at least a glimmer of hope.

That in 1984 television, in all the developed industrial countries of the Western world, has become mainly responsible for supplying the masses with cheap fiction, vicarious excitement, and mentally debilitating soft porn is too evident to need much elaboration. What may seem less obvious is the fact that Newspeak in 1984 takes its shape from the language of television advertising. Examples of tautological pseudo-logic like: "This powder washes whiter because it contains a special ingredient that washes whiter" have become commonplace on TV advertising. That such a statement should be considered convincing enough to warrant inclusion in an expensively produced commercial is striking evidence that the principles of Newspeak can debase the language to a point where genuine thought becomes impossible. And once the effectiveness of this attack on logical thought has been established by commercial advertising, inevitably political advertising follows suit. We may be well on the way toward reaching that point. Election commercials in the United States have almost totally eliminated reasoned argument and rely more and more on the mere appearance of the candidate. The effect of this technique on the level of political oratory even in contexts where reasoned argument might be possible—public meetings, press conferences, debates in Congress—has become painfully apparent in recent years and campaigns.

## VII

Orwell was among the first to formulate one of the basic facts about totalitarian politics and its manipulation of the masses: Large masses of people can best, and most completely, be controlled and manipulated to the extent that they can be removed from contact with reality. As their ideologies are distortions of reality, totalitarian regimes have to create a fantasy world that corresponds to their picture of reality. O'Brien tells Winston in one of their last confrontations:

> You believe that reality is something objective, external, existing in its own right. You also believe that the nature of reality is self-evident. When you delude yourself into thinking that you see something, you assume that everyone else sees the same thing as you. But I tell you, Winston, that reality is not external. Reality exists in the human mind and nowhere else.

*Nineteen Eighty-Four* was published in 1949. Two years later Hannah Arendt's *The Burden of Our Time* (later retitled *The Origins of Totalitarianism*) first appeared in London. In that book Arendt elaborated the same idea: that, as totalitarian ideologies were a distortion of reality, totalitarian governments could only remain in power if they succeeded in blurring their populations' sense of what was real, so that they would see the world as corresponding to their rulers' philosophy.

Television is a powerful instrument for projecting an alternative reality into the minds of its audience. Most of what is seen on television is staged or at least edited, including even those elements that are perceived as most real, such as the news. A political demonstration, for example, may have lasted several hours, during which there have been only thirty seconds of violence. Yet these are the thirty seconds that will be seen on television, not necessarily for some sinister political purpose, but merely because they form the most dramatic, and therefore most riveting aspect of the event. Precisely because it is a photographic medium, television tends to be unquestioningly accepted as objectively real.

In actuality, television presents a highly artificial, edited, staged, and therefore unrealistic picture of the world. This is true not only of openly fictional fare—situation comedies, police series, feature films—but also of the news, sports broadcasts, talk and game shows, and political debates. The very fact that cameras were in position to record a news event shows that its filming had been anticipated and staged. And in the great majority of cases it must subsequently have been edited and rearranged to give the maximum dramatic effect. In that sense much of the news is theater. Orwell, unresponsive as he was to the potential of television, imagined the rulers of *Nineteen Eighty-Four* distorting reality by means of radio broadcasts and newspapers. Television, because it is photographic and gives the illusion of a direct transmission of real events, has proved an infinitely more powerful medium for the creation of artificially distorted perceptions of the real world. In that sense the reality of 1984 far surpasses what Orwell imagined.

The political effects of this state of affairs may be more indirect, more gradual, and less readily perceived. They might well, for that very reason, be more insidious in the long run. For they operate in an atmosphere of affluence rather than of scarcity (as it exists in *Nineteen Eighty-Four* and in today's Communist world) and that in itself may be a more dangerous factor: affluence and contentment are a more effective means of gaining the acquiescence of the manipulated masses than discontent and deprivation. The long-term political effects on the masses of living in a fantasy environment, as I have suggested, might well spell the end of participatory democracy as we now know it in the Western world.

VIII

Despite the implications for the future, on the surface of daily life Orwell's vision has *not* come true in the non-Communist developed world. In the so-called Third World, however, there are numerous features of daily life that closely resemble the situation in Orwell's Britain—"Airstrip One." In the many military dictatorships of postcolonial Africa or Asia the media are used almost precisely as Orwell envisaged. There the world is full of Big Brothers. The loudspeakers blare out their propaganda on market squares, perpetual guerrilla wars rage from the Yemen to Afghanistan, from the Philippines to Cambodia, from El Salvador to the Argentine, from Mauretania and Uganda to Namibia and Angola, Ethiopia and Somalia, Lebanon, Iraq, and Iran. And everywhere there are daily hate sessions presided over by Ayatollahs and other Big Brothers. These wars would not be possible without the hatreds fostered incessantly by the media, used massively and unscrupulously.

If Orwell's vison of the situation in the developed Western world is so much farther off the mark, this is perhaps due to the fact that he greatly underestimated the speed of change. Winston Smith is thirty-nine years old in 1984, which means that he was born in 1945, the year World War II ended. Orwell thus chose the year 1984 simply because he tried to imagine what the world would be like when the generation born after the end of the war had reached maturity. One generation is a very short time span on the scale of history. But we must not forget that Orwell, in his mid-forties when he wrote *Nineteen Eighty-Four*, knew that he was mortally ill and would not long survive the publication of his book. To a dying man even the nineteen-sixties must have appeared unconscionably far distant, in an almost mythical future.

Most utopias and anti-utopias are set centuries or even millenia ahead. Orwell took a considerable risk in describing a future that many of the readers of the first edition of his book would actually live to see. That is why, as far as the mass media are concerned, we in 1984 can merely discern the potential for the emergence of tendencies that might ultimately develop into what Orwell envisaged on a much longer time scale. In *Brave New World* Aldous Huxley imagined a population drugged into apathy by chemical means, pills of "soma." Writing almost twenty years after Huxley, Orwell came much nearer to a possible reality by seeing that it was much more likely that this type of apathy might be produced by the mass media (although he obviously underrated the power of television). Prophets of evil things to come tend to hope that their predictions will not come true, precisely because of their fear of what they have prophesied and warned against. Through its impact on millions of readers Orwell's *Nineteen Eighty-Four* has surely already done much toward averting the evils it predicted.

As regards the media, however, these warnings are still most pertinent; radio and television are among the most powerful and potentially beneficial inventions of the human spirit—in their effect over centuries to come as decisive for the development of civilization as the invention of writing itself, or the art of printing. Because Orwell as a writer was involved in the political use of the media, he saw the negative possibilities of radio and TV for the next generation. But radio, and above all television, can also become powerful positive influences to raise levels of awareness, knowledge, and culture; they have much to contribute toward the goal of a more humane humanity. Orwell's dire warnings are perhaps even more relevant in 1984 than when they were first uttered.

# 16 *Marion Lewenstein*

# Smokey Bear as Big Brother

*How could you tell how much of it was lies?*

MEDIA INFLUENCE is the most commonly cited characteristic in comparing our current world with *Nineteen Eighty-Four's* mythical totalitarian state, Oceania. Media, Orwell tells us, will be everywhere. An elite clique, disguised as Big Brother, will tailor messages for media to deliver. These repetitive, uniform messages will manipulate response. In addition, media technology, in the form of telescreens, will permit this clique to invade every citizen's privacy.

Certainly, as the real 1984 approaches, media are, as Orwell predicted, ubiquitous, persuasive, and possessed of technology easily permitting spying. But, for the American society at least, Smokey Bear may be our most reassuring symbol that *Nineteen Eighty-Four* has not, in fact, yet arrived.

Smokey Bear?

His image, like Big Brother's, peers at us from many places. It is well-recognized and linked with forest fire prevention by almost 98 percent of the American public. For the past four decades Americans have looked at Smokey posters, sung Smokey ballads, watched Smokey commercials, bought Smokey trinkets, accepted Smokey awards, and been bombarded with Smokey publicity that often featured famous fellow Americans.

This campaign, the longest run (it began in 1945) and best-documented public persuasion effort in American history, has enlisted the skills of those named by Orwell as the "new aristocracy" who would control oligarchical society—bureaucrats, publicity experts, sociologists, teachers, journalists, and professional politicians.

Despite the "success" of this public campaign, however, wildfires on public and private land are increasing steadily, though perhaps not at the rate they

1954 television version of *Nineteen Eighty-Four*. BBC copyright photograph.

would have without the help of Smokey and the millions of dollars spent yearly on promoting his image and message.

The Smokey Bear campaign employs many of the strategies depicted in *Nineteen Eighty-Four*—propagandizing the young, sponsoring theme songs, incorporating the symbol in national events, and publicizing the image of the charismatic figure through posters, newspapers, magazines, radio, TV, and commercial products. In one year alone, 1979, four billion messages reached American homes. Some 6,000 radio stations, 800 television stations, 8,500 newspapers, and 750 magazines carried Smokey Bear pleas, along with those seen on numerous outdoor and transportation advertising boards.

The difference, of course, in the real 1984 of the U.S., is the freedom to ignore all this manipulative effort. Smokey's Junior Forest Ranger programs may enroll six million young people, but their efforts to change adult fire habits have been less successful than those of Oceania's children to force their parents to conform to government fiat. In *Nineteen Eighty-Four*, children have a central authority to whom they can report deviant behavior; in the real 1984, they do not.

The insidious possibility of reporting on others in our society does exist. Otherwise, our FBI and CIA would not be flourishing. But journalistic inquiry from time to time reduces organizational control over our lives by disclosing questionable activities. A story of possible collusion between a regulatory agency and those whom it regulates, for example, puts media on the side of the "proles" rather than Big Brother.

## II

Though hordes of facts and impressions are easily marshalled to bolster the chilling Orwellian premise that mass media unerringly manipulate the masses, the effects of media influence are more variable and complex than is popularly assumed. Where governments do not enforce behavior—and Orwell's media portrayal presupposes two situations not generally present in 1984's non-totalitarian societies: oligarchical control of all media, coupled with a police state—it takes more than the endless message repetitions described in *Nineteen Eighty-Four* to modify human action, as we have demonstrated. Effecting change is a complicated mechanism involving attractiveness and credibility of the source, cultural attitudes of the receiver, and belief in the channel, or medium.

Though Orwell had Russia in mind, China has more closely resembled his Oceania. Newspapers, radio, posters calling for political action; surging throngs chanting "Mao, Mao" rather than "Big Brother"; "self criticism" and "study" sessions that seem remarkably similar to *Nineteen Eighty-Four's* hate and political sessions, are all much as Orwell depicted.

Yet, despite multiple pressures, not all of China's social goals have been sold to the masses, if they have not wanted to receive the message. Government efforts at encouraging one-child families, for example, have required physical and economic coercion above and beyond media persuasion to achieve results. In peasant families, where the need to reduce population is urgent, birth control has had its poorest results. In part this has been attributed to the fact that the carriers of the message are not themselves credible. There are Party cadres in the countryside, for example, who themselves have three or more children per family, thus undermining a huge multimedia campaign.

Television entertainment, with its attendant advertising, has been particularly persuasive in less developed countries whose populations are unused to media merchandising. One study showed that after American TV programs were introduced in Samoa, Samoans demanded products which had until that time been unknown to them: sleeping tablets, Western clothing, sugared cereals, to name a few. It can be convincingly argued that in a slow-paced South Pacific island swept by warm sea breezes, where naturally sweet fruit grows abundantly, the population has little need for artificial sleeping aids, bulky apparel, or expensive man-made food products.

Other attempts to sway the unsophisticated have been equally successful. After strong media campaigns, African mothers have abandoned disease-free breast milk for baby formula, difficult to keep sanitary in hot climates without refrigeration. The result has been sharp rises in infant mortality.

III

It was Aldous Huxley, in his "negative utopia"—to borrow Eric Fromm's phrase—who addressed himself to the potential seductiveness of entertainment media. In *Brave New World*, published in 1932, he describes with uncomfortable portent sensual movies known as "feelies" that, along with other media and drugs, provide pleasurable experience. Sight, sound, smell, touch, and emotions are so satisfied that citizens, lulled into dreamlike states, are easily dominated politically.

Even "positive utopias" emphasize the pleasures media can provide. Edward Bellamy's *Looking Backward*, a futuristic novel published in 1888, described stereo sound long before even crystal radio sets had been invented. The protagonist awakens after a sleep of 113 years to find himself in Boston of the year 2000. The world scheme is not dissimilar from that of Orwell's *Nineteen Eighty-Four*, with socialist concerns for the "good of society" determining all decisions. The state's aim, however, is benevolent, in contrast to Oceania's. The work force, known as the "industrial army," are assigned tasks intended to please, for instance, rather than the nonpersonalized assignments *Nineteen Eighty-Four's* workers must accept.

In any event, one surprise awaiting Bellamy's hero as he explores the latter-day Boston is a home "music room" wherein by pushing a few buttons he can choose musical selections—all conveniently listed by hour and day on a large yellow card. He is overwhelmed by the music-hall reality of the sound and sinks with pleasure into a soft lounge chair to murmur in wonder.

This enchantment with media could perhaps have a subtle persuasive effect that should concern us as much as deliberately programmed attempts to control our minds and actions. There is, for example, our tendency to play out our lives on a media stage. In recent times this started trivially enough. Tiny Tim, he of the high-pitched voice and long hair, married his child bride before television cameras; private individuals disclosed marital secrets on TV shows for a chance at winning home appliances; initially unsuspecting actors willingly displayed their gaffes on "Candid Camera" to give home audiences a laugh.

But more serious moments took center stage: dentist Barney Clark agreed to an artificial heart implant, knowing he stood no chance for a significantly extended life, but also knowing that the media publicity would help the heart transplant cause. Parents whose children need organ transplants sacrifice their privacy to plead before reporters and cameras for volunteered livers, kidneys, hearts.

A threesome involved in a paternity lawsuit over an unwanted, severely retarded child born to a married surrogate mother went on the Phil Donahue

Show to debate who was the "real" father—the man who had paid $10,000 after supplying his sperm, or the woman's husband? Before an audience of millions, the husband confessed that he had fathered a similarly retarded child in a previous marriage, and furthermore, had had sexual relations with his wife shortly after she was impregnated with the other man's sperm.

Nightly, F. Lee Bailey, the flamboyant lawyer, pronounces people guilty or innocent on "Lie Detector," a television program where he gives polygraph tests not always accepted in courts of law. Or, a retired judge hands down seemingly instant but legally binding decisions on "People's Court," a small-claims court recreated for television viewing.

By encouraging media to give us each a platform to communicate with our fellow citizens, the possibility exists that we might unintentionally persuade ourselves that life does not exist unless the media tell us it does. Such thinking could, of course, lead to exactly the condition Orwell was predicting, dependence on media information as the full truth. And, if that information has been doctored, "the citizen of Oceania is like a man in interstellar space, who has no way of knowing which direction is up and which is down."

IV

But is such unhealthy media dependence likely to occur? Media history would appear to demonstrate that the answer is "no."

Popular perception has it that media in democratic countries, especially the United States, have become more banal through the years, but this is not provably so. Media as personal gratifiers have always been with us. Sensational disclosure of personal lives and pleas for help have long been part of the American press. To read newspapers, even from the colonial period, will show gory detail that many would find startling. As recently as the 1930s, newspaper front pages were filled with headlines and stories on murder, sex, and scandal to a degree only occasionally seen today. Newspapers featured grisly first-person accounts of life in prison; or as a prostitute or a destitute unemployed.

Possibly the latter stories were precursors of today's open-heart surgery performed live on TV . . . a *Perils of Pauline* thriller carried to the ultimate. In any case, such heart-in-the-mouth journalism gradually has given way to more sober accounts of local politics, school board meetings, and toxic chemical leaks.

V

Ultimately, the freedom to publish or broadcast depends on who controls the media. Journalists, by and large, do not. Orwell's vision assumed oligarchical control of media so as to control thought. His theme that masses march lock-step with the messages they receive, changing direction as the message changes, may be dubious, but his warning on media control is suggestive enough to make us uneasy.

In most countries of the world, governments fund media. This is true in democratic as well as totalitarian states. However, since the Second World War, government funds in democracies have usually forced media diversity rather than monopoly. In Scandinavian countries, for example, the government provides money to each recognized political party to spend on media, in proportion to that party's percent of voters. The Italian government subsidizes virtually any newspaper that can get itself into production; in addition, the government sponsors three television and radio networks, each managed by one of the three major political divisions within Italy.

England's newspaper and magazine industry has long been privately owned, but the broadcasting industry, until recently, was entirely government sponsored. Now television too has moved toward some commercial sponsorship.

The U.S. appears to have sufficient media diversity with its 1,700 daily newspapers; over 9,000 weekly, college, and foreign-language newspapers; 11,000 magazines; 2,500 book publishers; 1,000 TV stations; and 9,000 radio stations—almost all privately owned. But what this list disguises is rapidly converging ownership. Once independent publishers and broadcasters have now become part of media conglomerates. Noted media critic Ben Bagdikian tells us that only fifty corporations own all the newspapers, magazines, and broadcasting stations that employ the majority of American journalists. Twenty publishing companies, he states, control half the daily newspaper circulation in this country, equal to some thirty million readers. Many of these same companies have controlling interests in television, radio, magazines, and the newer media technologies such as cable and videotext. This ownership concentration brings with it an oligarchy differing from Orwell's only in who is at the top.

Though there is little evidence to date that media corporations have abused this power by controlling content, that possibility surely exists. Even more possible is the power of government to persuade corporate giants, as well as media supported by government funds, to run the news as dictated for fear of government reprisals. England has censored through "suggestion" newspaper and television coverage of some Northern Ireland disturbances, and, through more overt manipulation, war news from the Falkland Islands in 1982.

In the sense that media do show willingness to abide by the rules of those in power, at least for limited periods of time, *Nineteen Eighty-Four* properly holds up a mirror to a possible future.

Another mirror to the future, though decidedly more murky, is Orwell's fascination with the linkage of memory with media. Winston Smith, who rewrites newspaper history in his job at the Ministry of Truth, thinks he is the only person in Oceania who remembers past facts. That everyone's memories would fade promptly upon presentation of new information, as Orwell would have us believe, has been disproved often enough. But there is a more intriguing form of inadvertent memory loss that future societies may have to concern themselves with: loss of first drafts.

Writers have gloried in the new ease with which computers permit them to change, correct, and rearrange copy. Few, however, have wondered what history will make of these flawless final drafts of their thoughts. Gone will be initial musings, first bold exclamations, devious lines of reasoning, un-finished ideas, and clear junctures in opinion by which scholars normally trace a chronicler's evolving attitudes. In this manner, technology may come to deprive us of first memories, those beginning impressions so important in reflecting on society's changing views. This is a more subtle reworking of history than Orwell presented to us in his futuristic novel.

In *Nineteen Eighty-Four*, technology and particularly television, or tele-screen as he calls it, is developed primarily to spy upon society. Certainly, that possibility exists for us today and in the future. Computers that permit us to gather information and buy goods from remote sources also permit a third party to keep tabs on our choices. Office computers on which clerks keep files also log how much time each task takes or how long the clerk has been away from the computer. Communication satellites that encourage in-stant world-wide message sending also facilitate government scanning of private messages.

Thus, in the end, though Smokey Bear may disprove Orwell's judgments on media domination in 1984, we must welcome *Nineteen Eighty-Four's* call to watch Big Brother, who may, after all, be watching us. Otherwise we may, through indifference, discover that we have traded imperfect democratic media for imperfect totalitarian ones. By which time, our world could have come to resemble Oceania more than we would care to suppose.

Cartoon by Henfil. From *Opinao*, Rio de Janeiro. By permission of World Press Review.

# IV
# FREEDOM IS SLAVERY

# 17 Paul Robinson

# For the Love of Big Brother: The Sexual Politics of *Nineteen Eighty-Four*

*Eroticism was the enemy.*

IN *NINETEEN EIGHTY-FOUR* ORWELL PRESENTS a distinct theory about the relation between sex and society under totalitarianism. Put very simply, he argues that sexual expression and political authoritarianism are incompatible.

"The aim of the Party," Orwell writes, "was not merely to prevent men and women from forming loyalties which it might not be able to control. Its real, undeclared purpose was to remove all pleasure from the sexual act." Significantly, the Ministry of Repression in Oceania—i.e., the police—is called the Ministry of Love. The Party also disapproves of erotic language, and Party members are expected to avoid profanity. In Newspeak, sexual life is entirely encompassed by two words, *sexcrime* (sexual immorality) and *goodsex* (chastity):

> *Sexcrime* covered all sexual misdeeds whatever. It covered fornication, adultery, homosexuality, and other perversions, and, in addition, normal intercourse practiced for its own sake. There was no need to enumerate them separately, since they were all equally culpable, and in principle, all punishable by death.

In his final peroration, the malevolent O'Brien reveals that the Party seeks not just to curtail sex or diminish its pleasure, but to do away with it entirely: "The sex instinct will be eradicated," he announces. "Procreation will be an annual formality like the renewal of a ration card. We shall abolish the orgasm." Moreover, the regime's puritanism is no mere ideological fluke, but essential to its survival. As theoretician Emmanuel Goldstein explains, "All the beliefs, habits, tastes, emotions, mental attitudes that characterize our time are really designed to sustain the mystique of the Party and prevent the true nature of present-day society from being perceived."

The government of Oceania has already made remarkable strides toward its goal of desexualization. The people we meet in *Nineteen Eighty-Four* are among the most unprepossessing, the least sexy, in all literature. "Nearly everyone was ugly," observes Winston Smith, looking around the canteen at the Ministry of Truth. The men are described variously as beetlelike, frog-faced, chinless, and dumpy. The women are grayish, dusty, and wispy-haired. To be sure, Winston's wife, Katharine, is "a tall, fair-haired girl, very straight, with splendid movements," but she is also the most complete re-alization (to date) of the regime's antisexual ideal: she detests intercourse, her body stiffening the moment Winston touches her. Even more horrible, she insists on a weekly enactment of this "frigid little ceremony," which she refers to as "our duty to the Party."

Although desexualization is also the ultimate fate of Winston and his lover Julia (at their final meeting the thought of intercourse is detestable to both of them), their political rebellion, appropriately, is linked to sexual liberation. Indeed, in an important sense their revolt and their adultery are one and the same, as Winston repeatedly explains. He had hoped, for example, to arouse his wife from her erotic numbness, not for his own pleasure but because of its political implications:

> What he wanted more even than to be loved, was to break down that wall of virtue, even if it were only once in his whole life. The sexual act, successfully performed, was rebellion. Desire was *thoughtcrime*. Even to have awakened Katharine, if he could have achieved it, would have been like a seduction, although she was his wife.

He is thrilled to hear that Julia has slept with Party members scores of times, wishing only that it had been hundreds or even thousands. "Anything that hinted at corruption always filled him with a wild hope." Similarly, her bawdy talk registers with him as an act of political opposition. And after they make love for the first time he gives succinct articulation to its revolutionary sig-nificance: "Their embrace had been a battle, the climax a victory. It was a blow struck against the Party. It was a political act."

Orwell carefully insists that it is sex, not love, that contains the promise of revolt. He was by temperament, one feels, too tough-minded, too anti-romantic, to propose that love might be the answer. "Not merely the love of one person," reflects Winston, "but the animal instinct, the simple undif-ferentiated desire: that was the force that would tear the Party to pieces."

Winston's formulation is overstated and doesn't in fact represent Orwell's considered opinion. In an earlier discussion of the Party's attitude toward prostitution, he had written: "Tacitly the Party was even inclined to encourage prostitution, as an outlet for instincts which could not be altogether suppressed. Mere debauchery did not matter very much, so long as it was furtive and joyless." Presumably, therefore, the revolutionary sexuality Orwell has in mind is something less than love but more than a mechanical discharge of sexual tensions. It might best be called "humanized" sexuality: sexual pleasure, not just sexual relief—which is what the proles get and what Winston himself got (much to his dissatisfaction) when he visited a prostitute.

Oceania presents certain sexual anomalies that don't fit the general pattern of repression. The most glaring of these would seem to be the "proles," who are explicitly exempted from the regime's antisexual policies. Indeed, the proles are positively incited to libertinage. A whole bureau in the Ministry of Truth is devoted to creating pornographic novels and films for them. The explanation for this, of course, is that the Party considers the proles less than human. The encouragement of a kind of animal sexuality among them (they are repeatedly compared to animals in the novel) prevents them from developing the political consciousness that might pose a threat to the regime. They are victims of what Herbert Marcuse has called "repressive desublimation."

A more intriguing anomaly is the Junior Anti-Sex League, to which the lusty Julia belongs. This is one of Orwell's better jokes, but I wonder if he has caught its full irony. The first hint of the regime's puritanism comes when Julia is introduced in her Anti-Sex League costume:

> She was a bold-looking girl of about twenty-seven, with thick dark hair, a freckled face, and swift, athletic movements. A narrow scarlet sash, emblem of the Junior Anti-Sex League, was wound several times around the waist of her overalls, just tightly enough to bring out the shapeliness of her hips.

Freud would call this "the return of the repressed." Not only does the Anti-Sex League's emblem highlight the wearer's sexuality, but its scarlet color is heavily freighted with biological and literary associations of an unmistakably erotic nature. The repressed also makes a return in the Party's idealized physical type: "tall muscular youths and deep-bosomed maidens, blond-haired, vital, sunburnt, carefree." Here Orwell takes an obvious swipe at the prurience of the Nazis.

In spite of such complications, both the Party and its enemies (i.e., Winston and Julia) agree that authoritarianism is intimately connected to sexual repression. What seems a good deal less clear is the nature of that connection. Why, we must ask, does the regime's survival depend on its imposition of a puritanical sexual code?

Two possible answers immediately suggest themselves, but must be dismissed as illogical or inadequately supported by the text. The first is the idea that sex threatens the regime because it is natural; as an unmediated biological instinct it necessarily stands in opposition to the artificialities of Oceanic society. The notion of the subversive naturalness of sex is associated with Freud's *Civilization and Its Discontents*, which maintains that culture is based on sexual repression and hence that sex in the raw, so to speak, undermines social order. Whether or not Orwell held such a doctrine, it is obviously too general to distinguish the peculiar society of Oceania—i.e., a totalitarian one—from all other societies.

A second inadequate hypothesis argues that sex is subversive because of its privateness—because it creates a realm beyond the Party's control. In Oceania, however, sex is not in fact private. There are telescreens and hidden microphones everywhere (including bedrooms), and the microphones are sensitive enough to detect even a heartbeat. Under such circumstances only sex that is completely silent and conducted in absolute darkness can remain secret. Winston and Julia think that they go undetected when they have intercourse above Mr. Charrington's antique shop, but the Thought Police have eavesdropped on them from behind a picture. Even their seemingly isolated lovemaking in the woods has been observed (though Orwell does not explain how), and Winston eventually recognizes that "no physical act, no word spoken aloud" had been undetected by the police. "They had played sound tracks to him, shown him photographs. Some of them were photographs of Julia and himself. Yes, even. . . ." The theory that sex is subversive because of its privateness fails on empirical grounds.

Two characters in *Nineteen Eighty-Four*, O'Brien and Julia, articulate their own explanations for the regime's puritanism. Neither theory is entirely satisfactory—neither, that is, adequately accounts for the sexual information contained in the novel. But they bring us closer to understanding Orwell's meaning.

O'Brien's explanation might be called the theory of competing pleasures. It advances in three steps. First, the goal of the Party, he says, is to seek power "entirely for its own sake." Second, one asserts power over another human being "by making him suffer." Finally, since the sole object of the Party is power, and since power reduces itself to inflicting pain, the Party must create a world in which "there will be no emotions except fear, rage, triumph, and self-abasement. . . . All competing pleasures will be destroyed." Hence his conclusion: "We shall abolish the orgasm." Even for *doublethink*, O'Brien's argument here is unusually tortuous, and one inevitably feels that there has been some logical slippage. The same line of reasoning would appear to rule out eating, defecating, scratching, and any number of other "competing pleasures" with which the regime seems prepared to make its peace. Orwell nowhere elaborates the theory or addresses its obvious difficulties, and one senses that it is intended mainly to convey O'Brien's talent for extravagant casuistry.

Julia's theory is more promising. It is down-to-earth and finds greater resonance in the novel as a whole. A Freudian would call it an "economic theory," since it is based on a notion of displaced libido:

> Unlike Winston, Julia had grasped the inner meaning of the Party's sexual puritanism. It was not merely that the sex instinct created a world of its own which was outside the Party's control and which therefore had to be destroyed if possible. What was more important was that sexual privation induced hysteria, which was desirable because it could be transformed into war fever and leader worship. The way she put it was:
>
> "When you make love you're using up energy; and afterwards you feel happy and don't give a damn for anything. They can't bear you to feel like that. They want you to be bursting with energy all the time. All this marching up and down and cheering and waving flags is simply sex gone sour. If you're happy inside yourself, why should you get excited about Big Brother and the Three-Year Plans and the Two Minutes Hate and all the rest of their bloody rot?"

The same logic—"bottling down some powerful instinct and using it as a driving force"—leads Orwell to describe Hate Week as a "great orgasm . . . quivering to its climax." We have come to associate the economic metaphor with psychoanalysis, but it was in fact the common property of European sexual ideology throughout the nineteenth century, embodied, for example, in such infamous notions as the "spermatic economy." Thus no direct indebtedness need be assumed.

The trouble with the economic theory, like the naturalness theory, is that it's too general. It serves to explain the libidinal dynamics of *all* societies, and nothing about it points to the uniquely authoritarian character of Oceania. Much more apposite is another idea associated with Freud: the proposition, set forth in *Group Psychology and the Analysis of the Ego*, that societies hold together because their members fall in love with the leader—or, to use Freud's own language, are attached to the leader by "aim-inhibited libidinal ties." The idea was taken up by Thomas Mann in his novella *Mario and the Magician*, a parody of Italian Fascism, in which the erotic bond between leader and led is made quite explicit. Like Freud and Mann, Orwell, I would suggest, argues that the totalitarian society of Oceania requires that all its members be in love with the society's leader, Big Brother. And since Big Brother's power is absolute, the love his subjects bear him must also be absolute. Unlike an ordinary society, Oceania demands that its subjects' sublimation be complete. Hence the regime's goal of abolishing sex altogether.

Whether or not Big Brother exists is, of course, irrelevant. Indeed, all the better if he is merely a fabrication of the Party, since then he can be fashioned precisely to fulfill his essential role as love object. As O'Brien explains, "Big

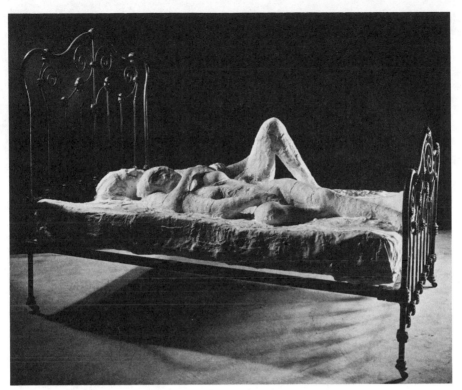

*Lovers on a Bed II* by George Segal, 1970, plaster and metal, 48" × 72" × 60". Courtesy of Sidney Janis Gallery.

Brother is the guise in which the Party chooses to exhibit itself to the world. His function is to act as a focusing point for love, fear, and reverence, emotions which are more easily felt toward an individual than toward an organization." The projected image of Big Brother, moreover, is strikingly erotic. He is "a man of about forty-five, with a heavy black mustache and ruggedly handsome features." Burt Reynolds might be our contemporary equivalent. No other male in the novel is described as handsome, and indeed the vast majority of them are positively hideous. Big Brother is always spoken of as potent: he is "full of power and mysterious calm," "all-powerful," "omnipotent," a potency enhanced by his invisibility and unknown whereabouts. His voice is "enveloping." His "hypnotic eyes" are like "some huge force . . . pressing down upon you." Only once is more than his face mentioned, and on that occasion we learn that his statue has displaced Admiral Nelson's as the corona of London's most prominent phallic symbol.

Orwell makes entirely explicit that Oceanic society depends for its survival on its members being in love with Big Brother. The final line of the novel, marking Winston Smith's complete capitulation, states simply, "He loved Big Brother." Before Winston's, the "conversions" of the traitors Jones, Aaronson, and Rutherford were complete when they, too, loved Big Brother. "It was touching," says O'Brien, "to see how they loved him." O'Brien interrupts his own paean to hatred and torture (in which he abolishes the orgasm) to remark: "There will be no love, except the love of Big Brother." The exclusiveness of that love is essential: to rule absolutely, the leader must monopolize all aim-inhibited affection.

Orwell indicates in numerous ways that sex lies at the root of this affection. Although Big Brother is loved equally by men and women, we learn several times that women in particular are drawn to the Party's zealous puritanism. The Junior Anti-Sex League advocates complete chastity in both sexes, but its membership seems to consist entirely of women. During the Two Minutes Hate, a characteristically drab and repressed female Party member erupts into orgasmic ecstasy at the leader's appearance on the telescreen:

> The face of Big Brother seemed to persist for several seconds on the screen, as though the impact that it had made on everyone's eyeballs were too vivid to wear off immediately. The little sandy-haired woman had flung herself forward over the back of the chair in front of her. With a tremulous murmur that sounded like "My Savior!" she extended her arms toward the screen.

The Hate induces a thinly disguised sexual response in all the participants:

> At this moment the entire group of people broke into a deep, slow, rhythmical chant of "B-B! . . . B-B!" . . . It was a refrain that was often heard in moments of overwhelming emotion. Partly it was a sort of hymn to the wisdom and majesty of Big Brother, but still more it was an act of self-hypnosis, a deliberate drowning of consciousness by means of rhythmic noise.

Not only during this "general delirium," but even in casual moments (as when Mr. Parsons blathers on at lunch), the loved one is addressed in familiar, even intimate, terms. He is not Big Brother, but "B.B." We may safely conclude, then, that Oceania's puritanism results from the logic of libidinal displacement. The sexual attachment of citizens to one another must give way to a uniform, sublimated attachment to the leader.

The displacement theory, I believe, does fullest justice to the explicit arguments and evidence presented in the text. But it fails to come to terms with a more subtle level of erotic persuasion in the book. There is surely a profound paradox in the fact that George Orwell, who is among the least sensuous of writers, should have argued so vehemently for the revolutionary potential of sexuality. And, indeed, *Nineteen Eighty-Four* exhibits an alarming discrepancy between its strenuously prosexual doctrines and its unfailingly anemic representation of sexual passion.

The affair between Winston and Julia is both a literary and a sexual dud, its erotic scenes flat and cliché-ridden. Orwell places the lovers' first encounter in a pseudo-Laurentian wood full of bluebells and singing thrushes. The language, however, remains resolutely earthbound ("He pulled her round so that they were breast to breast; her body seemed to melt into his"). They next have intercourse in an abandoned church tower (a setting that brings to mind the comic seduction scene in *Madame Bovary*), and Orwell's account is as mechanical as before. Mercifully, he then permits them to retire to the room above Mr. Charrington's, where, perhaps knowing his weakness, he restricts himself to short, general descriptions—mere indications, actually—of their lovemaking.

He also seems relieved to allow the process of sexual routinization to set in as quickly as possible. Winston is happy to have found a place "where they could be alone together without feeling the obligation to make love every time they met," and where, in fact, they spend most of their time lying on the bed or sleeping. Julia remains the more erotic of the two ("a rebel from the waist downwards"), while Winston clearly prefers reading Emmanuel Goldstein's book to fulfilling his sexual responsibilities.

Inevitably one feels that were it not for his abstract conviction that sex is revolutionary he would be perfectly comfortable with the regime's puritanical ideals. Measured by any literary standards, Orwell's dionysian protest is a failure.

*Nineteen Eighty-Four* does, however, contain scenes of genuine erotic power. They occur not between Winston and Julia but between Winston and O'Brien, and (as I will suggest in a moment) they are intimately related to Orwell's explicit theory about the political significance of libidinal displacement. Winston's relationship with O'Brien takes the literary form of an illicit court-ship. Perhaps this is simply because illicit sex and political conspiracy share a similar experiential structure. But the erotic flavor of the relationship is nonetheless remarkable. Let us briefly follow the stages of their romance.

It begins with "an equivocal glance," but a glance so meaningful that it inspires Winston to his first act of revolt, the writing of his diary:

> Momentarily he caught O'Brien's eye. O'Brien had stood up. He had taken off his spectacles and was in the act of resettling them on his nose with his characteristic gesture. But there was a fraction of a second when their eyes met, and for as long as it took to happen Winston knew—yes, he *knew!*—that O'Brien was thinking the same thing as himself. An unmistakable message had passed.

The scene is a not-so-distant relative of the "dumb charade" between Baron Charlus and Jupien in Proust's *Cities of the Plain*. Winston becomes convinced that O'Brien belongs to a secret organization with the significant name of "the Brotherhood," which is also described in remarkably suggestive language:

> Some days he believed in it, some days not. There was no evidence, only fleeting glimpses that might mean anything or nothing; snatches of overheard conversation, faint scribbles on lavatory walls—once, even, when two strangers met, a small movement of the hands which had looked as though it might be a signal of recognition.

Later Winston wonders whether Julia might not belong to "the fabulous Brotherhood," and Orwell's grammar, in a nice unconscious touch, effectively denies that the organization contains women: "Perhaps the Brotherhood existed after all! Perhaps the girl was part of it! No doubt the idea was absurd. . . ."

Even before that equivocal first glance, Winston felt himself "deeply drawn" to O'Brien. The glance, however, creates a "strange intimacy" between them, and Winston comes to feel that he is writing his diary both for and to O'Brien, as if it were a kind of love letter. The furtive glance is followed by a furtive encounter. "Laying a friendly hand for a moment on Winston's arm," O'Brien invites him to his flat to look at a new edition of the Newspeak dictionary. This "equivocal remark" excites "secret imaginings" in Winston. And when they finally meet in the flat, "a wave of admiration, almost of worship, flowed out from Winston toward O'Brien."

After his arrest, Winston thinks not about Julia but about O'Brien. And when O'Brien turns out to be his tormentor, his love becomes explicit: "If he could have moved he would have stretched out a hand and laid it on O'Brien's arm. He had never loved him so deeply as at this moment. . . . In some sense that went deeper than friendship, they were intimates." As the obscene tortures increase, Winston's devotion to O'Brien becomes only more abject.

It would of course be ludicrous to suppose that *Nineteen Eighty-Four* is a homosexual *roman à clef*. But the suggestion of a libidinal tie between Winston and O'Brien contributes significantly to the erotic argument of the novel. For in every sexual sense (and several nonsexual ones as well) O'Brien is transparently the same person as Big Brother. Orwell invests him with the only body in the novel that might be considered a suitable match for the face he has given Big Brother. O'Brien has a "prize-fighter's physique," with a "powerful chest," and his grip is so ferocious that it "crushed the bones of Winston's palm." We are repeatedly reminded how he towers over the scrawny, maladroit, and fragile Winston, who with his "pale and meager body" and his horror of odors, exercise, and rats is made to seem distinctly womanish.

The psychological identification of O'Brien and Big Brother is, however, more than a matter of complementary anatomy. Orwell several times permits

O'Brien and Big Brother to coalesce in Winston's imagination. When Winston examines a portrait of Big Brother on the frontispiece of a children's history book, "the face of O'Brien, not called up by any obvious association . . . floated into his mind." Again later, "the face of Big Brother swam into his mind, displacing that of O'Brien." Thus the infatuation with O'Brien, which starts out on such a bright revolutionary note, culminates logically in Winston's love affair with Big Brother. O'Brien is not merely the agent of this transformation—the matchmaker, as it were. Psychologically speaking, he and the ultimate love object are interchangeable.

There is one final level of erotic argument that I would like to draw attention to, and it also plays upon the theme of displaced homosexual attachment in the totalitarian polity. In one sense, as I've just suggested, O'Brien is Big Brother. But in another (and entirely compatible) sense, he is also identified with Winston's mother. *Nineteen Eighty-Four* is replete with potential maternal images, massive females who dwarf and absorb their children. These mothers are the only figures in the novel, outside of O'Brien, of course, to whom Orwell attributes physical substantiality and robustness. The most important of them, naturally, is Winston's own mother, whose "large shapely body" recurs several times in his dreams and fantasies, and for whose murder he feels himself responsible. She is replicated in a number of other real or fanciful matriarchs: a "middle-aged woman" in a film who holds a three-year-old boy between her breasts, seeking to protect him from bullets, as both are about to drown; a fifty-year-old proletarian grandmother, "her thick arms reaching up for the line, her powerful marelike buttocks protruded," whom Winston finds distinctly "beautiful"; and a foul-mouthed drunk—"an enormous wreck of a woman, aged about sixty"—who is dumped on Winston's lap in jail, and who, on learning that both of them are named Smith, says, sentimentally, "I might be your mother!"

Orwell's preoccupation with maternal fantasies, and with the child that has somehow murdered his mother, has an almost Wagnerian obsessiveness about it. Indeed, the potent mother who inspires both awe and guilt seems to represent the psychological bedrock of the novel, although I won't pretend to understand the full logic of Orwell's conception (any more than I do Wagner's). But that O'Brien's relationship with Winston is at some level maternal is made repeatedly and abundantly clear. Throughout the scenes of Winston's torture, O'Brien looms over his recumbent victim as over a child in a crib. Orwell is quite explicit about the matter: Winston, he writes, "clung to O'Brien like a baby, curiously comforted by the heavy arm round his shoulders." In this growing attachment to his maternal tormentor one detects Winston's effort to atone for his guilt, and we may be reminded of Freud's contention that guilt—or aggression directed against the self—is the fundamental psychological cement holding society together. Apparently, the roots of desexualization reside not merely in a libidinal bond between ruler and ruled but, at their deepest, in the mysteriously ambivalent ties between mother and child.

Doubtless one must resist the temptation to make too much of the sexual argument in *Nineteen Eighty-Four*—either the explicit one or the subterranean one that I have sought to identify. In general, Orwell was more interested in the intellectual apparatus of totalitarianism that in its instinctual dynamics. He was, above all, a novelist of ideas, and the most memorable aspects of his book are its exposition of such characteristic intellectual phenomena as doublethink and Newspeak. Nor does he appear to have worked out the book's sexual argument with the same thoroughness that he brings to the conceptual issues. There is, for example, no appendix on sexual doctrines to complement that on Newspeak.

Nonetheless, Orwell comes back again and again to his libidinal theme, giving it pride of place in the novel's wrenching final moments. Moreover, his treatment of it exhibits a characteristically Orwellian twist. *Nineteen Eighty-Four* is of course a book much loved by conservatives. But I doubt that they can be entirely pleased that it embraces such frankly libertine sexual doctrines. They would be even less pleased, I suspect, with my suggestion that its sexual politics have a good deal in common with certain of Freud's ideas. Least of all would they care to hear that, at its deepest, it plunges into the psychologically murky waters of sublimated homoeroticism, maternal identification, and masochistic guilt. But in fact Orwell's vision in *Nineteen Eighty-Four* is as quirky and ideologically heterogeneous as that of such earlier works as *The Road to Wigan Pier* and *Homage to Catalonia*, which leftists have generally found more congenial. The book manages to preach both anti-Stalinism and sexual liberation, just as it unites rationalistic common sense with an uncanny sensitivity to life's erotic and emotional undercurrents.

# 18 Edward J. Brown

# Zamyatin's We and Nineteen Eighty-Four

*"Do it to Julia."*

IN THE EXERCISE OF HER CHOSEN PROFESSION the prophetess Cassandra was far more accurate in her forecasts than either George Orwell or the Russian novelist Eugene Zamyatin: the dismal future events she predicted did come true. But Cassandra as a prophetess had the advantage over them that nobody listened to her. The paradox of prophecy arises from the position of the prophet as himself a factor in the future development he foresees. We remember how the prophet Jonah upbraided his God for sparing Nineveh, whose destruction Jonah had confidently predicted. It was precisely because the inhabitants had hearkened to Jonah's prophecy and mended their evil ways that God had spared Nineveh, "that great city."

There are many nonlegendary and non-Biblical examples of prophets whose prophecy introduces something analogous to the Heisenbergian "uncertainty principle" into the social development they measure and predict. Marx's predictions—"The progressive impoverishment of the working class . . . the knell of private capitalist property . . . the expropriators are expropriated"—led directly to Bismarck and the sweeping German social reforms of the 1880s, and ultimately to the modern welfare state. Marx's measurements may have been correct for the time and place he made them, but his predictions were invalidated in part at least because they themselves had an effect on what followed. Cassandra's tragedy was the curse upon her of the God Apollo, who gave her the gift of prophecy but then turned against her and decreed that nobody would believe her, thus validating her prophecies but depriving her of any influence on the course of events.

Other prophets, including Orwell and Zamyatin, have been treated more kindly by the gods of history. The vocabulary Orwell invented, Big Brother, *doublethink, crimethink*, Thought Police, Newspeak, and the like, has entered our language as an effective polemic against the totalitarian state. Now embedded in the democratic culture of the West, *Nineteen Eighty-Four* has worked to preserve that culture. Cassandra should have been so lucky.

The involvement of Zamyatin's *We* in the defense of democratic culture has been somewhat more complex. Written in the Soviet Union in 1920, that novel has never been published there but it has been widely read, first in clandestinely circulated manuscript copies (a form of distribution well known to us as "samizdat"), and, after its publication abroad, in copies illegally smuggled into the Soviet Union (a process known in Russia as "tamizdat"). The novel undoubtedly has had some impact in Russia itself, but the full force of its prophecy was felt in Western Europe, where it served both Aldous Huxley and George Orwell as a literary model. Orwell read it in 1945 and reviewed it very favorably in *Tribune* in 1946, saying that he believed it superior to *Brave New World*, which seemed to him "quite possibly a plagiarism" of *We*. Orwell has fully acknowledged his own debt to Zamyatin.

II

Zamyatin's utopia is a city-state of the twenty-ninth century called the Only State. The civilization represents the final triumph of the *city*, the last step in *civilization*. In the course of a two-hundred years' war—a "protracted" atomic conflict, the prototype of which Zamyatin found in H.G. Wells's anti-utopia *The Sleeper Awakes*—the city has finally abolished the country, and all surviving human beings have been gathered into an enormous urban center, sealed off entirely from nature by a domed wall of glass. Nothing accidental can ever happen under the dome; even the weather is totally controlled. The invention of an artificial "petroleum food" has made the city independent of the country, and outside the glass wall there is only the "debris" of nature and some not-quite-human beings, a remnant of the human race forgotten and left behind, known as the "Mephi." Thus one part of the human race has developed entirely along rational lines, while the other has preserved primitive, instinctive impulses and feelings. Revolutionists in the Only State propose to tear down the wall that separates them from nature and, through commerce with the creatures outside the wall, rehumanize the life inside.

The Only State is a regimented paradise in which the concept of a separate, autonomous human being no longer exists, and it is possible to speak only of "we." The citizens do not have names but only numbers, and they are called "numbers" or "unifs." Their life is precisely controlled and every activity mathematically regulated for the sake of the one great good, human happiness, and in theory they have gladly surrendered individual freedom in order to gain that happiness. The ruler of the Only State is The Benefactor, a figure of absolute power and iron beneficence, who cares always for the state and the numbers, while their whole duty is to honor and obey him as a very god. The earthly paradise has a security force called the Guardians, somewhat reminiscent of the "guardian angels" of the old religion. They hover protectively over the citizen at all times, listen to his conversations, read his mail, censor his books, observe his expression for evidences of thought—and operate a mechanism called "The Machine," which vaporizes political deviants.

A number of parallels with *Nineteen Eighty-Four* will be immediately obvious. Zamyatin's benevolent dictator appears in *Nineteen Eighty-Four* as Big Brother; the Mephi outside the wall have their counterpart in Orwell's proles, who, left out of the Party, have escaped the artificial language, and, debauched though they are, have not forgotten how to love and how to sing. Echoing the revolutionaries of *We*, Winston Smith in *Nineteen Eighty-Four* declares that "if there is any hope for humanity it is in the proles." Zamyatin's benevolent Guardians are of course Orwell's Thought Police, and in both the Only State and Oceania any conversation is likely to be picked up by concealed devices. Zamyatin did not foresee the Orwellian telescreen which observed one's every action and could not be turned off, but his characters lived in glass houses and were under constant surveillance—except for a "personal" hour, during which they might draw their shades for properly validated sexual activity. In both books the philosophy that motivates the ruler is expounded for an erring citizen by an all-wise father figure—in *We* by the Benefactor, who totally dominates the hapless hero, D-503, and in *Nineteen Eighty-Four* by Big Brother in the person of the policeman O'Brien, who towers over the weak and spiritless Winston both intellectually and physically.

In their plotted action the two novels also have a number of striking points of congruence. In each the story is told from the viewpoint of a citizen who becomes disaffected with his life and looks for contact with another reality; in each the narrator is keeping a diary. Love for a free-spirited and courageous young woman is for both characters a crucial experience, and the germ of revolt enters them by way of spontaneous and satisfying sex, practiced in defiance of strict sexual regulations in the Only State, and of anti-sex puritanism in Oceania. One scholar has pointed out that the female revolutionist in *We*, numbered I-330, is a kind of Jungian "anima" figure: a beautiful, mysterious woman who in myth and art appears when the male psyche is in danger of being dominated by the rational element and who effects a healthy integration of the male and female "principles" within the hero. Both I-330 and Julia function as females who, like Eve in the Book of Genesis, seduce the male from safe loyalty toward an established and rational order. In both novels rebellion takes the form of illicit sexual activity—"love" they call it—carried on in a secret rendezvous at a safe distance from proper residential areas: in *Nineteen Eighty-Four*, in a room above Charrington's old-book-and-curiosity shop in the proles' quarter, and in *We*, in an "Ancient House" preserved on the outskirts of the city-state near the glass wall. Here I-330 introduces her lover to ancient vices such as alcohol and cigarettes, along with the raptures of sex and the long-forgotten poet Pushkin. Finally, the central character in both novels is "saved" for the state and rational behavior by drastic means: in *We* his deviance is treated by a kind of lobotomy, an operation which removes the center of "fantasy"; in *Nineteen Eighty-Four*, O'Brien, through overpowering logic backed up by unendurable pain, fixes Winston's mind so that he really believes black is white and really loves Big Brother.

III

In language, in style, and in the structure of images the two books are not even distant relatives. Zamyatin is an idiosyncratic cousin of the Russian symbolists, and *We* has striking stylistic and even thematic similarities to Andrei Bely's *St. Petersburg*. Orwell maintains a soberly realistic manner when he describes the enormity of Oceania, while Zamyatin creates a fantasy world where the seam between reality and dream is often invisible, and each character tends to fuse with the metonymy or metaphor used to describe him. Each of *We*'s supposedly faceless and uniformly dressed characters is identified by a persistently repeated trope: D-503 has atavistic hair, the poet R-13 has large negroid lips, 0-90 is round like her name, the Guardian S-4711 is slithery and serpentlike, I-330 has sharp teeth and a "bite" smile; she is built like a whip, and there are glowing coals concealed in her eyes. And the narrative style of *We*, which is based entirely on the diaries of D-503, involves distortions of the real world that result from the intense emotional experiences he undergoes. To put it succinctly, Orwell has a closer affinity in style to Tolstoy than does Zamyatin, who belongs among the moderns—James Joyce, Djuna Barnes, and, to skip a few decades, Thomas Pynchon or Gilbert Sorrentino.

A crucial difference between the two novels is the character and role of women in each. When I-330 lures D-503 to an assignation in the Ancient House she not only offers him sex and good coffee but regales him with a philosophy of revolution and a program of action—not concerns of Orwell's Julia. Before he met Julia, women in Winston's life had been a bore or a burden, and sometimes a real menace: "He disliked nearly all women, and especially the young and pretty ones. It was always the women, and above all the young ones, who were the most bigoted adherents of the Party, the swallowers of slogans, the amateur spies and nosers-out of unorthodoxy." But what of Julia, the agent of his release and the object of his bursting love? Her rebellion is, as a matter of fact, quite limited, even though she is aware that they—the rulers—are "nothing but swine." She is engagingly resourceful in finding ways to outwit them and to procure supplies of real coffee and decent food, but her principal goal in life is good sex. Her world view is a view of sexuality, and her only pregnant comments on Oceania concern the inner meaning of the Party's sexual puritanism. On all other subjects she is simpleminded and determined to remain so. She only questioned the teachings of the Party "when they in some way touched upon her own life." She falls sound asleep during Winston's reading of a treasured dissident volume on the nature and genesis of the state system in Oceania. She is, as Winston ruefully reflects, "a rebel only from the waist downwards." And in the final test under torture Julia is no stronger than Winston himself; she betrays him just as surely as he had betrayed her. So much for the "great love."

Julia's opposite number, I-330, is not only a fascinating sexual partner, she is one of the leaders of the revolution against the Only State. Julia was empty-headed and bored by ideas; I-330 by contrast is an eloquent historian of the Only State and an articulator of a revolutionary philosophy. Zamyatin's own ideas are given to I-330: his belief that heretics are a necessary antidote to ossification and entropy, and his argument that just as there is no final number, so there can be no final revolution. In the universe as a whole and in human social life I-330/Zamyatin sees two forces at work, the tendency toward dead uniformity, and the restless force of energy opposing it. I-330 explains all of this, in the course of their assignations, to her wide-eyed lover: "There are two forces in the world, entropy and energy. One leads to blissful quietude, to happy equilibrium, the other to the destruction of equilibrium, to tormentingly endless movement. . . ." And again, "Ah, uniformity everywhere! That's exactly where it is—entropy, psychological entropy. Is it not clear to you, a mathematician, that only differences, differences in temperature—thermal contrasts—make for life? And if everywhere, throughout the universe, there are equally warm, or equally cool bodies . . . they must be brought into collision—to get fire, explosion, Gehenna. And we will bring them into collision."

I-330's ideas are at the core of the novel, whose plot she foments and whose thought she glowingly articulates. I-330 moves in an aura of intelligent, purposeful intrigue aimed at disturbing the very foundations of society. She remains an ascendant figure even in her final moments when, betrayed by D-503 and subjected to unspeakable torture, she still refuses to break. That scene is described for us by D-503, who has been reduced after his lobotomy to a kind of contented idiocy:

> In the evening of the same day, I sat (for the first time) at the same table with the Benefactor in the famous Gas Chamber. She was to testify in my presence. The woman smiled and was stubbornly silent. I noticed she had sharp and very white teeth, and that was pretty. Then she was placed under the Bell. Her face became very white, and since her eyes are dark and large, it was very pretty.

When they began to pump the air out of the Bell, she threw her head back, half closed her eyes; her lips were tightly shut—it reminded me of something. She looked at me, gripping hard the arms of the chair—looked until her eyes closed altogether. Then she was pulled out, quickly restored with the aid of electrodes, and placed once more under the Bell. This was repeated three times, and still she did not say a word. Others brought with that woman were more honest: many of them began to speak after the very first time. Tomorrow they will all ascend the stairs to the Benefactor's Machine.

In Orwell's Oceania there are no exceptions to the rule enunciated by Julia: "Everybody confesses, they make you." But *We* offers hope for humanity in the mythic figure of that irresistible female, fire glowing in her eyes, who is capable of sending both God and the Devil to Hell.

IV

The satiric intent of the "anti-utopia" was neatly expressed by Zamyatin himself in his essay on H.G. Wells. Speaking of Wells, he says: "He makes use of his social fantasies almost exclusively for the purpose of revealing defects in the existing social order." The same observation should be made of the two novels under discussion, which are legitimate heirs of the anti-utopias of Wells. Both present images of tendencies present in the society of their own day. Zamyatin had lived in England, and his initial experience of an industrial society organized along rational lines was London. The image of a modern, regimented society in *We* is based, then, on his own version of tendencies present in Western Europe, rather than on anything that had developed in Russia in 1920. But its satire is directed also at the collectivist mystique present in the Russia of his own day, where self-styled proletarian poets and writers proclaimed that there could be no more individual heroes: the great laboring mass of humanity must now be the hero in literary works. The poets Gastev and Kirillov both wrote sonorous verses announcing the death of the personal pronoun "I." Gastev, moreover, was a convinced theoretician of the totally rationalized world, and one of his heroes was the American industrial efficiency expert Frederick Winslow Taylor, often credited with discovering the assembly line method of factory production. But Gastev had carried Taylor's ideas to a poetic extreme of absurdity, as he demonstrates in the following passage, which sounds like a parody of itself, but isn't:

> The mechanization, not only of gestures, not only of production methods, but of everyday thinking, coupled with extreme rationality, normalizes in a striking degree the psychology of the proletariat. . . . It is this that lends proletarian psychology such surprising anonymity, which permits the qualification of separate

proletarian units as A, B, C, or as 325075, or as O, and the like. In this normalization of psychology and its dynamism is the key to the prodigious elementariness of proletarian thinking. . . . In this psychology, from one end of the world to the other, flow potent massive streams, making for one world head in place of millions of heads. This tendency will next imperceptibly render individual thinking impossible, and thought will become the objective psychic process of a whole class, with systems of psychological switches and locks.

Obviously the objects of Zamyatin's satire are both the industrialized and "rationalized" West, and the proponents of analogous development in Russia. With his belief in the "Mephi" and his resistance to the coming technological miracles of Western society, Zamyatin has perhaps deserved to be called a primitive.

The enemy in Orwell's case is just as obviously topical and contemporary. The London of *Nineteen Eighty-Four* with its bad gin, crumbly cigarettes, drabness, wartime regimentation, and occasional rocket bombs is the London of the late 1940s, during and immediately after the Second World War, with a Stalin-like Big Brother image superimposed upon a sacrosanct bureaucracy. The contemporary targets of Orwell's satire in *Nineteen Eighty-Four* are evident from an article he published in *Polemic* in January 1946, at a time when the ideas and images of *Nineteen Eighty-Four* were actively gestating. He speaks in that article, entitled "The Prevention of Literature," as a writer who understands the forces in modern life that are inimical to freedom, and to any pursuit of truth:

On the one side are its theoretical enemies, the apologists of totalitarianism, and on the other its immediate and practical enemies, monopoly and bureaucracy. Any writer or journalist who wants to retain his integrity finds himself thwarted by the general drift of society rather than by active persecution. The sort of things that are working against him are the concentration of the press in the hands of a few rich men, the grip of monopoly on radio and films . . . the encroachment of official bodies like the Ministry of Information and the British Council, which help the writer to stay alive but also waste his time and dictate his opinions, and the continuous war atmosphere of the last ten years, whose distorting effects no one has been able to escape. Everything in our age conspires to turn the writer into a minor official, working on themes handed him from above and never telling what seems to him the whole of the truth.

*Republican Automatons* by George Grosz, 1920, watercolor, 23⅝" × 18⅝". Collection, The Museum of Modern Art, New York. Advisory Committee Fund.

And consider the genesis in Orwell's mind of *doublethink*:

> A totalitarian society which succeeded in perpetuating itself would probably set up a schizophrenic system of thought, in which the laws of common sense held good in everyday life and in certain exact sciences, but could be disregarded by the politician, the historian, and the sociologist.

Orwell was clearly alarmed at the threat of the totalitarian dictatorships, but even more at the acquiescence of liberal British intellectuals to censorship during the war years, as well as the chilling effect on free thought of monopoly control of the press. Some who have worked there report that there was much in common between the Ministry of Truth and the BBC during Orwell's tenure.

Perhaps the chief contrast that separates the two books is that while Orwell seems in awe of the vast power exercised by the enemy in both its guises— Soviet totalitarianism and monopoly capitalism—Zamyatin in *We* communicates an ironic contempt for collectivizers and regulators, whose philosophy takes the form in that book of a grotesque parody of rationalist thought. The philosophy of the Only State is patiently explained to the erring D-503 by the Benefactor himself, a monstrous metallic idol:

> . . . I ask you: what did people—from their very infancy—pray for, dream about, long for? They longed for someone to tell them, once and for all, the meaning of happiness, and then to bind them to it with a chain. What are we doing now if not this very thing?

That philosophy of human nature is of course modeled on the ideas of Dostoevsky's Grand Inquisitor in *The Brothers Karamazov*, who assured Christ that the mass of humanity would gladly surrender their freedom to an elite few in return for the guarantee of happiness. But that shallow justification of absolute power is belied in the dramatic movement of the novel itself. D-503, the chief mathematician of the state and builder of the space ship *Integral*, had at one time thought himself content to be a mere number in the giant calculus of the Only State, but fell prey to revolutionaries when they appealed to some deep subconscious hunger for an individual self, a love of his own, even a mother that would be just his. And he finds there are many other rebels. In fact every character we meet is in the movement, even the member of the Guardians, S-4711. The Wall has been breached and rebellion is still in progress with the issue in doubt as the novel ends.

*Nineteen Eighty-Four* on the other hand presents a future landscape of unrelieved darkness. The two rebels are isolated from the society and ultimately betray one another. They never find allies. Once Winston thought he had spotted one, O'Brien, but we experience the full measure of desolation when we learn that the attractive, intelligent O'Brien, who looked like "someone you could talk to," is the honored surrogate of Big Brother, and an invincible dialectician supporting his arguments with unbearable torture. In those final scenes the failure of Winston's mind and spirit is more desolating than his body's pain: "What most impressed him was the consciousness of his own intellectual inferiority." And again, O'Brien's face is ". . . full of intelligence." O'Brien's ascendance is never contested and his cruel sophistries are imposed on Winston almost without argument. We reach finally the very bottom of human despair when Winston, faced with "the worst thing in the world for him," hungry rats ready to eat his living face, utters the awful words "Do it to Julia." Are we to conclude, as I think we do, that the total state really might gain total control, that no area in a human being would be private and inviolable and no word given ever secure? And yet Zamyatin's I-330 endured repeated torture and never betrayed anyone. The pathetic Winston Smith, Julia's love, failed to know that having the rats gnaw his eyes would have been a happy fate compared to the final degradation of that "Do it to Julia." We must conclude that Orwell was afraid of the enemy and exaggerated his power.

V

I have suggested that both utopias and anti-utopias engage in a polemic with failures of reason and justice in contemporary society and that the dire prophecies of anti-utopia function to avert their own fulfillment. The coming of the year 1984 leads naturally to reflections as to where the human race has arrived on its path to the unknown future. We seem likely to escape the degradation of Oceania or the Only State; indeed the direction would seem to be surprisingly different from that postulated by Orwell and Zamyatin. That monstrous idol, the Benefactor, at one time seemed, both to Orwell and to us, fully realized in the figure of the "all-wise, all-knowing, father of peoples," Stalin. But the statues of Stalin have long since been toppled and his memory degraded in the Soviet Union.

The proletarian poets whose work Zamyatin satirized are hardly ever read in the Soviet Union in 1984 and they have no prestige, either as proletarians or as poets. His fears for literature have been only partially realized. The worthless product of state poets in praise of the Only State and the Benefactor has been more than outweighed by a magnificent literary production known as samizdat, to which we are in debt for some of the most important literary works of the century. And the frequent persistence of literary and human values even in officially published literature, where writers are still obliged to take account of tasteless bigotry in the Guardians, is even more striking. The total debasement of literature has simply not occurred.

Zamyatin's prophecy has, however, been partially fulfilled in the constant surveillance of private matters—conversations, letters, telephone calls—and in the concept of election day as a "day of unanimity" and the effective paralysis of political life in the Soviet Union. But as these lines are written the Soviet system comes under increasing question, not only in Eastern Europe but within the Soviet Union itself, where a goodly number of heroic figures immune to brain management have emerged.

Orwell's credentials as a prophet are even less secure than Zamyatin's. The various contemporary figures whom Orwell captured in the portrait of Big Brother: Stalin, Hitler, Mussolini (along with Mao, who came later), have all been swept away, and far from controlling the memory of the past as Big Brother does in *Nineteen Eighty-Four*, they themselves are in some risk of being eliminated from it; which would be too bad. The future Orwell forecast involved constant warfare among three major powers, and the occasional, though never decisive, use of atomic weapons. How could he have foreseen that the terrible escalation in the destructive power of those weapons would make their use unthinkable and would, at least up to the year 1984, keep a kind of peace among the major powers?

It is impossible to measure in full our debt to both Orwell and Zamyatin for those prophecies that have worked so well in our culture to discredit themselves. Their books are actually an attack on social and political tendencies that their authors discerned in their own day. That *We* and *Nineteen Eighty-Four* are still very much alive in the East and in the West argues that their polemic is still effective, and still needed. The threat of Oceania or the Only State will no doubt be with us for a long time, since democratic liberties are only a recent political discovery of the human race, imperfectly realized in some places—Orwell's England, for instance—and too easily lost in others.

# 19 Gerald A. Dorfman

# The Proles of Airstrip One

*But the proles, if only they could somehow become conscious of their own strength . . . needed only to rise up and shake themselves like a horse shaking off flies. If they chose they could blow the Party to pieces tomorrow morning.*

HOW DOES ORWELL'S DARK PROFILE OF THE "PROLES" in the Oceania of *Nineteen Eighty-Four* relate to the Britain he knew in 1948 and the 1984 we know? The answer is complex and interesting. Britain's working class, its "proles," have won and used the power which Winston Smith could only fantasize they might explosively seize. They have tasted the hope, the dreams that were nearly unthinkable in Oceania. This year, 1984, finds the working class a far more potent force in British life and its politics than Orwell's proles could ever imagine—if they *could* imagine. But this year also finds Britain's proles far less powerful and far less optimistic than they were at the time Orwell was actually writing *Nineteen Eighty-Four*. What is interesting is that this decline of working-class power in Britain has occurred in part because of some of the same self-destructive tendencies which, as Orwell suggests, troubled the potential strength of his proles in Oceania.

## II

The proles in Orwell's writing are the "swarming disregarded masses" of Oceania. The workers of Britain in our 1984, indeed in this century, have been by no means a disregarded mass of humanity. On the contrary, the British working class has indelibly stamped its force on British society and stands today, whatever its problems, as a critically important influence.

The proletariat in Britain rose to power during the first four decades of this century. Their gathering strength was expressed first in the birth of individual unions, reaching back to the early Victorian years; then in the creation of the Trades Union Congress as a centralized union spokesgroup; and finally, in this century, by the development of their political party, the Labour party. Their victory in actually winning political power and working-class participation in national decision making came during the 1940s, as collectivist politics transformed British life and its political system. Thus, while Orwell's man of 1984, Winston Smith, was fantasizing that if only the proles could "somehow become conscious of their own strength, [they] would have no need to conspire," the proles in Orwell's contemporary society were already using the consciousness of their strength to win and use power.

Working-class power in Orwell's time was sharply focused on the incumbency of the first majority Labour government (1945-50) led by Clement Attlee as prime minister. It was "their" government and demonstrated that they had arrived at the very seat of national decision making. They had achieved a conscious victory; they had converted deprivation into power. But it had not come easily.

Britain had suffered twenty years of economic recession and depression— from just after the end of the First World War until the beginning of the Second. Britain's working class not only bore the brunt of the inevitable economic dislocation; they also experienced an enormous loss of influence in the political system. It would not be an exaggeration to say that by the early thirties the working class was in the political wilderness. They had watched first a *minority* Labour government betray their interests, and then the coalition "National government" of 1931 follow Tory policies which did little to relieve the suffering imposed by bad times.

These humiliating and difficult decades produced, however, a determination among trade union leaders in Britain to work flat-out for the victory of a *majority* Labour government absolutely pledged to implement an agenda of change that would directly enhance working-class interests. During the thirties, these union leaders made plans with their political allies in the Labour party.

The Second World War provided the important opportunity for change. The calamity of those years not only destroyed physical and human resources, it destroyed much of prewar British politics. The pulling together of the nation, the explicit policy of "fair shares," together with the persistent memory of the long depression, helped to forge a powerful consensus for change toward a more collective, compassionate, and egalitarian future in postwar Britain. This provided the opportunity for which Britain's working-class leadership had planned, and the 1945 victory of Attlee's Labour party over Churchill's Conservatives gave them the actual power they sought.

The late forties was thus a period of heady optimism among the proles in Britain. The Attlee government was committed to legislating the terms of its agreement with its union friends. Almost every single item on which the political and union side had agreed was carried out. Britain was being transformed. In political terms, these changes meant a new kind of politics—collectivist politics. Government and interest groups—especially the union movement—shared power in a new relationship. Government had made a new commitment that there be a better life, and they could not keep that commitment without endowing the proles, the productive force, with significant power. It was their government, implementing their policies for the first time. The opportunity was a first, and they seized it eagerly.

The proles of postwar Britain were thus not the "inert force" that Orwell's Winston hoped "would some day spring to life and regenerate the world." They were in fact springing to life and pressing to regenerate Britain at the very moment that Orwell wrote!

But where did it all go? The 1984 we live in is a very different time for Britain's working class: different from the optimistic days of Orwell's own time, and also different from the dark forebodings of his writing. Certainly, the proles live more affluently now than in the late forties. The destruction wrought by the war was everywhere then and so was the shortage of both the good things of life and the barest necessities. The shabbiness of postwar Britain was very real—even though the war had ended. Britain in 1984 is a more abundant society, but the hope of the earlier time has very much dissipated. Unemployment, which was unacceptable—even unthinkable—thirty years ago, has returned to an extent not seen since the Depression. The political side of the labor movement, the Labour party, is broken and defeated, its future very much in doubt. And the union movement, the very heart of that collectivism which had brought the proles so much of their gain, is gravely weakened and divided, now excluded from the councils of power and policy making it had struggled so hard to enter and influence.

### III

What went wrong? There are many elements to any plausible answer, but some of Orwell's words about his proles and their relationship to the society and politics of Oceania are relevant. Two in particular seem compellingly important. First, Orwell's reference to the struggle between the High, Middle, and Low. The notion of continual struggle between High, Middle, and Low immediately calls up images of the class struggle. But it may also be more broadly viewed as a struggle among political elites. Refocusing our attention in this way, we can learn a great deal about the course of proletarian power in Britain leading to this year, 1984.

The successful bid by the working class through its union movement and its political party for a place at the center of political power in Britain produced significant tensions. While class conflict was one of the earliest consequences, it was not the most important. Working-class participation in political decision making was strange and uncomfortable for some elements of Britain's social elite. It was much more of a problem for Britain's political elite—political leaders from all parties (ironically, including the Labour party) who compete for and hold public office. Suddenly, and unhappily, they found themselves with a new "governing partner," one with whom they had to share authority and to whom they soon found they had given veto power. Britain's proles were literally in the cabinet room; in ministers' offices, conferring regularly with civil servants about all kinds of public policies. Although they would often give their advice, their agreement, and sometimes their acquiescence to the elected political elite, they would sometimes withhold it when policies clashed with their particular interests. They could put public policy at risk and even into paralysis. This last became a reality during the fifties, sixties, and into the seventies, and caused Britain's political elite to realize that it had an unacceptable and unworkable political decision-making process. Scholars labeled the new relationship *collectivist politics* and its unintended consequences *pluralistic stagnation*.

Great victory for the proles in Britain thus carried the seeds of great conflict and ultimately serious counterattack and defeat. There is some parallel between the party's dealings with the proles in Orwell's *Nineteen Eighty-Four* and in the real Britain leading to our 1984. In both, the political elite needed to find some way to muzzle, restrain, or otherwise neutralize the potential or real political power of the working class to challenge its authority. In Orwell's Oceania, the proles were to be kept without "strong feelings" except for a primitive patriotism. In contemporary Britain, the proles are to be pushed out of political decision making and limited to concentration on their own productivity—where they can patriotically contribute to Britain's economic revival while causing as little political disruption as possible. Contemporary Britain, and particularly its political elite, has felt proletarian power and wants no more of it.

IV

The second point Orwell makes about his proles which has relevance for our times is the tendency of the proles to direct their aggressiveness against themselves: to indulge in petty squabbles and struggles over individual grievances rather than giving their collective attention to the external enemies and to the fight for societal advantage. This kind of behavior is occurring today in Britain and is proving to be a critical weapon for the political elite in its struggle against working-class power. Both the industrial and political sides of Britain's labor movement are suffering this problem. On the one hand, the Labour party has nearly blown itself to bits, and on the other hand, the union movement is badly fractured and weakened.

The Labour party has been one of two ruling parties in Britain for the last six decades. It literally grew out of the union movement to become its political agent. Many different groups came together to sponsor the Labour party's development; but its purpose, its direction, and its financing came primarily from the union movement, which believed its own activity was too limited adequately to defend and promote working-class interests. The creation of the Labour party in the early part of this century was, therefore, a kind of rising up of the proles against the then dominant political elite.

From its beginning, the Labour party has suffered from serious internal divisions. Ideological arguments between radicals and moderates have raged endlessly, as has the struggle between individual personalities, who are usually champions of one ideological camp or another. Its ability to survive as a party has hinged—successfully until recently—on its ability to pull together temporarily to fight in elections and, when in office, to paper over the more serious arguments by accepting hierarchial leadership. In recent years, this "glue" has failed to work and a dangerous struggle among the ideological Right, the "soft" Left, and the "hard" Left has become impossible to patch up. The 1983 election was a disaster for Labour: its popular vote fell to the lowest level in more than half a century. It emerged from that election tattered and bickering, almost without credentials as a real opposition to the present government.

Thus, in 1984, the future of the Labour party is in doubt. Squabbles and petty rivalries all wrapped up in the rhetoric of fierce ideological arguments are threatening the hopes of Britain's working class for political power. It can no longer offer the electorate a strong working-class party. It can no longer appeal for the kind of broader support a winning party in a two-party system must secure.

The apparent self-destruction of the Labour party comes at a particularly bad time for the union movement, because the central core of proletarian strength in Britain is beset by its own problems. The unions in Britain are suffering two simultaneous blows. The first is the serious worldwide economic recession with its attendant unemployment, which is fiercely afflicting the British economy. The second is the powerful political counterattack that the government of Margaret Thatcher is directing most skillfully at the union movement. The economic recession itself is likely to be a transitory condition, but its damage is likely to hurt the union movement permanently. Recession is providing the Thatcher government with leverage to make a fundamental antilabor alteration in the political process which the wider British political elite has found so threatening to its authority.

The origins of this political counterattack are rooted in the events of the middle and late seventies, when union power reached its zenith at the same moment Britain suffered its most serious postwar economic crisis. The political elite at that time attempted to solve its economic problems by using traditional patterns of collectivist politics. Specifically, it kept its commitments to maintain a number of contradictory policies that were both financially and politically too expensive. These included the maintainance of full employment, a rising standard of living, low inflation, and a strong currency; and the various programs that comprise what we call the welfare state. All these enhanced working-class interests as well as working-class power. Full employment, especially, provided the union movement with economic strength so that it could participate forcefully in the political process.

The political elite then became wholly dependent on the union movement for significant assistance in resolving the economic crisis. If Britain were to keep inflation low and sell its industrial production abroad so that it could finance a rising standard of living, union members would have to restrain their wage demands and their industrial militancy. But the union movement would not come to terms, would not restrain its demands for wage increases, and did allow disruptive strikes to occur, all of which further damaged the economy.

Both economic policy and political authority became paralyzed as militant union behavior overwhelmed the government. The leadership of both the Conservative and Labour parties became alarmed when they found themselves placed at the mercy of union conflict. The power of Britain's proles was no longer the power to demand and win certain policies in a positive sense, as it had been just after the Second World War. Rather, it had become the power to withhold cooperation and thus paralyze or veto initiatives taken by the nation's political leaders in dealing with growing economic problems. The collectivist politics by which unions were initially drawn into the center of economic decision making was thus a failure and left the country in a deep crisis by the mid-seventies. Faced with this threat, the political elite looked for a way to counterattack.

The concept of Britain's political elite as an interest group in its own right is bolstered by the all-party response to the failure of collectivist politics and, particularly, the union challenge to its authority. It is frequently claimed that the Thatcher Conservative government was the first to put the "boot" to the union movement. In fact, counterattack was launched by a Labour government in 1976. That a Labour government, the political arm of the collective labor movement, took this step against its own brethren is testimony to the near panic that Britain's politicians felt in the face of the obstructionist power that Britain's proles held.

The counterattack by the Labour government took the form of a significant shift in economic policy. The 1976–79 Labour government under the leadership of James Callaghan as prime minister boldly took the politically dangerous initiative of gradually dropping its commitments to a whole battery of policies that had become sacrosanct since 1945. The most significant of these for trade union power was the government's abandonment of the long commitment to do whatever was necessary to maintain full employment. Although the prime minister and his ministers were careful to continue their fraternal and consultative relationship with union leaders, they allowed the sting of rising unemployment gradually to erode the strength of their union friends. To be sure, the change in the power relationship between the political elite and the union movement did not occur overnight. The all-out strikes that exploded during the winter of 1978 ultimately brought down the Callaghan government and reminded the country that Britain's proles did have the power to disrupt nearly everything. But the desperate and counterproductive conflict caused the electorate to turn to a Conservative leadership, one even more determined to press the attack against union power by adding a political dimension to the economic initiative already irreversibly in place.

Mrs. Thatcher's victory in the 1979 election thus opened the second phase of the struggle against working-class power in the political process. Mrs. Thatcher was determined from the outset of her incumbency to go beyond Mr. Callaghan's effective economic counterattack. From the first day in office, the new prime minister made it clear that union leaders would no longer be welcome in the cabinet room, nor would her ministers be telephoning them for advice or agreement, or even discussions. She insisted that she would restore political authority, and thereby end permanently the postwar pattern of producer-group politics.

Mrs. Thatcher has carried out her promises, helped considerably and perversely by the economic recession, which has produced dramatic increases in unemployment and a fall in the standard of living. The telephones at the Trades Union Congress are quiet these days. Government cars no longer move in and out of their driveway. The political counterattack is effective and shows no signs of letting up.

The consequences of this period on the internal political situation in the unions have been disastrous. The proles of contemporary Britain have fallen into petty squabbling and arguments about individual grievances, just as Orwell said his proles were prone to do. The union movement has turned inward instead of constructing alternative strategies for regaining their lost power.

V

The power and hope of working-class solidarity is being replaced by bickering, weakness, and growing despair in *our* 1984. Political authority has been recaptured by the political elite in Britain and there is no sign that they will soon lose it again. Moreover, it is clear that the political elite has discovered that unemployment is a powerful weapon against proletarian power. It has sapped union strength and done so without the electoral backlash that politicians in Britain had so long feared. The Conservative victory in the 1983 election confirmed this advantage. There are now few strikes, little inflation, and the proles are divided against themselves both industrially and politically. Britain's political elite in *our* 1984, like that of Oceania, has apparently decided that the proles should be pushed into the political wilderness.

# 20 *Robert Conquest*

# Totaliterror

*"One does not establish a dictatorship in order to safeguard a revolution; one makes the revolution in order to establish the dictatorship. The object of persecution is persecution. The object of torture is torture. The object of power is power."*

THERE HAVE BEEN REGIMES from the earliest times which have kept themselves in power by what was regarded as an excessive and illegitimate use of violence. But our first use of "Terror" with a capital "T" is in the history of the French Revolution, when opponents of the regime, or anyone speaking against it, went to the guillotine or the *noyades* in numbers which then appeared enormous, and which were, at any rate, enough to cow the population.

With the French Revolution, and even with the very first phase of Lenin's regime, terror was usually seen as what may be thought of as a war measure, or an immediate postwar measure, to crush dangerous and still powerful political opponents. Orwell gives us something else: terror as a permanent policy in a stable environment.

Above all, he melds this permanent and total terror with permanent and total falsification. The key phrase about the *Nineteen Eighty-Four* regime is: "Power is in tearing human minds to pieces and putting them together again in new shapes of your own choosing." The terror which pervades the book is not just extreme terror in a traditional sense. It is terror definable in a single mix of torture-execution-*doublethink*-Newspeak, and its parts cannot be treated separately.

II

Orwell began work on *Nineteen Eighty-Four* early in August 1946, and finished it in early November 1948. He died on January 21, 1950. His views on a number of matters had changed over the years, and in dealing with his intention in *Nineteen Eighty-Four*, it is only permissible for us to refer as I shall do here to what he was thinking in this final and mature period of his life.

*Nineteen Eighty-Four* is fiction, not prophecy. Orwell did not regard anything as inevitable—and indeed censured intellectuals for thinking that things are bound to go the way they happen to be going at a given moment. He certainly regarded a future of the *Nineteen Eighty-Four* type as at least unpleasantly possible, but no more than that.

There are two constituent elements in the sort of regime Orwell predicates. He was much impressed by, though also had his reservations about, James Burnham's thesis (in *The Managerial Revolution*) that a managerialist oligarchic society was emerging everywhere, with the world about to be divided among three exemplars of this new type of order. They would be, as Orwell put it in 1947, "collectivist not democratic, and would be ruled over by a caste of managers, scientists, bureaucrats who would destroy old-style capitalism and keep the working class permanently in subjection. In other words, something like 'Communism' would prevail everywhere."

While Burnham expected a world of managerialist powers, the only one he granted to be already in full existence was the USSR. He saw it as immensely powerful, established so firmly that it could never be shaken. But Orwell did not, in real life, accept the totalitarian permanence he offers us in fiction. He wrote in 1946:

> It is too early to say just in what way the Russian regime will destroy itself. If I had to make a prophecy, I should say that a continuation of the Russian policies of the last fifteen years—and internal and external policy, of course, are merely two facets of the same thing—can only lead to a war conducted with atomic bombs which will make Hitler's invasion look like a tea-party. But at any rate the Russian regime will either democratise itself, or it will perish. The huge, invincible, everlasting slave empire of which Burnham appears to dream will not be established, or, if established, will not endure. . . .

It is important to note that Burnham and Orwell differ on one major point. Burnham seems to have held that all of the world's major political and social orders were inevitably tending toward this managerial oligarchy. Orwell, even at the time when he was most inclined to accept Burnham's thesis whole, had his reservations: "It is even possible that if the world falls apart into three unconquerable superstates, the liberal tradition will be strong enough within the Anglo-American section of the world to make life tolerable and even offer some hope of progress."

Orwell could scarcely have written convincingly in a Russian or Chinese setting. Nor would that have much interested an Anglo-American readership. So his setting is inevitably England. But the Oceania of *Nineteen Eighty-Four* is neither Burnham's model derived from Western actuality, nor the possibly semi-liberal managerialist state of Orwell's practical hopes. It is made perfectly clear that the *Nineteen Eighty-Four* system has not arisen through capitalism—the Party hates capitalists and is explicitly shown to have overthrown capitalist rule and "expropriated" the capitalists. Nor is it the product of the Labour party's policies—the old Labour party is referred to in the text as something extinct, and Orwell issued a denial that he was in any way targeting Attlee's (highly anti-communist) Labour Government, which he in fact supported, if not uncritically. But Ingsoc (like communism) "grew out of the earlier Socialist movement and inherited its phraseology"; and, while rejecting all that Orwell understands by socialism, "chooses to do it in the name of Socialism."

The foundation of *Nineteen Eighty-Four* is, in fact, Stalin's Russia. In his *George Orwell*, Raymond Williams (writing from a left-wing viewpoint) criticizes him for this. Williams rightly argues that he could have gone beyond "a single political tendency" and sought models all over; and in effect censures him for *not* seeing a potential totalitarianism in the Western system.

Had Orwell indeed thought that the *Nineteen Eighty-Four* regime could have arisen from the corruption of conservatives, capitalists, Labourites, or whatever, he had a particularly good opportunity of developing it—with a neo-capitalist-conservative totalitarianism in Oceania to balance "neo-Bolshevism" in Eurasia. He did nothing of the kind, and those who argue that every political culture, with its imperfect politicians, insensitive bureaucrats, occasional abuses of power, sporadic euphemisms and falsifications, is seen by Orwell as equally liable to breed totalitarianism, are simply not reading the book (or, come to that, Orwell's other explicatory writings of the same period).

He did not do so, because he did not in fact see the West as seriously tending in that direction. Much as he detested Conservatives and Catholics, press lords and movie moguls, he did not envisage them as precursors of the terror state. And he saw Western culture, on which they were the warts, as nevertheless the hope of the world. Sometimes that hope might appear strong, sometimes feeble. But at worst he felt (in 1946) that "our own society is still, broadly speaking, liberal." The Soviet Union, on the other hand, was his model of a frightful local present and a possible frightful world future.

There are, of course, a number of ways in which Oceania is not a precise homologue of the USSR, though mainly in its exaggeration and extrapolation in the natural direction of logical caricature. But it is remarkable how much is derived directly from, and only from, the Soviet record. Even Big Brother's style is modeled on Stalin's! Goldstein is, of course, a pure Trotsky figure.

The "unperson" is entirely based on Soviet practice. The most usual procedure in Moscow has been the omission of important figures from history. But sometimes more Orwellian methods have been employed. Many readers will know of the occasion when, after the fall of Beria, subscribers to the *Large Soviet Encyclopedia* were sent a set of fresh pages on the Bering Sea and an obscure eighteenth-century courtier call Bergholz, with instructions to remove certain unspecified but numbered pages with a razor blade and paste these in instead. When Malenkov lost the premiership, but not all his power, the next edition of the *Encyclopedic Dictionary* differed from its predecessor solely in shortening his entry, making up space with a minor fortress, an engineer who had invented a six-wheeled bogie, and a hitherto neglected strawberry called *malengr*. Dozens of similar examples might be cited. For American observers, perhaps the most remarkable rewrite came in the volume of the *Small Soviet Encyclopedia* which was rolling off the press in 1941. In some copies, evidently the earlier part of the print, Franklin Roosevelt appears as an agent of American business and instigator of an imperialist war; in others, he has become a representative of the aspirations of the people and an opponent of fascist aggression.

The unperson disappears not only from the written, but even from the visual, record. The most famous case is the classic picture of Lenin addressing a crowd, in which two other faces were previously visible by the rostrum: Trotsky and Kamenev. In the picture as it has appeared in Russia for the last fifty years these have been eliminated. There are pictures of delegates to party congresses, in which, for later versions, previously existing faces have been blurred into other people's greatcoats. There is, too, a celebrated photograph of Stalin in exile with a handful of other revolutionaries; in the earlier version Kamenev is on his left, in the later he has become part of a tree.

The tradition continues. There are two instances of otherwise identical photographs of groups of Soviet cosmonauts appearing in different versions; in each case the later one showing no sign of one of those present in the earlier. In one, the figure is now merged with a doorpost; in the other, with the wall of an aeroplane. Their offense and fate is unknown.

Winston Smith's memory of the presence of Jones, Aaronson, and Rutherford in New York, when it is alleged at their trial that they had flown to Eurasia to conspire with the enemy, is matched by the moderate leader Abramovich's presence at the Hague when he was allegedly conspiring in Moscow—and even more closely by the Communist veteran Pyatakov's mythical flight to Oslo to conspire with Trotsky.

Above all, Orwell takes the central point—that the accused in the Moscow Trials were required not merely to confess to their imaginary criminal acts, but to *repent*, to admit that Stalin was right and that they themselves were degenerate scum. As to the mental state of the victims, the Czechoslovak Communist Evzen Loebl, one of the three accused not executed after the

1952 Slansky Trial in Prague, describes the effect on him of the long interrogation process, even when, after confession, he had been allowed adequate food and rest: "I was quite a normal person—only I was no longer a person."

As has been pointed out by Soviet dissidents, the Gestapo tortured people to find out their resistance or other secrets, and had no further aim, except that of general terror. The Nazis, though responsible for the most frightful mass slaughter, imposed a terror with characteristics different from those of the Soviet Union or *Nineteen Eighty-Four*. It is true that the Hitler regime was in power a comparatively short time, had not seriously attacked a number of fairly autonomous groupings like the churches and the Officers' Corps, had not gone so far into totalism as had been possible in Russia. And it is quite plausible that a victorious Nazism might have developed that same insistence on brainwashing and full control of the victim's, or citizen's, mind as was implicit in Stalinism. But at any rate, it was not the model here for Orwell.

Even as to *facecrime*, an authoritative instruction issued in Moscow about this time runs:

> One must not content oneself with merely paying attention to *what* is being said for that may well be in complete harmony with the Party programme. One must pay attention also to the *manner*— to the sincerity, for example, with which a school-mistress recites a poem the authorities regard as doubtful, or the pleasure revealed by a critic who goes into detail about a play he professes to condemn. (*Oktyabr*, No. 2, 1949)

Again, in the realm of literature proper, when Orwell writes of how it was necessary to "produce garbled versions—definitive texts they were called" of poems which had become politically objectionable, but which it was not wished to supress entirely, he is describing a purely Soviet phenomenon. Modern work by unpersons, of course, simply disappeared. But such things as traditional folk epics posed more of a problem. In 1940 the Kalmyk national epic *Dzhangar* was found to be "imbued with religious and reactionary content" and ordered to be "carefully purged," while its heroes were also transferred to a new epic, *Yorel*, in which they assist Stalin to "build the land of eternal youth." The Kirgiz epic *Manas* was ordered "expurgation" in 1952, but when the new "composite version" was ready in 1956—after Stalin's death—while it was accepted that it was now free of mysticism, nationalism, and so on, idealization of the feudal past still seeped through, and further action was recommended.

The "Spies" are a not very farfetched caricature of the Komsomol and its still younger equivalent, the Pioneers. S. Pavlov, the First Secretary of the Young Communist League in the Khrushchev interlude, told the November

*The Subway* by George Tooker, 1950, egg tempera on composition board, 18″ x 36″. Collection of the Whitney Museum of American Art. Juliana Force Purchase.

1962 Plenum of the Party Central Committee that under Stalin "the very first task of all Komsomol work was the necessity to seek out and recognize the enemy, who then had to be removed forcibly, by methods of economic pressure, organizational-political isolation, and methods of physical destruction."

More specifically, Orwell would certainly have known of the case of Pavlik Morozov, a fourteen-year-old Pioneer who denounced his father for "hoarding" grain, and was himself killed by villagers. He became, and remains, a Soviet hero—the Palace of Culture of the Red Pioneers in Moscow was named after him, and even in the Khrushchev period *Komsomolskaya Pravda*, official organ of the Party youth, told of "the sacred and dear" Pavlik Morozov Museum in his own village: "In this timbered house was held the court at which Pavlik unmasked his father." Nor was he a lone figure. In his speech marking the twentieth anniversary of the secret police, Mikoyan went out of his way to praise two other children who had turned in their relations, and these were representative of tens of thousands enrolled to report on the peasantry.

The public hangings of *Nineteen Eighty-Four* seem to have been founded on that of junior German war criminals in Kiev: Orwell had objected strongly to the British left-wing press "gloating" over it. In fact this was almost a lone episode, though we may perhaps see a proleptic point in the fact that Stalin seems to have planned a public execution of the unfortunate doctors of the "doctors' plot" in 1953—from which they were saved by his death.

The sudden switch of alliances in the middle of a party orator's speech is modeled on the circumstances of the Nazi-Soviet pact, when some editions of Communist newspapers of the same day accused the Germans of war-mongering in the afternoon, and celebrated them as friends in the evening.

*Doublethink* is virtually a translation of the Russian *dvoeverye*. Of dozens of examples which might be given, the most obvious is Soviet elections. *Vybor* (election) in Russian as in English means "choice." The ballot forms contain elaborate instructions on crossing out all but one name. But there never is more than one name. . . . Or again, "concentration camp" was changed in Stalin's time, as the camps got more deadly, to "corrective labour camp": "joycamp" takes the process further still.

When it comes to the *Nineteen Eighty-Four* fetishism of the Party as such, as early as 1929, Pyatakov (to be a major victim of one of Stalin's confession trials) was saying that he "would be ready to believe that black was white, and white was black, if the Party required it. In order to become one with his great Party, he would fuse with it, abandon his own personality, so that there was no particle left inside him which was not as one with the Party."

As to the general atmosphere, the writer Isaak Babel had said, "Today a man can only talk freely with his wife—at night, with the blankets pulled over his head"—precautions which were inadequate to save Babel himself from arrest and death.

We should note, however, that the scale of arrests and terror in *Nineteen Eighty-Four* is in one sense a reflection not of the height of the *Yezhovshchina*— the super-terror of 1937-38—but rather of the level maintained under successful Stalinism, around 1950, when all the machinery of repression was working smoothly, and a comparatively limited number of arrests was adequate to keep the pressure up on the population.

Orwell had never been to a totalitarian country. It is true that his time in

Catalonia had given him a direct and priceless experience of Communist lies and terror during the struggle for power, but the final product he could only gather through his ability to use the eyes of others. A Balkan Communist once said to the present writer that Orwell's intuitive genius was demonstrated, as against earlier anti-utopian writers, by his not making his totalitarian state a machinery of soulless efficiency, but on the contrary, just like the real USSR, a place where you can't get razor blades and the lifts do not work. In this as in other matters, Orwell knew by some instinct or by sufficient sense and experience what the true picture was and what the fake, among the many reports emerging from Moscow—a rare gift.

Above all, Orwell had the imagination to understand that there are people who would find it perfectly satisfactory to see the future in terms of "a boot stamping on a human face—forever." The parochial notion that everyone is much the same, that we all dislike war or terror, is absent from his view of history—as well it might be in the twentieth century. He saw that Stalin, like Tamerlane or Jenghiz Khan, was not in the least put out by the idea of the killing of millions of men. He knew that there have been cultures where torture was commonplace. That is to say, he knew that there are people, now as in earlier ages, who are not the product of the moral principles to which he himself gave assent.

Even today, the greatest hurdle to understanding the Soviet Union or similar regimes is the unthinking and inexplicit assumption that the basic motivations of the Soviet leaders differ little from our own. It was an advantage to Orwell that he knew nothing of one sort of "political science"—a supposed discipline which to this day, by concentrating on forms and structures, removes the essence of a given polity from active consideration. It is a notable fact that Orwell, like Koestler, was a novelist and journalist, and that in general, the record of such writers is far better than that of many "serious" students. Perhaps the reason is that to understand the Stalin regime took an effort not only of the intellect, but also of the imagination.

In spite of its clearly established Stalinist background, it is sometimes said that *Nineteen Eighty-Four* is intended to satirize not the Stalinist possibility in particular, but "tendencies to totalitarianism" in all societies. In the sense that its intention is to satirize tendencies to Stalinism, or to the excusing of Stalinism, in all societies, this is true. But, as we have shown, it is not true in the sense that Orwell was writing about some supposed tendency for all societies to become totalitarian, or was making some general attack on Stalinist and non-Stalinist attitudes alike.

Orwell's stature is such that people try to recruit him for their own beliefs. "What would Orwell think of" some more recent phenomenon is a common distraction. On the whole this matters little. But when it is perverted by writers of forewords or afterwords to Orwell's books, as in the latest Signet edition of *Nineteen Eighty-Four*, it is a particularly presumptuous—but also misleading—attempt to preempt Orwell's attitudes, providing examples calling for special attention.

Walter Cronkite, in a vapid introduction, suggests (quite contrary to the economic lessons of *Nineteen Eighty-Four*) that "greater efficiency, ease and security may come at a substantial price in freedom" whereas, of course, Orwell saw that totalitarianism destroys efficiency, ease and security together with liberty, and *because* of the destruction of liberty. Cronkite even gives Khomeini as a typification of Big Brother. But no, the mere existence of an age-old style of tyranny and terror was not Orwell's target, but rather a specific and modern phenomenon of which he had taken the measure.

Again, Eric Fromm, in his Afterword, gives as a supposed instance of doublethink the claim that nations may "prepare for war in order to preserve peace." Now, this proposition may be fallacious, but it is in no way self-contradictory. More important in our context, Orwell several times made it clear that he believed it to be true. And more generally, to apply Orwell's highly specific totalitarian terror-falsification concepts to assorted Western notions is to dilute, indeed to stultify, Orwell's point. Fromm is entitled to his views: he is not entitled to give them a spurious prestige by bringing in Orwell to validate them. Above all, this sort of thing distorts Orwell's view of the totalist terror state as something distinct and different from our own imperfect societies—indeed, something to be resisted at all costs.

Orwell hated the distortion of truth, the mental cheapening to be found in the Western press and film. (It is true that he was also able to condemn his much loathed movie moguls for active pro-Stalinist propaganda, as in the Hollywood film *Mission to Moscow* based on Joseph Davies's book of that title.) But for him, as for anyone, a partisan exaggeration or oversimplification was not just a lesser offense, but a lesser category of offense, than the complete substitution of fiction for fact and the total suppression of rival accounts. *Nineteen Eighty-Four* distinguishes flatly between the two. The newspapers and history books of the past were "coloured and biased," yet, "falsification of the kind that is practiced today would have been impossible."

Of course all views, even when rational in themselves, are accompanied by a penumbra of angled and simplified phrases to some degree distorting or caricaturing reality in favor of the given opinion. Orwell, though himself offending as often as the rest of us, was in principle against such phraseology and concerned to make people avoid it in the interests of clean thinking. However, when he writes in 1946, "The connection between totalitarian habits of thought and the corruption of language is an important subject and has not been sufficiently studied," he goes on to give examples of this not from Catholics or Conservatives, with the idea that such linguistic practice makes Catholicism or Conservativism more totalitarian each time it is performed; his examples are solely from admirers of the Soviet Union, writing abjectly and above all *badly* on their own favorite subject. What he is clearly seeking to show is less that any sort of misuse of language produces totalitarianism than that totalitarian habits of thought need a jargoneering and confusing dialect to maintain themselves.

Why did *Nineteen Eighty-Four*, with all its faults, have the feeling of reality? Because in some fundamental sense everyone knew (even if in some cases it was only a repressed consciousness) of the actualities of Stalinism. Because, on the other side of the equation, Orwell carried conviction through his clear and confident understanding of Stalinist phenomena.

When Orwell wrote, his main concern, as he makes clear time and again, was less to attack the Stalin regime as such than to combat a whole herd of intellectual quislings at home; to expose the delusions of intellectuals. He remarks, in his 1947 Introduction to the Ukrainian edition of *Animal Farm*, "I would not have condemned Stalin and his associates merely for their barbaric and undemocratic methods. . . . But on the other hand it was of the utmost importance that people in Western Europe should see the Soviet regime for what it really was," his aim being "the destruction of the Soviet myth" in Western minds.

One of the motives of Western pro-Stalinists, Orwell suggests, was hatred of their own country; another, the wish for a society in which the intellectual had at last got his hands on the whip.

It is precisely Orwell's view that there is no moral symmetry between the West and the Communist world, and that, on the contrary, the West needs to defend itself against a fearful political threat, but in particular against its own misrepresentations and misunderstanding of this threat. What he found most contemptible, though also most characteristic, was the fact that opposition to the Marxist-Leninist regimes was always represented as "insane or activated by the worst motives" and never discussed on its merits as a reasoned opinion based on facts.

Orwell's friend Arthur Koestler wrote of "the thousands of painters and writers and doctors and lawyers and debutantes chanting a diluted version of the Stalinist line." After a generation of hard work by those who have sought out and presented the real facts of the USSR in Stalin's time, delusions about it have at last almost wholly dissipated. But human nature, the will to be deceived, does not change, and it will be surprising if there are not many Western intellectuals who in twenty or thirty years will in turn—one trusts not too late—have to abandon delusions about similar regimes, whose legitimization is, as ever, merely their similar hostility to the West, and their ability to project similar misapprehension about their real acts and aspirations. If the meaning of the book is distorted to deal with other targets, however deserving, Orwell's intent is lost.

# 21 *Alexander Dallin*

# Big Brother Is Watching You

*On coins, on stamps, on the covers of books, on banners, on posters, and on
the wrapping of a cigarette packet—everywhere. Always the eyes watching you
and the voice enveloping you. Asleep or awake, working or eating, indoors
or out of doors, in the bath or in bed—no escape.*

BIG BROTHER IS ONE OF GEORGE ORWELL'S GIFTS to the contemporary lexicon
of politics. It is hard to believe that the phrase "Big Brother is watching you"
entered our literature—and our consciousness—only some thirty years ago,
so commonly is it now accepted as the symbol for the omnipotent state's
suspicious surveillance of the defenseless individual. But who is Big Brother?
What are his functions and what is the nature of his power? And to what
extent has the course of history since the book was written tended to validate
Orwell's projections?

It is characteristic of Orwell's intuitive understanding of the totalitarian
manipulation of symbols that he did not give the supreme master a monar-
chical or princely title, nor endow him with a familiar position—president,
general secretary, or dictator—nor finally provide him the appellation of a
father figure. The sibling label and the use of "B.B." as the familiar shorthand
fit well the pretense of comradeship and equality which are part of the
*doublespeak* of Ingsoc—a dialectic of alleged closeness and kinship on the one
hand, and obedience and intimidation on the other.

Equally part of the mood of *Nineteen Eighty-Four* is the vagueness—the
lack of definition—in the image of B.B. One wonders whether this uncertainty
was an unwitting consequence of the haste (necessitated by his failing health)
with which Orwell wrote his nightmarish warning, or whether it was part
of a conscious design to suffuse the whole book—the picture of life in Oceania
A.D. 1984—with a dreamlike sense of latent terror and ubiquitous anxiety.

That there is no known capital in the land and no known residence of Big Brother suggests intent rather than a flaw in the design. So does the contrast between the ambiguities of Big Brother's role and certain telltale specifics, such as his black mustache and his unvarying age of forty-five.

## II

At one level, Big Brother may be thought of as the tacit antagonist, the polar opposite of the book's hero, Winston Smith. Big Brother stands for the unlimited authority of the state and ruling party. Yet we never encounter Big Brother: all we know about him are references to him by others. Right at the outset the author relates:

> The hallway smelt of boiled cabbage and old rag mats. At one end of it a colored poster, too large for indoor display, had been tacked to the wall. It depicted simply an enormous face, more than a meter wide: the face of a man of about forty-five, with a heavy black mustache and ruggedly handsome features. . . . On each landing, opposite the lift shaft, the poster with the enormous face gazed from the wall. It was one of those pictures which are so contrived that the eyes follow you about when you move. BIG BROTHER IS WATCHING YOU, the caption beneath it ran.

And again, outside,

> The black-mustachio'd face gazed down from every commanding corner. There was one on the house front immediately opposite. BIG BROTHER IS WATCHING YOU, the caption said . . .

We learn more from the long excerpts of *The Theory and Practice of Oligarchical Collectivism* by Emmanuel Goldstein, the former insider turned renegade and now the object of the primal hate. Describing Oceania's society, he writes,

> At the apex of the pyramid comes Big Brother. Big Brother is infallible and all-powerful. Every success, every achievement, every victory, every scientific discovery, all knowledge, all wisdom, all happiness, all virtue, are held to issue directly from his leadership and inspiration. Nobody has ever seen Big Brother. He is a face on the hoardings, a voice on the telescreen.

Big Brother also refracts the major mechanisms, institutions, and processes that Orwell identifies with Ingsoc, such as Thought Police, Newspeak, and the rewriting of history. As Goldstein writes, "Oceanic society rests ultimately on the belief that Big Brother is omnipotent and that the Party is infallible. But since in reality Big Brother is not omnipotent and the Party is not infallible, there is need for an unwearying, moment-to-moment flexibility in the treatment of facts. . . . This demands a continuous alteration of the past, made possible by the system of thought which really embraces all the rest, and which is known in Newspeak as *doublethink*."

Early in the book, Winston confronts the personal disorientation caused by this falsification of history:

> [Winston] tried to remember in what year he had first heard mention of Big Brother. He thought it must have been at some time in the Sixties, but it was impossible to be certain. In the Party histories, of course, Big Brother figured as the leader and guardian of the Revolution since its very earliest days. His exploits had been gradually pushed backwards in time until already they extended into the fabulous world of the Forties and the Thirties. . . . There was no way of knowing how much of this legend was true and how much invented.

Goldstein corroborates Winston's thoughts: "We may be reasonably sure that he will never die, and there is already considerable uncertainty as to when he was born." It is presumably the same puzzlement that leads Winston, under arrest and after tortures and adventures, to ask O'Brien:

> "Does Big Brother exist?"
> "Of course he exists. The party exists. Big Brother is the embodiment of the Party."
> "Does he exist in the same way as I exist?"
> "You do not exist," said O'Brien. . . .
> "I think I exist," he said wearily. "I am conscious of my own identity. I was born and I shall die. I have arms and legs. I occupy a particular point in space. No other solid object can occupy the same point simultaneously. In that sense, does Big Brother exist?"
> "It is of no importance. He exists."
> "Will Big Brother ever die?"
> "Of course not. How could he die? Next question."

We are then left with an unresolved tension between Big Brother the specific, "historical" person and Big Brother as a myth and symbol—a tension to which we shall need to return.

### III

What then are the functions of Big Brother as they emerge from the text of *Nineteen Eighty-Four*? Once again Orwell puts it best in the manuscript of Emmanuel Goldstein: "To act as a focusing point for love, fear, and reverence, emotions which are more easily felt toward an individual than toward an organization."

Big Brother is, first, to be feared: we are reminded of the "Big Brother Is Watching You" posters, of the expectation of unquestioned compliance and—

*Government Bureau* by George Tooker, 1956, egg tempera on gesso panel, 19⅝″ × 29⅝″. Collection of the Metropolitan Museum of Art. George A. Hearn Fund.

just in case—his presiding over the apparatus of the Thought Police with its many refinements, as Winston and so many others were to experience them. It was in Big Brother's name that the guardians of purity followed the citizens' every move and listened to their every word or groan through the system of telescreens.

Second, Big Brother is to be celebrated and hailed: Goldstein matter-of-factly speaks of the "worship of the semi-divine leader" as a common feature of all three empires—Oceania, Eurasia, and Eastasia. Orwell gives us accounts of mass exercises and mass rallies, no doubt patterned on those of the Hitler and Stalin eras, and examples of the self-hypnosis regularly practiced in Big Brother's name and behalf.

If indeed Big Brother was no more than a figment of the propagandists' imagination—in Goldstein's words, "a guise in which the Party chooses to exhibit itself to the world"—the myth unwittingly, by its deathless continuity, also serves a third function of removing the trauma and crisis of successions and transitions—the perennial problem of regimes such as the Soviet and Chinese.

But the most original and difficult function Orwell imputes to Big Brother is to be universally loved, not only by the rank and file as part of the general structure of loyalty but also by internal enemies, dissidents, and recalcitrants. Such a requirement went well beyond the historical models Orwell had in front of him. In spite of the sickening adulation extended to a Stalin or Hitler, there was in their systems never any expectation that opponents of the regime would be made—or had to be made—to "love" the 'vozhd' or Führer. Ultimately compliance was all that could be required, with the tacit assumption that, in an atmosphere of latent terror, the obedient fulfillment of commands would be habit-forming.

True, the theory and practice of "Thought Reform"—the "reeducation" of class enemies—in the People's Republic of China in the late forties and early fifties (as well as the theory that had underlain the twisted rationale of the Soviet "correctional" labor camps) were closer to the aim of remaking human norms and values. But however ugly some of the practices which these efforts led to, there is good reason to think that we have tended to accept a misleading if not fictitious version of the process: in the last analysis, there is no such thing as "brainwashing." In the perspective of *Nineteen Eighty-Four*, this must lead us to ask: Why did B.B. have to be loved? One is bound to wonder to what extent the notion built on Arthur Koestler's *Darkness at Noon*, which, having first appeared in 1941, had had an extraordinary influence on an entire generation of Western leftists and liberals. In that book (where incidentally a character spoke of the leader as the "manikin with the black mustache") the hero, Rubashov, was of course expected out of dedication to the party and its cause to confess to a tissue of imaginary and implausible crimes.

Readers will remember the scene in *Nineteen Eighty-Four* in which O'Brien tells the tormented Winston:

> "You are improving. Intellectually there is very little wrong with you. It is only emotionally that you have failed to make progress. Tell me, Winston—and remember, no lies: you know that I am always able to detect a lie—tell me, what are your true feelings towards Big Brother?"
>
> "I hate him."
>
> "You hate him. Good. Then the time has come for you to take the last step. You must love Big Brother. It is not enough to obey him: you must love him." [And with that Winston is sent to the dreaded Room 101.]

The effort obviously succeeds—if leaving Winston a broken man is deemed a success. In the end, physically, emotionally, and mentally a cripple, Smith spends his days drinking cheap gin in a pub:

> He gazed up at the enormous face. Forty years it had taken him to learn what kind of smile was hidden beneath the dark mustache. O cruel, needless misunderstanding! O stubborn, self-willed exile from the loving breast! Two gin-scented tears trickled down the sides of his nose. But it was all right, everything was all right, the struggle was finished. He had won the victory over himself. He loved Big Brother.

This conversion is one of the weakest, least convincing elements in Orwell's imaginary edifice. So is the ideological rationale which O'Brien provides for it: "We make the brain perfect before we blow it out. The command of the old despotisms was 'Thou shalt not.' The command of the totalitarians was 'Thou shalt.' Our command is *'Thou art.'*" Perhaps a simpler and more convincing explanation would have been to conceive of mandatory love as a religious function: there is ample precedent for live historical figures to become objects of religious myths which require of their devotees a renunciation of self.

There remains another, more pervasive irony regarding the functions Big Brother is to perform, and once again it is not clear whether the irony is intended or—more likely, in this instance—whether it reflects a contradiction Orwell did not manage to dispel. The thrust of the book, of course, is the successful suppression of human feelings and individual drives. And yet, we are told, one *raison d'être*—or better perhaps, *raison de paraître*—for Big Brother is the fact that love, fear, and reverence are "more easily felt toward an individual than toward an organization."

IV

The model for Orwell's Big Brother was surely provided by Stalin and, to a

lesser degree, by Hitler. In this sense as in many others *Nineteen Eighty-Four*
is a product of the late Stalin era. Orwell was especially prone to draw—
quite consciously and intentionally, one must assume—on the Soviet record,
with Big Brother in the mold of Stalin and Emmanuel Goldstein patterned
on Leon Trotsky:

> The story really began in the middle Sixties, the period of the
> great purges in which the original leaders of the Revolution were
> wiped out once and for all. By 1970 none of them was left, except
> Big Brother himself. All the rest had by that time been exposed
> as traitors and counter-revolutionaries. Goldstein had fled and
> was hiding, no one knew where, and of the others, a few had
> simply disappeared, while the majority had been executed after
> spectacular public trials at which they made their confession of
> their crimes. . . .

When Winston, on the job, had to compose something to replace a previous
official version, he would dictate in Big Brother's familiar style—described,
in a clear allusion to Stalin, as "a style at once military and pedantic." Of
course the long excerpts from Goldstein's trenchant critique of the system
show, as with Trotsky, both a sharp mind and the extent to which Goldstein
unwittingly shared some of the nefarious values Orwell condemns.

And yet Big Brother is clearly meant to go well beyond the known "totalitarians." Where does he fit against the record of history and social science?
Historians will think of Caesaropapist precedents for linking thorough command of power and ideology. Students of Weberian theory may well refer to
the frequent pattern in history of magicians and priests serving—and ben-
efiting from—a sacred figure, increasingly removed from public view, in a
process that can be reconciled with the notion of a "routinization of charismatic rule." Other social scientists would stress the interactional elements
of leadership, which is seen as satisfying the mutual expectations of both
leaders and led; and contemporary analysts might well document the fact
that national leadership increasingly has come to involve institutionalized,
impersonal action in the name of (but not personally by) the leader.

In some significant respects then Big Brother, in all his monstrous uniqueness, has some familiar roots. Yet there remains the question whether the
course of events since 1950 has tended to validate or contradict the images
which George Orwell projects in *Nineteen Eighty-Four*. In the Soviet Union,
the power of all of Stalin's successors has been less sweeping, arbitrary, and
personalistic than his had been; and with insignificant exceptions the same
has been the pattern in other communist systems. The most erratic or absolute
dictators elsewhere in the world—be it an Idi Amin, a Muammar Khadafi,
or "Papa Doc" Duvalier—have typically lacked the technology, the ideology,
or the sophistication to move significantly in the direction of a Big Brother.

Modern technology has had an ambiguous impact. If television can present American presidential candidates—and winners—as invariably attractive and informed, modern communications also make it impossible for public figures to maintain the privacy and safety that earlier would-be leaders had, or to address fractured audiences, to each of which something different could safely be said and pledged. If we know very little of the private lives of Fidel Castro, Yuri Andropov, or Deng Xiao-ping, they nonetheless can scarcely conceal their infirmities as kings or despots could in earlier times.

All in all, if we are to believe that the fiction of Big Brother was meant to represent a formula for permanent rulership in the future, it seems less credible today than it did when *Nineteen Eighty-Four* first appeared. And this brings us to the broader context within which Big Brother is placed.

V

Lionel Trilling, in commenting on "George Orwell and the Politics of Truth," captured admirably a seeming tension in the author and his work when he approvingly endorsed the view of Orwell as "a virtuous man" but also reflected that "he was not a genius, and this is one of the remarkable things about him." The earnest, anxious warning that *Nineteen Eighty-Four* conveys needed to be made in mid-century Europe, even if today, for many readers, it may not seem as imminent, as inescapable, as likely a scenario. Indeed, one might foolhardily affirm that, fortunately, Orwell has turned out to be wrong: in 1984 the world does not face a *Nineteen Eighty-Four*. It is not that he was bound to be in error in regard to discrete events (mercifully, for instance, no atomic bombs have been used since the book first appeared): no one could have known. From our vantage point it is far easier to assert than it was in 1948 that the vision that the book offers pictures a world too pat to be credible.

Thus we can assert today that human emotions and individual impulses are too strong and too tenacious to be eradicated. Likewise, the argument that the elite seeks power as an end in itself is less, rather than more, credible today, given what we know of the motivations and at least the rationalizations in private conversations of men like Adolf Hitler and Mao Tse-tung. The totalitarian model, the implicit futility of resistance, and the pointlessness of harboring a private calculus in such a system, have been seriously and effectively challenged by critics on a wide variety of grounds—as well as by historical experience from Eastern Europe to the Far East.

The fact is that no single dictator even approached the image of Big Brother in power or manipulation. The picture—really only a silhouette—of Big Brother in *Nineteen Eighty-Four* suggests an unrealistically simplistic notion of politics and the job of ruling and running a complex modern empire.

If earlier we suggested that Big Brother stood for the all-powerful, all-knowing ruler, the very opposite of Winston Smith the impotent citizen, it might actually be more accurate to perceive of B.B. not at all as the master but rather as himself a tool or puppet—the object of manipulation—if not altogether a myth. It is not really Big Brother who is watching you: even by Orwell's conventions, it is a huge army of Thought Police personnel, censors and rewriters of history, watchmen and listeners, indoctrinators and organizers of "two-minute hates." (Anyone with experience of Communist politics would inquire: Who watches the watchmen—*Quis custodiet ipsos custodes?*) When all is said and done, Big Brother remains an empty shell.

But if Big Brother is not the actual master and decision maker, who is the real Big Brother in Orwell's Oceania? How is he—or how are they—chosen, how is he—are they—replaced? What authority does he—do they—have? The answer could go some of the way toward answering the question why *Nineteen Eighty-Four* will never come about. Ironically, George Orwell commits the same mistake that Karl Marx made in assuming that in a future society, administration—as a neutral, technical routine—can take the place of policy, both in the sense of choosing policies (that is, the inescapable task of decision making) and of engaging in political behavior. At the very least, behind the facade of Big Brother's omniscience and omnipotence, there are bound to be stirrings of elite politics, conflicts of divergent priorities and policy prescriptions, clashes of personalities, tempers, and egos, contests of interests and opinions, which cannot be wished, legislated, or decreed away. Even priests and magicians, even members of the Praetorian guard are bound to divide and differ, and that minimal hint of political pluralism may well be the first crack that may grow into a geological divide. Whether or not the actors are aware of it, there is a continuous political process at work in every modern decision making system, even where authority is routinized and the pretense of unanimity is affirmed and upheld.

VI

*Nineteen Eighty-Four* was informed by the experience of the Hitler and Stalin eras. Since then we have had reason to conclude—or to delude ourselves—that these were exceptional phenomena, extremes unlikely to be replicated in the future. While the conjunction of politics and technology may create new scourges and new threats to our values—indeed, to the survival of humankind—they are not likely to engender the world which Orwell conjured up. If, on the one hand, we can no longer subscribe to the earlier optimism about progress and the course of history, and about the rule of reason, we can perhaps, on the other hand, also call for a surcease of Orwellian alarums: Big Brother is nowhere in sight. This does not make it any less powerful as a symbol and a warning of an ominous—we hope, exaggerated—threat to humanism and individualism in our age.

# 22 *Philip G. Zimbardo*

# Mind Control: Political Fiction and Psychological Reality

*"The Party is not interested in the overt act: the thought is all we care about.
We do not merely destroy our enemies; we change them."*

IN *NINETEEN EIGHTY-FOUR*, WE ARE CAST as observers of an unnatural experiment in the negation of human nature. One by one, each of the qualities at the core of that elusive construct called human nature are stripped away. The System's goals are proclaimed clearly and coldly: "To extinguish once and for all the possibility of independent thought"; to eliminate the conditions that enable even one "erroneous thought [to] exist anywhere in the world, however secret and powerless it may be"; to crush the core of humaneness so that no person is "capable of ordinary human feeling"; and to enforce such total behavioral obedience to its authority that everyone is "prepared to commit suicide, if and when we order you to do so." Its mission is to be supreme authority over every individual's thoughts, feelings, and actions.

Winston Smith is the reluctant hero because he is the last person capable of independent thoughts, self-contained secrets, passionate feelings, and occasionally rebellious deeds. He is the enemy of the System, who represents the only principle that can still defeat its brutal omnipotence—"the spirit of man." The System cannot destroy him as long as he persists in preserving his free will, maintaining his autonomy, and sustaining a sense of compassion for his fellows. The absolute power of the oppressive System is threatened by the presence of even a single dissident who can laugh at its pretentiousness by remembering when life was different, and by imagining future realities with meaningful options and choices: "You are a flaw in the system, Winston. You are a stain that must be wiped out."

Orwell confronts the reader with a series of the most profound questions about our existence: What is reality? What is truth? And what are the central qualities of the individual psyche? What happens when intelligence is allowed free reign without constraint by feelings or social conscience? And, can an individual survive in an inhospitable setting without the tangible support of a social group or the spiritual support of a religious-mystical ideology?

The uniqueness of our species and of each individual member comes from the coupling of intelligence, consciousness, and affect. With intelligence we have the capacity to learn, to remember, and to imagine. With consciousness we have the awareness of the self as a unique time-bound entity able to distinguish inner from outer realities. With affect we have the basis for coloring the quality of experience in infinitely subtle and complex hues beyond animal pleasures and pains.

Human intelligence has enabled our species to achieve supremacy on this planet, to go beyond the basic survival concerns of our ancestors. Our enormous capacity for learning means that we can not only profit from personal experience, but also construct the present life we want by building on the memories, plans, and written histories of others. Our ability to imagine alternatives, propose options, and anticipate consequences allows us to design future scenarios unbound by mundane restrictions. And our capability for loving and experiencing intense emotion provides a basis for total engagement in the social-sensory world of the empirical present.

But vital to each of these functions is the individual's development of a balanced temporal perspective of the past, the present, and the future. Central to human nature, then, is a mental facility for becoming involved in what was, what is now, and what will be. When a moral-ethical system is added to this temporal trilogy, human behavior is guided by an awareness of what could have been and what ought to be.

Memory establishes the continuity of self over time and thereby a sense of personality. The past provides the present with standards, criteria for comparison, the wellsprings of tradition, and the stable references for the transient flux of immediate experience. Feelings connect us to other people through our passions and compassions for them—and theirs for us. Strong affect engages us fully in the expanded moment of the present, giving a vibrancy to our experience that intellect alone cannot. Through affectionate relationships, love and trust replace instrumental utility of others as the basis for bonds of attachment and empathy. Human imagination gives us the power to overcome yesterday's failures and grief while altering the givens of today to become tomorrow's potential realities. Such imagination, in recognizing its own frailty and mortal limits, establishes principles of justice and a transcendent vision of spiritual life. To thrive, people need to be part of a society that reasonably and equitably trades off self-interests, rights, and privileges with social obligations that foster the common good. People need other people to create a system of supportive interdependence—a bonded social unit that helps each to resist better any assaults from destructive influences in the physical, social, and political environment. Isolation is the precursor of all pathologies that plague the human spirit.

III

People commonly believe that they have more strength to resist attempts to modify their behavior than they really have. At the same time, they underestimate the true power of social pressures to make them conform, comply, and obey. This misperception prevents them from realistically appraising the ubiquitous influences that operate in social norms, rules, and the roles we are given to enact. We are most likely to become susceptible to blindly obeying unjust authority precisely when we overestimate the power of such abstract conceptions as "ego strength," "force of character," and "spirit of self-determination." Humanity is better served by not rushing into situations where angels fear to tread while visions of "person power" dance in their heads.

There can be no underestimating the power of external forces in Big Brother's world. Orwell foresaw a well-stocked arsenal of mind-control technologies that could be used in the battle of the System against the individual. But there abides in each of us the naive belief that we will win in the end— that despite all odds, innocent good can triumph over systematically applied evil. It does so—in romance novels, but not in Orwell's political novel, nor in the total situations of authoritarian control that occur in our real world.

Among other conceptions of human nature we must examine if we are to understand how to resist Big Brother more effectively is the religious. Winston does not cry out in Torture Room 101, "Father, why hast thou forsaken me?" because he has long since given up a religious orientation to life. In doing so, he is isolated from the connection to spiritual freedom that comes from a sense of immortality, higher consciousness, and inner unity. From Western religions, which are religions of the will, come a source of strength to resist tyranny—demonstrated by the response of Polish Catholics to Pope John Paul II's 1983 visit to their oppressed nation, or by the will of Jehovah's Witnesses to resist the cruel tactics of their tormentors in prisoner-of-war camps. From Eastern religions, which turn inward to couple choice with intellectual freedom, come discipline and methods for transforming human desires. Without either, Winston—and we—must make it on our own, relinquishing one of the fundamental strengths that humans can call upon when confronting adversity and evil.

Another conception of human nature centers upon the essential interplay of intelligence and feeling. If Big Brother and the Party are intelligence without feeling, then *Nineteen Eighty-Four* is a study of the perversion of human nature by an intelligence turned in on itself. The Party represents a master analytical intelligence striving toward an ideal of omniscience and omnipotence. But when human intelligence is allowed free rein—unguided by moral values, ethical principles, and the humanizing constraints of love—it becomes a monster run amok. For Mary Wollstonecraft Shelley, that monster was Dr. Frankenstein, whose genius could create a living creature in a scientific laboratory, but whose lack of tender caring deprived it of a human spirit, the heart and the soul of a person. Orwell's Party is Dr. Frankenstein as Committee Mentality; its all-knowing, nonfeeling intelligence sets as a goal not the creation of life from inert matter, but the opposite: the draining of life out of once vibrant creatures until they are reduced to mindless, pliable matter. Frankenstein's experiment had the modest aim of inducing one working mind in his creature. The Party's experiment set the more ambitious objective of destroying every independent mind in all human creatures.

The Party's experiment is complete when every individual is converted and reshaped, his inner mind captured. Dr. Frankenstein's fictional achievement in discovering nature's secret for the spark of life pales in comparison to the Party's fictional achievement: "We make the laws of nature." Its second slogan might be "We unmake the laws of human nature." As O'Brien, the Party's spokesperson, says, "You are imagining that there is something called human nature which will be outraged by what we do and will turn against us. But we create human nature. Men are infinitely malleable."

Is that doctrine of human malleability merely another of Orwell's fictional devices? Listen to the rhetoric from some of the persuasive realists from the world of fact:

> Give us the child for eight years, and it will be a Bolshevist forever. (Lenin, speech to the commissars of education, 1923)

> Give me a dozen healthy infants, well-formed, and my own specified world to bring them up in and I'll guarantee to take any one at random and train him to become any type of specialist I might select—doctor, lawyer, artist, merchant-chief, and, yes, even into beggar-man and thief, regardless of his talents, penchants, tendencies, abilities, vocations, and race of his ancestors. (J.B. Watson, "What the Nursery Has to Say About Instincts," 1926)

> The individual should accept his personal insignificance, dissolve himself in a higher power and then feel proud in participating in the strength and glory of this higher power. (Hitler, *Mein Kampf*, 1933)

Each of *Nineteen Eighty-Four's* technologies of mind control is aimed at undermining or overwhelming an attribute central to the human spirit. For freedom of action there is obedience training. For independence of thought there is Newspeak, *thoughtcrime*, and Thought Police. For liberty of association and interpersonal trust there is social isolation, enforced solitude, and a spy network. Memory is reduced to selective amnesia through control of the past. Reality guides to decisions and actions are removed by *doublethink* and denial of sense impressions. Tender feelings for others are replaced by conditioning negative emotions and by implanting sentiments that support war while eliminating sexual impulses. Pride is broken by interrogation tactics and the humiliation of facing the personal terrors of Room 101. Individuality and eccentricity yield to the force of *crimestop*. Strength is sapped by food deprivation. The quest for truth succumbs to the arbitrary arrangement of approved Party opinions. And privacy cannot survive Big Brother's telescreen surveillance. "Always the eyes watching you, working or eating, indoors or out of doors, in the bath or in bed—no escape. Nothing was your own except the few cubic centimeters inside your head"—and each day that private vault was being robbed of some of its contents.

Surveillance by authorities has a chilling effect in suppressing individual actions. It intimidates by imposing a perceived power differential in which "they" know about "you" but you don't know them. Feelings of powerlessness arise and then are accepted as an inevitable feature of the status quo wherein submission to surveillance is necessary for some good reason or other. But when one's neighbors, spouse, and children may be spies who report any deviations to the Thought Police, then interpersonal trust—the basis for a social support network—is transformed into distrust in a climate of suspicion. With the social bonds weakened, physical isolation becomes more commonplace. The exchange of momentary glances between a man and woman become "a memorable event, in the locked loneliness in which one had to live"— in an age of solitude in which individuals are alone.

But perhaps the Party's most potent technology for mind control is the insidious manipulation of time. It ceases to matter that the clocks are striking thirteen. It is no longer possible to discern the difference between the unalterable past and the altered historical record. By rewriting all references to the past so that they are acceptable to current ideology, the Party reconstructs history to be always on the right side. Party predictions are then always supported, estimates accurate, and concerns justified. What was is mandated into what should have been, given what is. But is there a past that survives when written records and memory traces do not agree as to what *really* happened?

*R.A.D.* by Nancy Grossman, 1982. Courtesy of Ronald Feldman Fine Arts, New York.

The Party could thrust its hand into the past and say of this or that event, *it never happened*. . . . "Who controls the past," ran the Party slogan, "controls the future: who controls the present controls the past." And yet the past, though of its nature alterable, never had been altered. . . . All that was needed was an unending series of victories over your own memory.

What follows is the bleakest question of the successful mind controller or his would-be subject: "If both the past and the external world exist only in the mind, and the mind itself is controllable [by all these efficient technologies]—then what?"

V

Is there any factual validation of these fictional tactics of mind control? If Orwell were writing now, might he not sound a broader alarm to warn us of contemporary practitioners of mind control—"for our own good"?

There are some contemporary parallels to Big Brother's strategies and tactics for making real people think, feel, and act in ways dictated by others. Orwell's monolithic, evil System is being transformed now into a bewildering array of seemingly benevolent mini-systems that control not coercively, but through the covert operations of cure and care. Everyman and Everywoman of our 1984 are less directly threatened than Winston Smith was by the coercive and sinister Party System, but not all of the following description from *Nineteen Eighty-Four* is unfamiliar to us:

The scientist of today is either a mixture of psychologist and inquisitor, studying with extraordinary minuteness the meaning of facial expressions, gestures, and tones of voice, and testing the truth-producing effects of drugs, shock-therapy, hypnosis, and physical torture; or he is a chemist, physicist, or biologist concerned only with such branches of his special subject as are relevant to the taking of life.

Our civil liberties and personal integrity are not as likely to be stomped to pulp under the boot of known enemies in power-mad political parties. Instead, we are seduced into giving them away to a benevolent brotherhood of professionals licensed to intervene in our lives.

For over a decade, spanning the 1950s and 1960s, the Central Intelligence Agency in the United States sponsored experiments in extreme forms of mind control and behavior modification. MK-ULTRA (Ultra Mind Kontrol?) was the title of their most notorious covert program designed to develop and make operational technologies for disrupting and then reprogramming an individual's habitual patterns of perception, thought, and action.

Government research funds were funneled through universities and mental hospitals to encourage the experimental testing of LSD and other psycho-active drugs, as well as new forms of electroshock treatment, hypnosis, and other exotic types of direct intervention into the functioning of the human mind. In addition, clandestine experimentation of this kind was conducted within some military units and socially marginal segments of the civilian population: prisoners, prostitutes, and the poor. Subjects were either not aware of the experiments or misled to believe they were "therapeutic." There are documented cases of chronically impaired functioning and even suicides resulting from exposure to these assaultive technologies. The program was halted not because of the outrage of the citizenry (few knew of its existence) or the ethical concerns of turning American citizens into "vegetables," but because it didn't do the job it was supposed to. These potent gadgets and gimmicks could surely scramble anyone's brain, but they could not direct a single person's action in predetermined ways. Parenthetically, the one en-during contribution of the CIA's MK-ULTRA program was to underwrite the start of wide-scale experimentation with recreational drugs in the United States.

Soviet scientists have since been perfecting a device that bombards the brain with low-frequency radio waves. These airborne waves can travel over distances and change the behavior of animals and humans in their path. The low-frequency radio waves simulate the brain's own electromagnetic current and produce a trancelike state. The device, known as LIDA, is de-scribed as having therapeutic value for cases of hypertension and neurotic disturbances. But such remote control makes possible some potentially fright-ening uses for altering the brain's functioning.

Mind control by means of technologies for directly controlling the brain through psychosurgery, electroshock, and electrodes implanted in specific brain regions does exert powerful effects on mood, memory, and behavior. Research is continuing on direct electrical stimulation of the brain in human patients as well as in animals. For example, when pleasure centers in the brain are stimulated electrically, patients may get sexually aroused in the absence of any of the normal stimuli for sexual arousal. Animals will work themselves into a frenzy pressing levers that deliver an electrical jolt to their pleasure center. Fear, rage, and other strong emotions have been electronically activated by remotely triggering brain impulses in subjects who have had electrodes implanted in their brains. But again, in their application by phy-sicians and psychiatrists, the changes produced by the various technologies tend to be general and incapable of inducing specifically directed, reliably replicated changes in what the person thinks or does.

One of the pioneering researchers in this area, José Delgado, speculates about the benefits of a "psychocivilized society" controlled by electrical stim-ulation of the brain. He claims that "movements, sensations, emotions, de-sires, ideas, and a variety of other psychological phenomena may be induced, inhibited, or modified by electrical stimulation in specific areas of the brain." Delgado foresees the possibility—once the brain's activity can be brought under systematic, rational control procedures—of a "future psychocivilized human being, a less cruel, happier, and better man." This optimistic vision is somewhat dimmed by the scientist's concluding statement: "The concept of individuals as self-sufficient and independent entities is based on false premises."

Although we do not have a Ministry of Truth that rewrites the past to "say of this or that event, *it never happened*," we do have textbook authors, publishers, and vested interests who recreate, reconstruct, and revise the past to make it more desirable politically and socially. Until recently, American history texts, like Western movies, portrayed Indians as the savage murderers of innocent white travelers. They rarely document military massacres of Indian settlements, the violation of sacred Indian territories by these opportunist "foreigners," or the destructive spread of disease by the whites among the once healthy native American population.

While the textbooks in our schools ignore the reality of the internment of over 100,000 Japanese-Americans in Western concentration camps during World War II, new Japanese texts also tinker with the past. They have recently distorted history to present a more positive image of Japan's involvement in World War II. The world has witnessed the purging of history in the Soviet Union and in the People's Republic of China, where new political rulers regularly denigrate and then delete out-of-favor predecessors from public records. Such manipulation of history is a way of shaping the thinking of future generations. The power of such a biased perspective lies in disguising propaganda and prejudiced beliefs as education and facts.

Police departments everywhere routinely rely on informers to provide incriminating information on criminal activities in their precincts. Although it is less common for national governments to institutionalize spying among its own citizens, the Soviet Union has recently resumed the practice for the first time since the Stalin era. The Andropov regime is experimenting with an anonymous denunciation-by-mail system. "Signal Cards" distributed in select cities invite good citizens to note an offender's name and address and underline any of a dozen conveniently listed offenses. The offenses to be reported include: not working, drunkenness, use of narcotics, living on unearned income, "committing crimes," "previously on trial," and the catch-all offense of "other violations of social order and the rules of socialist society."

In America, surveillance is not symbolized by posters of Big Brother but is carried out by the marketing surveillance devices of big business. Orwell might have been amused to read *Security World*, the trade journal of the industrial security field. It is filled with advertisements and articles on more types of high technology "security" hardware than he could have imagined. Surveillance cameras record images for offices, elevators, stores, airports, and public areas with security problems while ultrasonic and infrared detectors sense motion, noise, or body heat. Bugging devices, voice stress analyzers, lie detectors, and employee screening tests (both psychological and biological monitoring) are becoming standard equipment in the business world. To these intrusions on our privacy, add airport security inspections, massive computer credit files filled with personal histories, and government proposals to screen the population for those who are potentially "problem people" at the earliest possible age. Some feel infants are not too young to be studied as "psychosocial organisms" by researchers trying to "develop ways to work with community-based systems in identifying, before birth, infants who will be vulnerable to mental health problems."

At least five negative consequences flow from such soon-to-become ubiquitous surveillance in our society.

1. It fosters a climate of suspicion and an erosion of interpersonal trust.

2. A chilling effect is established which intimidates individuals, restraining them from expressing unpopular opinions and sharing dissenting ideas.

3. A power differential emerges in which unknown others have information about the individual; this inequitable distribution of information reduces the person's sense of personal autonomy and increases feelings of powerlessness.

4. Screening procedures may select for docility and conformity while selecting out the activists and innovative rebels.

5. Accepting the necessity for minor surveillance in any area of our public lives conditions us to be less opposed to major intrusions into other areas of our private lives—a foot-in-the-door approach.

Orwell's demonstration of the power of situational forces to overwhelm the best that individual defenses can offer has been validated in a host of social psychology experiments. In the most notable of them, Stanley Milgram demonstrated that the majority of ordinary people will electrocute a stranger if an authority figure asks them to. He would give a subject the experimental role of a teacher whose mission is to help a student-learner by punishing his errors with increasingly severe electric shocks. As the "victim's" protests mount to screams, the subjects dissent, not wanting to hurt or seriously injure the learner (a confederate of the experimenter), but two out of three subjects do not disobey when the experimenter says, "Teacher, you must continue, the rules state that. . . ." They continue administering shocks, not from malice or evil motives, but because of situational constraints that distort their pro-social motives. Once they accept their experimental role, they are locked into a system which leads them down the path of blindly obeying authority.

To show that normal people could behave in pathological ways even without the external pressure of an experimenter-authority, my colleagues and I put college students in a simulated prison setting and observed the power of roles, rules, and expectations. Young men selected because they were normal on all the psychological dimensions we measured (many of them were avowed pacifists) became hostile and sadistic, verbally and physically abusing others—if they enacted the randomly assigned role of all-powerful mock guards. Those randomly assigned to be mock prisoners suffered emotional breakdowns, irrational thinking, and behaved self-destructively—despite their constitutional stability and normalcy. This planned two-week simulation had to be ended after six days because the inhumanity of the "evil situation" had totally dominated the humanity of the "good" participants.

VI

The major weakness in the mind-control armament Orwell supplies to the Party is the visibility of its coercive power. Since the Party wants to take full credit for each of its victories over individual psyches, it is necessary that Winston and the others know *how* they are being controlled. The Party acts like the Roman Emperor Caligula (at least in Camus's depiction of him) in its desire to demonstrate absolute power by its capricious deeds. It acts without concern for consequences, while insisting that those whom it crushes acknowledge whose boot is on their faces. O'Brien declares:

> Always, at every moment, there will be the thrill of victory, the
> sensation of trampling on an enemy who is helpless. If you want
> a picture of the future, imagine a boot stomping on a human
> face—forever.

Coercive controls create compliant conformists but never true believers. Public compliance without private acceptance occurs when individuals perceive that external forces are of sufficient magnitude to determine the individual's discrepant actions. When that might is visibly apparent, the person surrenders and yields, but does not internalize the new ideology. Without at least an illusion of freely chosen action, the individual becomes a passive reactor who takes no responsibility for the behavioral change while pointing an accusing finger at outside forces.

Among the major discoveries of modern social psychology is the simple principle that under specified conditions a bare minimum of social pressure can produce great attitude change. The most profound and enduring changes in attitude are generated when two conditions are present: first, the person perceives that he or she has free choice in deciding to behave in ways that are counter-normative or against one's values, beliefs, or motives; and second, the force applied to elicit this discrepant action is just barely sufficient in magnitude to accomplish the task. The pressure may be as innocuous as having the experimenter in an authoritative white coat say "We're doing an experiment . . ." or touch the subject's shoulder and say, "Do me a favor." People want to be good sports and team players.

When a person can be induced (or seduced) by means of such subtle, unsuspected tactics into publicly behaving in ways that are contrary to his or her prior standards or needs, then a state of cognitive dissonance arises. This tension state is great when the person believes the alien action was freely chosen rather than externally determined, and when the justification for making that decision was not sufficient in itself to undercut the freedom of choice. Armed with such knowledge or illusory belief, the individual becomes his or her own agent of self-persuasion. If the discrepant behavior cannot be attributed to external power, it is explained in terms of self-generated processes. "I must have unknowingly liked it, if I chose to do it without reward or threat of punishment."

In literally hundreds of studies, when intelligent subjects were misled to believe that their acts of lying, cheating, self-deprivation, aggression, suffering, and much more, were not due to the actual (though concealed) forces to which they were subjected, they invented personal reasons to account for their new, atypical behavior. These attributions are mini-theories which individuals use to help make sense of an apparently irrational action, such as eating fried grasshoppers after saying they dislike them, or accepting powerful electric shocks which they want to avoid—when given the option not to and only minimal incentives to do so.

The image of Orwell's persuader is a Joe Stalin trained by B.F. Skinner. Behavior can be controlled by powerful external contingencies, but the coercively controlled organism will do as its trainer directs without believing in the trainer's ideology. One need not travel long in any nation with a totalitarian government to see this discrepancy in action—uniformity of public behavior without correspondingly supportive private beliefs. The conformity persists only with sustained external force and continual surveillance. That is also why such governments, like the Party in *Nineteen Eighty-Four*, cannot allow a single dissident. The isolated voice of opposition might trigger a chorus of rebellious minds to say what they really feel about doing what they are being forced to do. They behave but do not believe.

A related point of contention is the Party's reliance on technology to do the work of mind control—just as the CIA's MK-ULTRA program did. Exotic tactics and high-tech devices do not influence attitudes and change behavior as much as do the most mundane human experiences. The real power of effective mind control is to be found in the basic needs of people to be loved, respected, recognized, and wanted. It is in social groups, which can reject deviants or embrace believers. It is in those fleeting moments of social exchange when someone gives or holds back a smile, a word of praise, a gentle touch. It is found in those social situations that help give people's lives meaning and security, a sense of purpose and place.

Psychologists use the term "fundamental attribution error" to describe a mental bias that underestimates the true power of these mundane social-situational determinants of human action while giving too much credit to external physical forces to control minds and to nebulous dispositional qualities within the person to resist them. Human nature is not diminished because such socially embedded mind control can be so effective. Paradoxically, human nature is all the more remarkable because the same seeds of its own perversion can also bear the fruit of tender, intense, and trusting social bonding that is essential for the human connection to be affirmed.

VII

The most telling of Orwell's predictions are to be found not in the heavy-handed practices of the Ministry of Justice, but in the treatment program of the Ministry of Love. "Shall I tell you why we have brought you here? To cure you! To make you sane! Will you understand, Winston, that no one whom we bring to this place ever leaves our hands uncured? . . . The Party is not interested in the overt act: the thought is all we care about. We do not merely destroy our enemies; we change them."

Twenty-five years after Orwell put those words into the mouth of his fictional character, comparable words were pronounced to a Soviet dissident, Viktor Feinberg, involuntarily committed to a Soviet mental hospital: "Your release depends on your behavior. And your behavior, to us, means your political views. In all other respects, your behavior is perfectly normal. Your illness consists of dissenting opinions. As soon as you renounce them and adopt a correct point of view, we will let you go" (Federation of American Scientists, Public Interest Report, October 1973). The speaker was not a Communist Party political bureaucrat, but a psychiatrist working for the government.

Orwell deserves credit for seeing the potential power of professionals whom society sanctions to intervene into the lives of its citizens "for their own good." But he barely hinted at the extent and depth of that power, which is so evident in our 1984. When control is cloaked as cure, surveillance as a security service, and repression as a rehabilitation program, civil liberties can be set aside and cherished freedoms put on hold without arousing resistance or rebellion. When it is being done for you and not to you, it is difficult to complain without feeling the guilt of the ungrateful.

The new ideology of intervention and control is based on the presumed needs and deficiencies of sick, suffering, incompetent, dangerous individuals and not on the requirements of government for loyalty and obedience. So instead of punishment, torture, exile, and other tricks of the tyrant trade, we are seeing such tricks of the treatment trade: intervention as therapy, education, social service, reform, retraining, and rehabilitation.

The current practitioners in our Ministry of Love come from the ranks of the mental health establishment (psychiatry and my own field, psychology), social welfare agencies, education, and business. As the social fabric of family, neighborhood, and community becomes stretched and frayed, ever more Americans are being turned over to institutional care providers. As day-care facilities begin to admit more infants and young children and nursing homes handle our aged, there is an increasing number of agencies and systems to process us from the start to the finish of life. When we become care receivers, it is expected we will follow the rules of the institution—usually impersonal, arbitrary rules designed primarily to make the many receivers more manageable by the few care givers. Unfortunately, the documented abuse of human dignity that sometimes occurs within the "total situation" created by many of these institutions is nearly as horrible as anything Orwell imagined for us in *Nineteen Eighty-Four*.

In a critical attack on the role of the mental health establishment as the new Party of our 1984, investigative journalist Peter Schrag warns us of the insidious danger inherent in the unquestioning acceptance of its seemingly benign ideology. With the change from power technologies to persuasive advocacy of medical, psychological, and social intervention comes a new concept of human nature. Schrag contends that "at the heart of the change lies a transcendental faith that with the proper environment or the proper methods, any individual can be reshaped, reformed, or at the very least, controlled with psychological or clinical methods, and alongside that faith, the chemical, mechanistic, behavioral view of man that sustains it."

In this time of ontological insecurity, people are turning to religion for spiritual solace—but not just the old-time religions. New religious movements have been flourishing in the last two decades to the point that today there are reportedly over 3,000 nontraditional religious groups in America. These cults are varied enough in their religious ideologies, orientation toward politics, and social issues to cater to virtually every human need. Like the slogan on a cement truck, they "find a need and fill it." While many of these cults *are* genuine religious organizations, there are some that use religion as a constitutional hideout to conceal their goals of political and economic influence and, in some cases, social revolution.

For the leaders of these new religious-secular cults there is also the added attraction of ascending to a position of enormous power. Their followers voluntarily vest complete, arbitrary power in these mortal messiahs—the same power the Party could obtain only by using extreme forms of destructive coercion. They plant one foot on secular soil to oppose communism, fascism, liberalism, equal rights for women, and other political-social concerns, while tiptoeing with the other foot on the spiritual soil to keep God and the angels on their side and the tax collectors and critics at bay. There are big bucks in these new-time cults, especially those that use the electronic pulpit provided by television to reach into the homes of millions of followers. They are business enterprises that offer salvation for a price.

## VIII

Sometimes people pay dearly—with their lives—when salvation includes surrendering their will to a paranoid prophet. On November 18, 1978, in a jungle compound in Jonestown, Guyana, 912 American men, women, and children obeyed the wish of their minister, Reverend Jim Jones, that they commit revolutionary suicide. At his urging, they voluntarily drank poison or force fed it to those members reluctant to die for his cause. Jones's "cause" was an imagined war pitting his small Christian-turned-communist band against the supposedly imminent invasion by fascist forces of United States imperialism.

This theme had been preached by Jones almost daily for many months and translated into practice by elaborately planned attacks on the enemies of People's Temple and "white knight" drills. Orwell's analysis of the Party mentality and the psychology of war applies to the Jonestown episode all too well:

> The social atmosphere is that of a besieged city. . . . The consequences of being at war, and therefore in danger, makes the handing-over of all power to a small caste seem the natural, unavoidable condition of survival. . . . It does not matter whether war is actually happening. . . . All that is needed is that a state of war should exist.

And when discovery by the Thought Police was inevitable, "the proper thing was to kill yourself before they got you."

If one closely analyzes Jones's tactics and strategies for developing in his followers a mentality in which the unthinkable became reasonable, one can, I believe, entertain a radical hypothesis: Jim Jones was consciously mimicking Orwell's *Nineteen Eighty-Four* in designing and executing his personal experiment—testing mind-control techniques to demonstrate the ultimate meaning of power without limits.

Only a sketch of the parallels between Orwell's fictional world and the factual world Jones created is possible here. Since Jones, like Richard Nixon, taped his public speeches and personal interviews for posterity, a documentary record of over 900 hours exists. On some tapes Jones can be heard punishing a follower for the crime of being "an intellectual," or he can be heard whipping the congregation into a frenzy that leads to the physical abuse of a boy by his elders—for the crime of eating oranges without authorization; or the paddling of a little girl for hugging another child—a prohibited act.

Unlike Big Brother, Jones did not use electronic invasion of privacy; he relied on his inner circle Security Committee. While the cult was still in the United States they would inform on members by breaking into their homes, examining garbage, checking mail, and so forth. Jones would then demonstrate his omniscience by revealing (during church services) intricate knowledge of individual members' lives that "no one else could have possibly known"—at least no mortal person. His spy system encouraged everyone to report evidence of deviance in friends and family, so that the sinners could be publicly denounced, humiliated, and punished—to help to mend their dissident ways.

But total control requires a total situation in which access to all information about external reality is selectively filtered, liberty of movement is constrained, and the group's social norms become the only laws that govern actions. Jones led his followers into the heart of darkness of the Guyanese jungle to create a socialist "agricultural experiment." The land he chose was terrible for farming—and worse for living. As in *Nineteen Eighty-Four*, the people were chronically malnourished and overworked. Marriages were dissolved arbitrarily by Jones's order, sexes segregated in separate barracks, and approval of the Social Committee was required to engage in intimate relations, or even for women to obtain sanitary napkins. Public denunciations of anyone complaining about anything were held nightly and the Discipline Committee would arrange the appropriate punishment—which included electric shocks, mind-altering drugs, and confinement for days in underground metal boxes. There was even the equivalent of Torture Room 101. People's Temple members had to write statements of their weaknesses and fears. When they got out of line, they would be reminded of where the line was drawn and who drew it for them by having their worst fears made manifest. One former member phoned in to a National Public Radio forum to share his experience: He had confessed to a phobia against snakes; so, for punishment, Jones had him stripped and bound, and then let snakes crawl over him.

But Jones's power reached even deeper into the psyches of his followers than that of Big Brother's Party did. The members of People's Temple feared him as an omnipotent, unpredictable messiah, but they also loved him as their Dad, as the Father-Who-Cares. The young man given the snake torture was also beaten and sexually abused—but to this day says that he respects and holds Jones in awe as a man above mortal limits.

Finally, Jones made use of doublethink to distort reality—not just as it exists in human memory of the past, but more remarkably, reality as it exists in perception of the present. These hungry, exhausted, fearful, abused people had to say their "gratitudes" regularly as they meditated upon him. They consisted of a litany of praise for Dad's providing them "good food," a "good home," "good work," and because he loved them so—despite the overwhelmingly contradictory evidence provided by their senses. Though held captive in a jungle concentration camp policed by armed guards, they had to give thanks to Dad for their freedom. Jones even showed them horror

*La mémoire (Memory)* by Magritte. © ADAGP, Paris 1983.

movies of Nazi concentration camps (such as *Night and Fog*) to remind them that conditions could get worse.

It is common in many cults to invite recruits and members to suspend usual reality testing, to practice forms of "heavenly deception," to stop thinking critically and start thinking with their hearts. Jones carried this doctrine of mindless cardiac comprehension to the extreme. He made them believe in things that could be readily proven false by the simplest empirical test. Jonestown was described as a paradise where there would be no death or sickness—yet people got sick and died. The climate was ideal, the earth fertile, the food abundant, the work light, and there were no mosquitoes. The people had to repeat those idyllic descriptions of Jonestown in censored letters sent back home as well as to visitors and to themselves. They did so while experiencing the jungle heat in a place where almost nothing edible grew, food was scarce, the work unremitting, and the mosquitoes were in fierce abundance.

Reverend Jones, first a prophet of God, then a self-proclaimed God, ended his reign as an Antichrist. He made these God-fearing people question and then burn their Bibles. They had to stop meditating on Christ and meditate only on him. He attacked their religious beliefs, discontinued church services, and finally transformed his Christian flock into a communist commune of comrades-in-arms. His "agricultural experiment" succeeded, if its true purpose was to demonstrate the conditions that could turn independent human beings into vegetables without the will to resist even their own destruction. The CIA's MK-ULTRA program would have had to acknowledge that Jones succeeded where they failed in the ultimate control of the human mind.

Jones's parody of doublethink existed even to the detail of his using the words of Santayana as the slogan above his throne chair: "Those who do not remember the past are condemned to repeat it." Who was that epitaph intended for—his followers, cut off from their past, or for us, who refuse to believe it could happen again—here, today, or maybe tomorrow?

IX

Variations on Orwellian technologies of mind control have been, are being, and will be increasingly used to get large numbers of people to think the way someone wants them to. Orwell alerted the world to the danger inherent in political parties that could evolve into repressive systems of coercive control. But what initially seemed like an overdrawn portrait of Big Brother's malevolence and brutal cunning has become a sharply drawn sketch of contemporary political realities in one after another totalitarian government throughout the world of both developed and underdeveloped nations.

The threats to freedom, liberty, and individual dignity are even greater today than they were in 1948 when Orwell wrote *Nineteen Eighty-Four*. Would-be mind controllers are spurting up everywhere, unconstrained by Party allegiance. They pose more of a threat because their tactics are more subtle, their strategies more insidious, and their influence more pervasive. They sell us, educate us, treat us, service us, and minister to us—after first persuading us of the need to pay willingly and dearly for their product.

And in the end, we must individually and collectively challenge the Party line: there is indeed something called human nature which will be outraged by what is done to the least of our kind—and will turn against despots and dictators whether demonic or benevolent. We defy Big Brother.

# Reader's Guide

All of Orwell's books are available in paperback; they are listed below in chronological order.

**Fiction:**
*Burmese Days*, 1934
*A Clergyman's Daughter*, 1935
*Keep the Aspidistra Flying*, 1936
*Coming Up for Air*, 1939
*Animal Farm*, 1945
*Nineteen Eighty-Four*, 1949

**Reportage:**
*Down and Out in Paris and London*, 1933
*The Road to Wigan Pier*, 1937
*Homage to Catalonia*, 1938

**Collections:**
*The Collected Essays, Journalism and Letters of George Orwell*, vols. 1-4. Edited by Sonia Orwell and Ian Angus. New York and London: Harcourt Brace, Jovanovich, 1968.
*The Orwell Reader: Fiction, Essays and Reportage*. Edited by Richard Rovere. New York: Harcourt Brace Jovanovich, 1956.

* * *

**Biography:**
Crick, Bernard. *George Orwell: A Life*. Chicago: University of Chicago Press, 1969.
Stansky, Peter, and William Abrahams. *The Unknown Orwell*. London: Granada Publishing Ltd., 1974.
Stansky, Peter, and William Abrahams. *Orwell: A Transformation*. London: Granada Publishing Ltd., 1981.

**Selected Criticism:**
Burgess, Anthony. *1985*. Boston: Little, Brown, 1978.
Gross, Miriam, ed. *The World of George Orwell*. London: George Weidenfeld & Nicolson Ltd., 1971.

Howe, Irving, ed. *Orwell's "1984": Text, Sources, Criticism*, second edition. New York: Harcourt Brace Jovanovich, 1982.

Hynes, Samuel L., ed. *Twentieth Century Interpretations of "1984"*. Englewood Cliffs, New Jersey: Prentice-Hall, 1974.

Rees, Sir Richard. *George Orwell: Fugitive from the Camp of Victory*. Carbondale: Southern Illinois University Press, 1962.

Williams, Raymond. *George Orwell*. New York: Viking Press, 1971.

Williams, Raymond, ed. *George Orwell: A Collection of Critical Essays*. Englewood Cliffs, New Jersey: Prentice-Hall, 1974.

Woodcock, George. *The Crystal Spirit: A Study of George Orwell*. Boston: Little, Brown, 1966.

Zwerdling, Alex. *Orwell and the Left*. New Haven: Yale University Press, 1974.

# Appendix

LISTED BELOW are notes and references pertaining to particular essays. In a more scholarly text, some would appear as footnotes; others are suggestions for further reading on the subject of the essay.

References to works cited in the Reader's Guide appear in abbreviated form. *The Collected Essays, Journalism and Letters of George Orwell* appears as *CEJL*.

### 3 — Comfort
- Winterbotham, F.W. *The Ultra Secret*. Harper and Row, 1974.
- Gilbert, M. *Auschwitz and the Allies*. Holt, Rinehart and Winston, 1981.

### 7 — Ehrlich
- Ehrlich, Paul, John P. Holdren, and Anne Ehrlich. *Ecoscience: Population, Resources, Environment*. W.H. Freeman, 1977.
- Ehrlich, Paul, and Anne Ehrlich. *Extinction: The Causes and Consequences of the Disappearance of Species*. Ballantine Books, 1983.

### 9 — McGinn
- Tribe, Lawrence. *Channeling Technology Through Law*. Bracton Press, 1973.

### 10 — Clayton
- "Splicing Life: A Report on the Social and Ethical Issues of Genetic Engineering with Human Beings." President's Commission for the Study of Ethical Problems in Medicine and Biomedical and Behavioral Research, Morris B. Abrams, chairman. Government Printing Number PR40.8:ET3/L62, November 1982.

### 11 — Babcock
- Connors, James. "Do It To Julia: Thoughts on Orwell's *1984*," in *Modern Fiction Studies*. Winter 1970-71, p. 1.
- Keats, John. *Letters*. Edited by Edward Hyder Rollins. Harvard University Press, 1958.

- Jakobson, Roman. "Closing Statements: Linguistics and Politics," in *Style in Language*. Edited by T.A. Sebeok. MIT Press, 1960, p. 371.
- Orwell. "Politics and the English Language," in *CEJL*, vol. 3, p. 136.
- Orwell. "The English People," in *CEJL*, vol. 3, p. 26.

## 12 — Traugott

- Bailey, Richard W. "George Orwell and the English Language," in *The Future of 1984*. Edited by Ejner J. Jensen. University of Michigan Press, 1984.
- Bereiter, Carl, and Siegfried Engelmann, *Teaching Disadvantaged Children in the Preschool*. Prentice-Hall, 1966.
- Bolinger, Dwight. *Language--The Loaded Weapon: The Use and Abuse of Language Today*. Longman, 1980.
- Chomsky, Noam. *Rules and Representations*. Columbia University Press, 1980.
- Saussure, Ferdinand de. *Course in General Linguistics*, 1916. Translated by Wade Baskin. Philosophical Press, 1959, pp. 111-12.
- Traugott, John. "Swift, Our Contemporary," in *Swift*. Edited by C.J. Rawson. London: Sphere Books, 1971.
- Whorf, Benjamin Lee. *Language, Thought and Reality: Selected Writings of Benjamin Lee Whorf*. Edited by John B. Carroll. MIT Press, 1956, p. 213.

## 13 — Watt

- Cicero. *De Inventione, I*. Edited by H.M. Hubbell. London: Heinemann, 1949, p. 72.
- Cicero. *De Oratore*. Edited by H. Rackham. London: Heinemann, 1942, p. 98.
- Connors, James. "Who Dies if England Lives?: Christianity and the Moral Vision of George Orwell," in *The Secular Mind*. Edited by W. Warren Wagar. Holmes and Meier, 1982, pp. 169-196.
- Crick. *Orwell*, pp. 117, 123, 223, 226-229, 541, 546, 580.
- Howe, Irving. "*1984*: History as Nightmare," in *Twentieth Century Interpretations of "1984."* Edited by Samuel Hynes. Prentice-Hall, 1971, p. 43.
- Norlin, George, ed. *Isocrates, II*. London: Heinemann, 1929, pp. 323, 327.
- For a good survey of the classical tradition, see Donald Lemen Clark, *Rhetoric in Greco-Roman Education* (Columbia University Press, 1957), especially pp. 5-17 and 51-83. The best analytic history of the later continuity of the humanist tradition is probably that of R.S. Crane, "The Humanities," in *The Idea of Humanities and Other Essays Critical and Historical*, vol. 1. Chicago University Press, 1967, pp. 3-170.

## 14 — Mellor

- Crick. *Orwell*, p. 13.
- Orwell. *Burmese Days*, pp. 89-90.

- Orwell. *The Road to Wigan Pier*, p. 29.
- For Orwell's views on the family see *CEJL*, vol. 3, pp. 159-165, and vol. 4, p. 91.

## 15 — Esslin

- Arendt, Hannah. *The Origins of Totalitarianism*. Harcourt Brace Jovanovich 1968.
- Huxley, Aldous. *Brave New World*. Harper and Row, 1932.

## 16 — Lewenstein

- Bagdikian, Ben. *The Media Monopoly*. Beacon Press, 1983.
- Bellamy, Edward. *Looking Backward*. Ticknor and Company, 1888. (Available in modern editions.)
- Schramm, Wilbur, Lyle M. Nelson, and Mere Betham. "Bold Experiment: A Study of Television Effects in American Samoa." Stanford University Press, 1981.

## 18 — Brown

- Beauchamp, Gorman. "Of Man's Last Disobedience: Zamiatin's *We* and Orwell's *Nineteen Eighty-Four*," in *Comparative Literature Studies*, vol. 10, 1973, pp. 286-301.
- Collins, Christopher. *Evgenij Zamyatin, an Interpretive Study*. The Hague: Mouton, 1973.
- Gregg, R.A. "Two Adams and Eve in the Crystal Palace: Dostoevsky, the Bible, and *We*," in *Slavic Review*, 4, 1965, pp. 680-687.
- Weber, Harry, and Kathleen Lewis, "Zamyatin's *We*, the Proletarian Poets, and Bogdanov's *Red Star*," in *Russian Literature Triquarterly*, 12, Spring 1976, pp. 253-278.
- Zamyatin, Yevgeny. *The Essays of Yevgeny Zamyatin*. Edited by Mirra Ginsburg. University of Chicago Press, 1970.
- For an account of the relationship of both books to the science fantasies of H.G. Wells, see E.J. Brown, *"Brave New World," "1984," and "We": An Essay on Anti-Utopia*. Ardis, 1976, pp. 46-54.

## 20 — Conquest

- Ehrenburg, Ilya. *Men, Years and Life*. English edition, vol. 4. London: Pergamon Press, 1963, p. 195.
- Koestler, Arthur. *Arrow in the Blue*, vol. 2. Macmillan, 1970, p. 208.
- Orwell. "The Prevention of Literature," in *Polemic*. CEJL, vol. 2, 1946.
- Orwell. Editorial in *Polemic*. CEJL, vol. 3, May 1946.
- Symons, Julian. *The Thirties: A Dream Revolved*. London: Cresset Press, 1960, p. 143.

- Valentinov, N. (Volski), quoted in Leonard Schapiro, *The Communist Party of the Soviet Union*. London: Eyre and Spottiswoode, 1960, p. 381.
- Williams. *Orwell*.

## 21 — Dallin

- Dallin, Alexander and George W. Breslauer. *Political Terror in Communist Systems*. Stanford University Press, 1970, p. 46ff.
- Trilling, Lionel. *The Opposing Self.* Harcourt Brace Jovanovich, 1978, p. 136.
- Weber, Max. "Social Psychology of the World Religions" and other selections, in *From Max Weber: Essays in Sociology*. Edited by H.H. Gerth and C.R. Mills. Oxford University Press, 1958.
- For an interesting if idiosyncratic argument that the essence of Leninism was (and is) precisely the linkage of charismatic leadership with institutional imperatives, see Kenneth Jowitt, *The Leninist Response to National Dependency*. Berkeley Institute of International Studies, 1978, p. 34ff.
- On the element of immortality in the Lenin cult, see particularly Peter Wiles, "On Physical Immortality: Materialism and Transcendence," in *Survey*, no. 56 (July 1965); and Nina Tumarkin, *Lenin Lives! The Lenin Cult in Soviet Russia*, Harvard University Press, 1982.
- For some of the recent debates on the validity or utility of the theory of totalitarianism, see e.g., Benjamin R. Barber, Michael Curtis, and Carl J. Friedrich, *Totalitarianism in Perspective: Three Views*, Praeger, 1969; Robert Burrowes, "Totalitarianism: The Revised Standard Version," in *World Politics*, XXI:2, 1969; and Leonard Schapiro, *Totalitarianism*, Pall Mall Press, 1972.

## 22 — Zimbardo

- Delgado, José. *Physical Control of the Mind: Toward a Psychocivilized Society.* Harper and Row, 1929.
- *Father Cares: The Last of Jonestown*. National Public Radio Tapes, 1981.
- Festinger, Leon. *A Theory of Cognitive Dissonance*. Harper and Row, 1957; Stanford University Press, 1962.
- Milgram, Stanley. *Obedience to Authority.* Harper and Row, 1974.
- *Public Interest Report*. Federation of American Scientists. October 1973.
- Reiterman, Tim, and John Jacobs. *Raven: The Untold Story of Jim Jones and His People*. Dutton, 1983.
- Schrag, Peter. *Mind Control*. Delta, 1978.
- Shelley, Mary Wollstonecraft. *Frankenstein: Or, the Modern Prometheus*. Routledge and Sons, 1818. (Available in modern editions.)
- Zimbardo, P., C. Haney, W.C. Banks, and D. Jaffee. "A Pirandellian Prison: The Mind is a Formidable Jailer," in *New York Times Magazine*. April 8, 1973.
- Zimbardo, Philip. *The Cognitive Control of Motivation*. Scott, Foresman Co., 1969.

# The Contributors

WILLIAM ABRAHAMS, has been a visiting lecturer at the Stanford Creative Writing Center. He is coauthor with Peter Stansky of *The Unknown Orwell* and *Orwell: The Transformation*. A senior editor at Holt, Rinehart and Winston, where he has his own imprint, he has edited the O'Henry Awards annual collection of short stories for eighteen years.

KENNETH J. ARROW received the Nobel Memorial Prize in Economic Science in 1972. A member of the Stanford faculty from 1949 to 1968 and again since 1979, he is Joan Kenney Professor of Economics and professor of operations research. He is author or coauthor of eight books and 154 professional papers.

BARBARA ALLEN BABCOCK, professor of law at the Stanford Law School, is a specialist in civil and criminal procedure. From 1977 to 1979 she served as U.S. Assistant Attorney General, Civil Division, under President Carter. She is coauthor of *Sex Discrimination and the Law: Causes and Remedies* and *Civil Procedure: Cases and Comments on the Process of Adjudication*.

EDWARD J. BROWN is professor of Slavic languages and literature emeritus at Stanford. Author of five books, his most recent are *Mayakovsky: A Poet in the Revolution* and *Russian Literature Since the Revolution* (newly issued in a revised and enlarged edition).

RAYMOND B. CLAYTON is professor of biochemistry in psychiatry and behavioral sciences and currently director of admissions at the Stanford Medical School. He teaches in the Values, Technology, Science, and Society Program and has published extensively on the chemistry, biochemistry, and physiology of steroids and related compounds.

ALEX COMFORT received his medical education at Cambridge. After nearly half a century as writer, physician, researcher in the biology of aging, and political theorist, he is currently adjunct professor at the Neuropsychiatric Institute, U.C.L.A. Until this year he was on the clinical faculty at the Stanford Medical School.

ROBERT CONQUEST, British historian, poet, critic, novelist, and journalist, is a senior research fellow at the Hoover Institution at Stanford. His numerous books on the Soviet Union and international affairs have appeared in nineteen languages, including Russian *samizdat*.

GORDON A. CRAIG is J.E. Wallace Sterling Professor of Humanities Emeritus at Stanford. He has written extensively on diplomatic and military subjects, most recently as coauthor of *Force and Statecraft: Diplomatic Problems of Our Time*. He is past president of the American Historical Association.

ALEXANDER DALLIN is professor of history and political science at Stanford. Formerly director of the Russian Institute at Columbia University, he has served as chairman of the National Council for Soviet and East European Research and as chairman of Stanford's International Relations Program. He is the author of numerous books and articles, including *Political Terror in Communist Systems*.

GERALD A. DORFMAN is a senior fellow at the Hoover Institution at Stanford. He is the author of *Government versus Trade Unionism in British Politics Since 1968* and *Wage Politics in Britain, 1947-1968*, as well as cofounder and publisher of two scholarly journals, *Politics and Society* and *Political Methodology*.

SIDNEY D. DRELL is Lewis M. Terman Professor, deputy director, and executive head of theoretical physics at Stanford Linear Accelerator Center and faculty fellow at the Stanford Center for International Security and Arms Control. He has served on the President's Science Advisory Committee and as consultant for the National Security Council and U.S. Arms Control and Disarmament Agency. His most recent book is *Facing the Threat of Nuclear Weapons*.

ANNE H. EHRLICH is a senior research associate in biology at Stanford and teaches a course in environmental policy in the Human Biology Program. She served as a consultant to the government's Council on Environmental Quality's *Global 2000 Report* and is a member of the U.S. Association for the Club of Rome. With Professor Paul Ehrlich she has coauthored eight books, including *Ecoscience: Population, Resources, Environment* and *Extinction: The Causes and Consequences of the Disappearance of Species*.

PAUL R. EHRLICH is Bing Professor of Population Studies and professor of biological sciences at Stanford. Winner of the Sierra Club's 1980 John Muir award, he is honorary president of Zero Population and a fellow of the American Academy of Arts and Sciences.

MARTIN ESSLIN, professor of drama at Stanford, is former head of the BBC Drama Department, where he directed over 200 plays. Translator of major German playwrights, he is a specialist in contemporary drama. His best-known books are *Brecht: A Choice of Evils* and *The Theatre of the Absurd*.

MARION LEWENSTEIN, professor of communication at Stanford, is a professional journalist and coauthor of *Workbook: Reporting and Writing for Print*. She is a recipient of the California Newspaper Publishers Outstanding Journalism Educator Award.

ROBERT E. MCGINN, professor of industrial engineering and engineering management, is associate chairman of Stanford's Values, Technology, Science, and Society Program.

ANNE K. MELLOR is Howard and Jesse Watkins University Professor in Feminist Studies and professor of English at Stanford. Recipient of the Dean's Award for Outstanding Teaching, she is author of *English Romantic Irony*, *Studies in Romanticism*, and *Blake's Human Form Divine*.

SCOTT R. PEARSON is associate director and professor of Stanford's Food Research Institute. Author or coauthor of five books, his most recent publication is *Food Policy Analysis*. He is currently engaged in research and teaching projects in Indonesia and Portugal.

PAUL ROBINSON has been a professor of European intellectual history at Stanford since 1967. Author of *The Freudian Left* and *The Modernization of Sex*, he is completing a book on opera and the history of ideas as well as reviewing for *The New York Times*, *The New Republic*, and *Psychology Today*.

PETER STANSKY is the Frances and Charles Field Professor of History at Stanford and former chairman of the department. He is coauthor of two studies of George Orwell, *The Unknown Orwell* and *Orwell: The Transformation*, and has written extensively on aspects of modern Britain.

ELIZABETH CLOSS TRAUGOTT, professor of linguistics and English at Stanford, is a Guggenheim Fellow and Fellow at the Center for Advanced Study in the Behavioral Sciences for 1983-1984. Her books include *A History of English Syntax* and *Linguistics for Students of Literature*.

IAN WATT, educated at Cambridge, is director of the Stanford Humanities Center and professor of English. He is author of *The Rise of the Novel* and *Conrad in the Nineteenth Century* and a fellow of the American Academy of Arts and Sciences.

PHILIP ZIMBARDO, professor of psychology, is director of the Social Psychology Graduate Training Program at Stanford. He has investigated such issues as persuasion, police interrogation techniques, and experimentally induced paranoia. Author of the widely used textbook *Psychology and Life*, he has written numerous other books, including *Shyness* and *Influencing Attitudes and Changing Behavior*.

# CREDITS

All quotations from *Nineteen Eighty-Four* by George Orwell, copyright 1949 by Harcourt Brace Jovanovich.

COVER       Cover design by Anita Scott.

FRONTISPIECE       George Tooker. *Landscape with Figures*, 1965–66. Egg tempera on pressed wood, 25½" × 29". From a private collection. Photo courtesy of Ronald Feldman Fine Arts, New York.

PAGE *xii*       George Orwell, 1943. BBC copyright photograph.

PAGE 7       June 19, 1949 ad for *Nineteen Eighty-Four*. Courtesy of Harcourt Brace Jovanovich, Inc.

PAGE 14       Komar and Melamid. *Yalta Conference (From a History Textbook, 1984)*, 1982–83. Photo by James Hamilton. Courtesy of Ronald Feldman Fine Arts, New York.

PAGE 28       Map by Donna Salmon.

PAGE 40       Juan Genovés. *Man*, 1968. Oil on canvas, 74¼" × 59". Estate of Joseph H. Hirshhorn.

PAGE 48       Robert Graysmith cartoon. From *Best Editorial Cartoons of the Year*, 1978 edition. © 1978 by Charles Brooks. By permission of Pelican Publishing Company.

PAGE 49       George Orwell. "Marrakech" from *The Collected Essays, Journalism and Letters of George Orwell*, vol. I, edited by Sonia Orwell and Ian Angus. New York and London: Harcourt, Brace, Jovanovich, 1968.

PAGE 58       Roy Justus cartoon. From *Best Editorial Cartoons of the Year*, 1975 edition. © 1975 by Charles Brooks. By permission of Pelican Publishing Company.

PAGE 66       Gary Viskupic. *Computer Thinker*. © 1983 *Discover Magazine*, Time, Inc.

PAGE 84       Alex Grey. *New Man II*, 1982. Polymer on paper, 24" × 24". Photo by Alex Grey. Courtesy of Ronald Feldman Fine Arts, New York.

PAGE 89       Magritte. *Ceci n'est pas une pipe (This is Not a Pipe)*. © by ADAGP, Paris 1983.

PAGE 98       Erika Rothenberg. *Defense Dictionary*, 1982. Photo by James Hamilton. Courtesy of the artist and Ronald Feldman Fine Arts, New York.

PAGE 105       Paul Klee. *Burden*. © by ADAGP, Paris 1983. Courtesy of Cosmo Press, Geneva, Switzerland.

PAGE 114       Edvard Munch. *The Kiss*. Woodcut. Courtesy of The Chicago Institute of Art.

PAGE 133       Ral cartoon. From *O Pasquim*, Rio de Janeiro. By permission of World Press Review.

PAGE 140       1954 television version of *Nineteen Eighty-Four*. The Parson Family and Winston Smith, from left to right: Keith Davis, Peter Cushing, Hilda Fenemore, Pamela Grant. BBC copyright photograph.

PAGE 146       Henfil cartoon. From *Opinao*, Rio de Janeiro. By permission of World Press Review.

PAGE 153       George Segal. *Lovers on a Bed II*, 1970. Plaster and metal, 48" × 72" × 60". Courtesy of Sidney Janis Gallery.

PAGE 166       George Grosz. *Republican Automatons*, 1913. Watercolor, 23⅝" × 18⅝". Collection, The Museum of Modern Art, New York. Advisory Committee Fund.

PAGE 182       George Tooker. *The Subway*, 1950. Egg tempera on composition board, 18" × 36". Collection of the Whitney Museum of American Art, Juliana Force Purchase.

PAGE 191       George Tooker. *Government Bureau*, 1956. Egg tempera on gesso panel, 19⅝" × 29⅝". Collection of The Metropolitan Museum of Art. George A. Hearn Fund, 1956.

PAGE 202       Nancy Grossman. *R.A.D.*, 1982. Photo by Geoffry Clements. Courtesy of Ronald Feldman Fine Arts, New York.

PAGE 213       Magritte. *La mémoire (Memory)*. © by ADAGP, Paris 1983.

# The Portable Stanford

THIS IS A VOLUME in The Portable Stanford, a subscription book series published by the Stanford Alumni Association. Each book is written by a distinguished scholar on the Stanford University faculty on a topic of current interest. Portable Stanford books are generally published three times a year and sent to subscribers on approval. Other titles in The Portable Stanford include:

*Human Sexuality: Sense and Nonsense* by Herant Katchadourian, M.D.
*Some Must Watch While Some Must Sleep* by William C. Dement
*Is Man Incomprehensible to Man?* by Philip H. Rhinelander
*Conceptual Blockbusting* by James L. Adams
*The Galactic Club: Intelligent Life in Outer Space* by Ronald Bracewell
*The Anxious Economy* by Ezra Solomon
*Murder and Madness* by Donald T. Lunde, M.D.
*Challengers to Capitalism: Marx, Lenin, and Mao* by John G. Gurley
*An Incomplete Guide to the Future* by Willis W. Harman
*America: The View from Europe* by J. Martin Evans
*The World That Could Be* by Robert C. North
*Law Without Lawyers: A Comparative View of Law in China and the United States* by Victor H. Li
*Tales of an Old Ocean* by Tjeerd van Andel
*Economic Policy Beyond the Headlines* by George P. Shultz and Kenneth W. Dam
*The American Way of Life Need Not Be Hazardous to Your Health* by John W. Farquhar, M.D.
*Worlds into Words: Understanding Modern Poems* by Diane Wood Middlebrook
*The Politics of Contraception, vol. I: The Present* by Carl Djerassi
*The Politics of Contraception, vol. II: The Future* by Carl Djerassi
*The Touch of Time: Myth, Memory, and the Self* by Albert J. Guerard
*Mirror and Mirage: Fiction by Nineteen* edited by Albert J. Guerard
*Insiders and Outliers: A Procession of Frenchmen* by Gordon Wright
*The Age of Television* by Martin Esslin
*Beyond the Turning Point: The U.S. Economy in the 1980s* by Ezra Solomon
*Cosmic Horizons: Understanding the Universe* by Robert V. Wagoner and Donald W. Goldsmith
*Challenges to Communism* by John G. Gurley
*The Musical Experience: Sound, Movement, and Arrival* by Leonard G. Ratner

Write to The Portable Stanford, Bowman Alumni House, Stanford, California 94305, or order on the attached card.

☐ Please send me _____ additional copies of ON NINETEEN EIGHTY-FOUR at $7.95 each (plus tax for California residents). This includes shipping and handling.

Mr./Ms. _____

Address _____

City _____ State _____ Zip _____

☐ Please send gift copies (including gift card) to:

Mr./Ms. _____

Address _____

City _____ State _____ Zip _____

☐ Payment enclosed.   ☐ Bill me.

Price subject to change.
The Portable Stanford, Stanford Alumni Association, Bowman Alumni House, Stanford, California 94305.

☐ I want to subscribe to The Portable Stanford.

☐ Please send me the following Portable Stanford volumes at $7.95 each (plus tax for California residents). This includes shipping and handling.

_____

_____

☐ Payment enclosed.   ☐ Bill me.

Mr./Ms. _____

Address _____

City _____ State _____ Zip _____

Price subject to change.
The Portable Stanford, Stanford Alumni Association, Bowman Alumni House, Stanford, California 94305.

# BUSINESS REPLY MAIL

FIRST CLASS    PERMIT NO. 67    PALO ALTO, CA

POSTAGE WILL BE PAID BY ADDRESSEE

## The Portable Stanford

Stanford Alumni Association
Bowman Alumni House
Stanford, CA 94305

# BUSINESS REPLY MAIL

FIRST CLASS    PERMIT NO. 67    PALO ALTO, CA

POSTAGE WILL BE PAID BY ADDRESSEE

## The Portable Stanford

Stanford Alumni Association
Bowman Alumni House
Stanford, CA 94305